Inhabiting the Earth

Inhabiting the Earth

Anarchist Political Ecology for Landscapes of Emancipation

Edited by
Martin Locret-Collet, Simon Springer,
Jennifer Mateer and Maleea Acker

ROWMAN & LITTLEFIELD
Lanham • Boulder • New York • London

Published by Rowman & Littlefield
An imprint of The Rowman & Littlefield Publishing Group, Inc.
4501 Forbes Boulevard, Suite 200, Lanham, Maryland 20706
www.rowman.com

86-90 Paul Street, London EC2A 4NE

British Library Cataloguing in Publication Information Available

Library of Congress Cataloguing-in-Publication Data

Names: Locret-Collet, Martin, editor. | Springer, Simon, editor. | Mateer, Jennifer, editor. | Acker, Maleea, 1975- editor.
Title: Inhabiting the Earth : anarchist political ecology for landscapes of emancipation / edited by Martin Locret-Collet, Simon Springer, Jennifer Mateer and Maleea Acker.
Description: Lanham : Rowman & Littlefield, [2021] | Includes bibliographical references and index.
Identifiers: LCCN 2021029553 (print) | LCCN 2021029554 (ebook) | ISBN 9781538159149 (cloth) | ISBN 9781538159156 (ebook)
Subjects: LCSH: Political ecology. | Environmental sociology. | Anarchism.
Classification: LCC JA75.8 .I54 2021 (print) | LCC JA75.8 (ebook) | DDC 320.5/7—dc23
LC record available at https://lccn.loc.gov/2021029553
LC ebook record available at https://lccn.loc.gov/2021029554

Contents

Preface

John P. Clark

REINHABITING THE LAND AND THE EARTH

This work, like the companion volume that preceded it, makes a major contribution to the creation of an explicitly anarchist political ecology. The concept of 'inhabiting the Earth' in the title points to the importance in anarchist social and ecological thought of place and region as the loci of meaning, value and the flourishing of life. Anarchist political ecology is the theoretical perspective that more than any other seeks to draw out the radical, and, indeed, revolutionary implications of bioregional thinking and of such key concepts as re-inhabitation and regeneration. It shows the disastrous consequences of the imposition on the Earth of artificial borders and other lines of demarcation based on political domination and instrumental rationality. As the Introduction to this volume points out, the issue of the relation between the universal and particular is a crucial one. Anarchist political ecology shows that true universality must be grounded in the rich, complex diversity of freely flourishing social and ecological communities. The alternative is the abstract universality and impoverished particularity of capital and the state, with their legacy of social alienation, possessive individualism and spiritual nihilism.

As this volume demonstrates, an integral part of re-inhabitation and social and ecological regeneration is the recreation (and, where it exists, the preservation) of the regenerative economy. Fiderŝek argues persuasively for such an arrangement in chapter 1 when he defends the need for a 'circular economy' that 'emulates natural systems' and makes use of 'simple, durable, reusable, and recyclable design'. Such a regenerative system is a subset of Nature's larger economy, which consists of the self-regulating and evolutionarily self-transcending metabolic activity of the Earth itself. The term 'economy' derives from *oikos*, the Greek word for the home or household, and from *nomos,* which is often translated as 'law', but in ancient Greece meant both law and custom. The term derives from the concept of 'allotment' or 'distribution' and is thus related to early ideas of natural justice, and specifically to what Heraclitus depicted as the common *logos* or discourse of nature.

According to this ancient wisdom, we must learn from the 'Great Book of Nature', which, contrary to Galileo, is written as much in the language of evolutionary biology and geohistory as it is in that of mathematics. What we learn from this primordial text is what the ancient Daoist sage Laozi expressed in his famous judgment that the 'Way of Nature' (that of the free community) is to take from where there is excess and to give to where there is deficiency, while the 'Way of Man' (that of the system of domination) is to take from where there is deficiency and to give to where there is excess. This is the truth that the regenerative economy, and indeed, the regenerative society, follows.

A commitment to such social and ecological regeneration looks to place-based, land-based and Earth-based cultures and value systems for examples and inspiration. This leads us to a rediscovery of the relevance today of historical practices of commoning, as is recognized here in both the Introduction and in a number of chapters. The commons cannot be dismissed as a merely abstract utopia, in view of its rich and expansive history, and the fact that it lives on today in many contemporary social practices, as noted by Auclair in chapter 2. It thus poses a materially and socially grounded challenge to the system of domination and inspires hope for the emergence of a broad sphere of mutual aid and social cooperation. Similarly, anarchist political ecology looks to living indigenous traditions as an embodied critique of domination and as a material basis for hope and regenerative praxis. Thomas and Figueroa-Helland present in chapter 4 an astute account of the significance of indigenous knowledge, practices and values. They note, for example, the presence of a 'care and response orientation' towards all beings, a recognition of the 'dynamic co-evolution' of all life forms, and the ethical and spiritual ideal of 'an integrated community of life'. One finds in this analysis and others in the collection an acute awareness of indigenous values as a powerful challenge to the ideological and existential roots of the system of domination.

OVERCOMING DUALISM

Underlying many of the diverse issues discussed in this work are deep ontological questions. These include what is perhaps the most fundamental one for any eco-political ontology, that of how we conceive of nature and of our place in nature. This encompasses not only how we conceptualize and experience *natural naturata* (natured natured), that is, the field of realized nature as we look upon and observe it but also *natura naturans* (nature naturing), that is, the activity of nature as an ongoing dynamic process of emergence and giving birth.

There are several references in this work to the ancient Ciceronian ideas of 'first' and 'second' natures. These concepts can be useful for challenging certain extreme dualisms between society and nature. However, it is important to realize that these ideas also have the potential to reinforce dualistic thinking if not developed into a more complex, dialectical view of emergence, continuity and difference in nature, and in the multiplicity of natures within nature. As is acknowledged in the Introduction, a key project for anarchist political ecology must be the overcoming of any dualistic conception of the relationship between social, and so-called 'environmental' problems.

We can begin by recognizing that in the most radical and strict sense, there are no 'environmental' problems. The *socius* and the *oikos* are not two separate spheres, and all social problems are, immediately, ecological problems. Furthermore, as part of its project of 'undoing human supremacy', a deeply non-anthropocentric anarchist political ecology will recognize that both the human and non-human exist at every level of being. This includes the levels of ontological nature, physical nature, chemical nature, biological nature, psychological nature and social nature. The present work is a notable advance in this direction, through its attention to the implications of animality and the ways in which other species share with humans diverse aspects of biological, psychological and social nature and through its recognition of our ethical and intellectual responsibility to acknowledge and act on these commonalities.

THE ECO-ANARCHIST CRITIQUE OF DOMINATION

Like the previous volume of the series, this one treats extensively the pre-eminently anarchist question of the nature of domination, which is identical to the question of the nature of liberation or emancipation. Authentic *anarchism* is always at the same time an authentic *libertarianism* in the most radical sense of that term. Anarchism is a quest not for abstract freedom, but, as is discussed in this work, for freedom as the full flourishing of interdependent and co-creative beings, in all their particularity and singularity. The title captures very well this geohistorical situatedness of freedom through the concept of 'landscapes of emancipation'.

A particularly strong point of this collection is the attention that it devotes to the problem of technological domination, as it interacts with other forms of domination. Pélenc, Grisoni, Milanesi, Sébastien and Marzal point out in chapter 3 the fateful arrival of a 'post-political' era in which 'technocratic mechanisms and consensual procedures' predominate, within an official but largely illusory 'framework of representative democracy, free market economics, and cosmopolitan liberalism'. The concept of 'consensual', as they employ it, should be interpreted in the sense of the 'neoliberal consensus' that has, according to conventional wisdom, prevailed since the collapse of the previous 'Keynesian consensus'. As we are now seeing throughout the world, the erstwhile triumph of this consensus and the pseudo-politics that accompanies it generates an authoritarian populist and even neo-fascist reaction. This reaction brings back the 'contestation and agonistic engagement' of the more authentically 'political', but now in its most twisted and demonic form.

Perhaps the most pertinent lesson that we can learn from the concept of 'post-politics' is that the political has been increasingly reduced to a superstructure in relation to a capitalist-statist-megamachinic base that is its ultimate determinant. This infrastructure of domination becomes ever more insidious as it progressively monopolizes not only social institutional structures but also forms of consciousness and sensibility. Thomas and Figueroa-Helland in chapter 4 indicate the depth of this process by depicting it as a process of 'epistemicide' that drives towards an 'episte-mological monoculture' in which technological rationality, along with other forms of instrumental rationality and irrationality, are universalized.

Needless to say, both the state and capital play a central role in such developments. Sporer and Suemnicht point out in chapter 8 that anarchist political ecology is essential to correct a mainstream political ecology that 'has had the misfortune of falling prey to state-thought'. In this, it reflects the reality of the larger society, in which state-thought is all-pervasive in large part because it is reinforced by so many other modes of experiencing. We think like a state not only because of overt ideological indoctrination but because we are taught to perceive, feel and imagine like a state.

Unless anarchist political ecology's critique of domination is heeded, we can expect even more of the same, especially under the pressures of intensifying social and ecological crisis. As Toro warns in chapter 10, 'the direction of national policies in a resource-scarce scenario will be likely managed by more technocratic governments'. He stresses the expansionist and cooptative powers not only of the state but also of capitalism, its sibling in domination, which is capable of turning even 'the discourse of degrowth' on behalf of 'concentration, monopolistic activities and oppression'.

FROM DENIAL AND DISAVOWAL
TO EMANCIPATORY PRAXIS

Another great strength of this volume is its forthright confrontation of the depth of the crisis of humanity and the Earth. It shows an awareness of our present period as the Necrocene, the new era of death on Earth, and of the pervasive denial of the reality of this tragic geohistorical reality and disavowal of its true implications. This is exemplified especially in Fischer's discussion in chapter 9 of the neglected ideas of psychologist and philosopher Erich Fromm, who framed the central world historical struggle as a fight between Eros and Thanatos, the forces of life, creativity and wholeness, on one side, and those of death, destruction and separation, on the other. As Fischer explains, Fromm describes a society in which masses of people do not love life, are attracted to death, and are somehow immune to the fear of 'total destruction'. Such 'necrophilia' develops in a society in which social alienation prevails and free, creative activity is suppressed, in short, in the society of domination, while 'bio-philia', the life-affirming orientation, thrives in a free and cooperative community. As this volume shows, anarchism is the political theory of just such a community. Accordingly, anarchist practice is the politics of eros, of being-toward-birth, of personal and social creativity.

The great irony and tragedy of history is that the dominant necrophiliac civilization that obsessively embraces the tools of annihilation of life on Earth is at the same time a profoundly death-denying culture. Fischer, in chapter 9, exposes the pervasive denial and disavowal of crisis and catastrophe by mainstream environmentalism and by much of the left, which can absurdly and tragically, 'celebrate a 0.7 per cent emissions reduction', a miniscule fraction of what is necessary to avoid collapse, as a 'step toward a true clean-energy revolution'. Similarly, Toro, in chapter 10, notes the astounding level of disavowal on the part of a left that recognizes that climate change above 1.5 to 2° will be catastrophic, yet supports policies that can only be expected to produce exactly such catastrophe. He warns that even proposals for de-growth can be turned into instrument of 'concentration, monopolistic activities and oppression' through an abstractly idealist and voluntarist ideology that promotes small steps in the right direction – measures that may be well-meaning, but in no way threaten the existence of a fundamentally ecocidal system. The task of anarchist political ecology is to demolish all illusions such as these that stand in the way of deep, and truly revolutionary, social ecological transformation.

The message of this important work, and of anarchist political ecology, in general, is quite literally one of life and death. Will we learn to become once again inhabitants of the Earth or will we cling to our delusions of being its masters and conquerors? Will we reclaim our role as organs through which the Earth promotes the flourishing of life or will we persist in our present self-destructive role as the exterminators of life?

Introduction

The Political Ecology of Inhabiting the Earth

Simon Springer, Martin Locret-Collet and Jennifer Mateer

> *we seek to integrate three broad elements: the ecology of people as organisms sharing the universe with many other organisms, the political economy of people as social beings reshaping nature and one another to produce their collective life, and the cultural values of people as storytelling creatures struggling to find the meaning of their place in the world.*
>
> – William Cronon, "Kennecott Journey: The Paths Out of Town" (1992: 32)

> *What's the use of a fine house if you haven't got a tolerable planet to put it on?*
>
> – Henry David Thoreau, *Familiar Letters* (1895)

FROM A BOUNDED ECOLOGY OF PLACE TO A GLOBAL LANDSCAPE, AND BACK

It was late October in Amsterdam and the weather was what you would expect from a typical Dutch autumn: cold, damp with intermittent sunny spells that turned the canals into mirrors. One of the members of this writing collective, Martin, was about to conduct an interview. He checked the address on his smartphone and made his way into the tiny, steamy corner café where his interviewee had arranged for them to meet. There is a reason why this meeting didn't happen in a more formal setting and why he would later have to deal with a background of reggae music on the recording. Far from having an office space, the friendly group-like structure the interviewee was representing didn't even have a legal status at the time of the interview. During the hour that followed, she explained in detail how she and a couple of dedicated volunteers had to work in a quasi-state of emergency. The hundred-year-old, one-hectare community garden they all had allotments in was about to be

1

turned into a surface-level car parking while waiting for future development. In a matter of months, they had assembled a community, held consultations, conducted research, gave interviews to local newspapers and sat through meetings with all the stakeholders including the major university that was to take ownership of the land, as well as the city council of Amsterdam, the current landowner. Even though the development of a new academic building was still planned for the following year at the time of the interview, the temporary surface-level car parking was now out of the picture and the site was being used as both a community garden and as a space of research and education on food and environment. Of course, the whole story is a little more complex – and still unfolding. But it is a textbook case of political ecology and one of the reasons why this book exists.

While half of the world population now live in cities, a proportion expected to reach 66 per cent by 2050 according to a recent United Nations report on World Urbanization Prospects (2014), the global stock of ecosystem services has decreased overall (Millennium Ecosystem Assessment 2005, Wu 2014, Dallimer *et al.* 2011). These figures may be common knowledge for anyone versed in urban and environmental studies, their juxtaposition nonetheless unravels one of the major challenges for any research concerned with human–environment interactions: a majority of human beings will now primarily access and interact with nature in urban areas. A side effect of such a radical and brutal change is that the emotional distance between citizens and nature is de facto increasing (Bertram and Redhanz 2015), therefore damaging an erstwhile organic connection when it is needed more than ever. Indeed, this increased distance means a dramatically reduced awareness of the fundamental interdependency between humankind and nature, threatening to dull the feeling of emergency which should be felt in the face of the aforementioned decline of ecosystems worldwide – and prompting us to address Thoreau's inquiry in the opening epigraph once again with a renewed feeling of urgency and existential implication.

Meanwhile, over the last several decades, scholars and practitioners have progressively acknowledged that we cannot consider cities as the place where nature stops anymore, resulting in urban environments being increasingly appreciated and theorized as hybrids between nature and culture, entities made of socio-ecological processes in constant transformation (Whatmore 2002, Murdoch 2006, Francis *et al.* 2008). This re-theorization has led to the recognition that there is not only one nature, but *natures* in the plural, historically, geographically and socially shaped, as well as discursively constructed by politics, activists, scientists and NGOs (Mac-Naghten and Urry 1998). No longer seen as an 'ornamental fashion' (Sukopp 2003: 301), nature has revealed itself in all its complexity and has recently made its way to the forefront of urban studies, unravelling how there is a multiplicity of urban natures that unfold as 'existing, possible, or practical socio-natural relations' (Kaika and Swyngedouw 2011: 02). Spanning the fields of political ecology, environmental studies and sociology, this new direction in urban theory emerged in concert with global concern for sustainability and environmental justice.

This convergence in urban and environmental thinking is worth noting for it emphasizes the *inter*-connectedness of the social and ecological spheres and the way the urban landscape integrates, interacts with and depends upon all other landscapes found within the wider environment, but is also responsible for its degradation through its activities. In fact, in Lefebvre's (2003 [1970]) view, the twentieth century has been marked by a major switch from people dwelling in cities to a global urban society, spreading far beyond city boundaries and making them obsolete in a way. There has been a disappearance of the rural/urban divide, as it used to be known, giving way to a global urban landscape within which cities are but one form of urbanization (Lefebvre 2003 [1970]). What we want our landscapes to look like accordingly becomes the pivotal question. There is an interesting and quite revealing synchronicity of the post-industrial world, which arose alongside the emergence of the geological era of people, the Anthropocene, where a fully urbanized society interacts with and impacts on an anthropic nature at a global scale. For better or sadly often for worse, humans now represent 'an integral part of virtually all ecosystems' (Redman *et al.* 2004: 161). All landscapes have become human ones in some capacity. In recognizing the impact of humans, there should also be an acknowledgement that post-modern cities are but one possible landscape, one form of urbanization – an epitome as much as a re-invention (Short 2006), but also much more. They are no longer the cities that subdue and master resources, they are the cities that fit in a wider world in which dependence on finite resources has grown, along with the threat that humankind might directly compromise its future ability to tap into these resources (Pickett *et al.* 2011). From a wider perspective, this echoes the growing environmental concern of the last fifty years, which at first smouldered as a slow burn, but has increasingly became widespread and now rage with all the fury of an inferno. The fires of anxiety about the current health of our planet are embodied by the many summits, conferences and landmark documents, such as the famous Bruntland Report titled 'Our Common Future' (Death 2014).

In this context, the commons have made a strong come back on the political agenda, along with the notion that natural resources are indeed our common good. This involves a re-imagination and reinvigoration of landscape along emancipatory lines. The notion of commons, through its original incarnation of common land, dates back to medieval England where it helped landless serfs sustain their livelihood. The 'modern' conceptualization of the commons (as common resources) has been extensively discussed for the last several decades (Eizenberg 2011), especially since Elinor Ostrom's Nobel prize winning work demonstrated that the so-called 'tragedy of the commons' can be avoided when actors favour co-operation in their management of common resources, ensuring a more sustainable development and equitable future (Vollan and Ostrom 2010). While Ostrom's work made important political strides, in many ways, it simply rearticulated and reinvigorated the ideas of mutual aid and cooperation that anarchists like Peter Kropotkin (1902) had laid down a century earlier. Nonetheless, the benefits of urban citizens' participation and involvement in urban green commons start to emerge: they help promote health and wellbeing, an improved quality of life (reduction of crime, sense of place, and an increase in social cohesion), but also the preservation of an ecological memory of place while helping to maintain the green infrastructure of cities (Dennis and

James 2016). In short, they are landscapes of emancipation. Beyond their already acknowledged environmental and ecological benefits, there is soaring evidence that ecosystem services and cultural ecosystem services also vastly benefit human life by improving physical health, mental health and overall wellbeing or by building up social cohesion (Keniger *et al.* 2013, Gaston 2013). In light of this research, the political ecological questions of production, accessibility, benefits and losses become even more imperative to reimagining the world that we inhabit and how we chose to inhabit it (Whitehead *in* Death 2014).

Unbalancing traditional modes of analysis, this emerging conception of the world, as a multiplicity of interlinked landscapes at a global scale, calls to develop new analytic tools, breaking down scales, hierarchies, dependencies and borders, as we have conceived them so far. The connection to anarchism in such a project should be clear, and it is precisely why we see so much value in articulating an anarchist political ecology. Common goods, resources, or lands constitute a profoundly disruptive idea in a capitalist, neoliberal environment that is premised upon individual property rights. But the commons is also increasingly perceived as a 'prime conceptual tool for ensuring sustainability and the rights of future generations' (Mishori 2014: 338), centred on intergenerational justice, transmission and preservation. The commons also offers new pathways to explore on all levels, including the political, the social, the environmental, and even in assisting us in resolving economic tensions. The commons is, after all, something that is meant to include us all regardless of age, gender, race, or species, where a multiplicity of diverse interest and ideas can and will find space to manifest. The commons is a living, breathing manifesto of how we are meant to inhabit the Earth. But it is not a fixed entity or a completed story but rather a continually unfolding narrative, a rugged and beautiful landscape, with many twists and turns, peaks and valleys as we negotiate our collective interests.

The commons is a call for action and resistance to protect what is not only our common good but our common responsibility and which enables our survival as a species, as highlighted in Pelenc *et al.*'s study of resistance to imposed mega structures in this volume. The commons act as a constant reminder that there is a need to take care of one another, as a community, while living in harmony with the planet we inhabit, enacting cooperation rather than competition for the survival and flourishing of all. The preservation and reinforcement of the commons is accordingly an essential and profoundly anarchist project. The commons reminds us of the anarchist guiding principle that theory should never be divorced from practice. Our conceptual efforts at reading and deciphering the world differently should always be aimed at transforming and bettering the conditions under which we inhabit this world (Auclair in this volume, Clough and Blumberg 2012). With theory and practice constantly informing each other, we can begin to solve the many challenges that face the future of humanity, such as food sovereignty (see Thomas and Figueiroa Helland in this volume), and furthering understandings of de-growth if we are to preserve natural resources and limit environmental damages. There also lies an invitation to depart from the rationalized, Western-centric conceptions and imaginaries that have been academia's mainstay for as long as academia has existed.

Indigenous, de-colonial, queer and other alternative epistemologies and ontologies are now blooming, which enhance and augment an anarchist endeavour to engage with the world (Barrera in this volume, Lawhon *et al.* 2014). Whenever we act in ways that break the mould, we can begin to push back against domination, the logic of profit and the exploitation of resources in ways that begin to map out our collective freedom and trace the contours of emancipation for all life on Earth (Springer *et al.* 2012, Springer 2016).

POLITICAL ECOLOGY AS EMANCIPATION

Political ecology affirms itself as a perfect intellectual toolbox to explore and chronicle the trajectory of common concern for the life of the commons. As a lens of inquiry, political ecology has gained a lot of traction and interest in the academic world in the last decades, where it remains a loosely defined term encompassing a large number of approaches (Clark 2012). Robbins astutely points out that political ecology, more than a strictly defined academic field, is 'a term that describes a community of practices united around a certain kind of text' (2012: 20). It is itself a narrative about the infinitely complex and yet exceedingly ordinary story of life. One could add that it also describes a community of interests and concerns and a certain way of appreciating the landscape. Political ecology is the study of the intertwined relationships between our contested political interests and our economic and social organization in concert with the environment, not merely as humans, but where 'our' should be read in reference to all earthlings in our 'endless forms most beautiful' (Darwin 2008 [1859]). In recognizing and foregrounding the power relations that play out through and with our fellow earthlings, political ecology explicitly aims to politicize environmental issues and the very idea of nature.

Despite the plurality of approaches that political ecology adopts, the genealogy of this idea is quite easily traced. Two major intellectual figures of the nineteenth century, Peter Kropotkin and Elisée Reclus, are widely acknowledged as its founding fathers. Both were respected albeit unorthodox geographers who got into troubles with the scientific and political establishments of their time owing to their affinity for anarchism, which was already being misrepresented and demonized in their time. Interestingly enough, the influence of their work somehow faded in the academic literature following their deaths, even if many anarchists continued to be inspired by their ideas. Within their discipline of geography, their work was all but ignored for over half-a-century, only to be rediscovered in the 1970s, and finally once again celebrated from the 2010s onwards (Springer *et al.* 2012). Following Humboldt, Kropotkin and Reclus broke with the long and prevailing tradition of environmental determinism which stated that the physical condition of any territory determines the moral and physical traits of the humans inhabiting that land, as well as their social organization and activities. Mirroring Darwin and Wallace, they also broke with deeply ingrained imperialist views on race and social domination (Robbins 2012). Most of their intellectual departure, theoretical insurgency and resultant advances in the field can be attributed to their philosophical and political thinking as much as to their concern for social justice and early environmental advocacy. Both prominent anarchists in their time, they rejected the concepts of centrality, the legitimacy of any kind of domination, and from evolutionary theory they had retained the idea that, beyond a dire competition, a certain level of cooperation and symbiotic living was necessary for any species to thrive (Robbins 2012, Springer 2013). As Darwin wrote in the concluding remarks of *On the Origin of Species*,

> these elaborately constructed forms, so different from each other, and dependent on each other in so complex a manner have all been produced by laws acting around us (Darwin 2008 [1859]: 360).

Neither Kropotkin nor Reclus ever characterized their work as political ecology, as the use of the term did not become widespread until the 1970s, but they most certainly laid its foundations with their conception of interdependent human–environment interactions, extensive and rigorous fieldwork and a decidedly non-centralist approach to viewing the world (Robbins 2012, Springer 2013).

The current state of the contemporary world is characterized by megaprojects, endless growth imperatives, hyper mechanization, ever-deepening industrialization, widespread dispossession and a broad range of technocratic approaches to virtually any given question that can be posed about how we dwell on this planet. If the answer is not packaged in a grandiose and broad ranging veneer, imposed from the top down and laboured over by legions of bureaucrats, officials and pencil pushers, then the vast majority of people now simply, and quite sadly, believe that it is invalid. We have accepted and even openly invited authority over our lives and the modes in which we organize ourselves, our families and our communities, in ways that would befuddle our ancestors. The world is more complex, but this is a condition of our own making, and it is something that can be unmade. In part, this is what a de-growth imperative demands. De-growth is fundamentally a call for reassessing our commitments to the planet. We can commit ecocide, as the cult of growth implores or we can commit ourselves to undoing this vicious and brutal assassination of the living world by aligning our priorities to undoing the sins of our fathers. It is a question of how we wish to dwell in the world. There are other ways of doing things. Other ways we can live upon this Earth that do not require an endless cycle of consumption, profit, exploitation and degradation. There are ways that we can organize that do not demand the voice of authority to guide us. But we must be willing to think and act beyond the depoliticizing discourse that attempts to placate us. The voices that implore us to position economic concerns over environmental ones are loud and imposing, with a great deal of money behind them to intimidate and stultify us into complacency, but we don't have to listen. We have the ability to skip to the tune of our own beat and sing songs of redemption, rehabilitation and rebirth. That is, we can contribute to a political ecology of inhabiting the Earth that is aligned with a demand for emancipation.

Yet in spite of the looming intertwined catastrophes of climate change and the rapid loss of biodiversity, we strangely cling to old modes, repeating the same mistakes again and again. Environmental issues that could be solved through alternatives means of organizing ourselves and the places in which we live our lives are instead turned back to our so-called 'leaders' to guide us. We appeal to authority for guidance, and more often than not, a Marxist political ecology perspective replicates this obsession. But more than ever, the sorry state of the natural world after a century of colonialism, industrialization and extraction exemplifies the need to think about how we would be better served by taking control of the process that shape our livelihoods and structure our lives for ourselves. When we begin to recognize our connectivity to the natural world, the very idea of the large-scale 'solutions' of the state become obvious affronts to our wellbeing. Grassroots initiatives put the power back within our own hands and demand that we work together, with and through our environments, to find answers. Right now the choice remains ours, but we are approaching a point of no return. We either start reorienting our social, political and economic structures towards small-scale systems of permaculture, free association, direct democracy and mutual aid, or the Earth will force our hand. Either way, the balance of the planet will inevitably return to the order and connectivity of anarchism. If we voluntarily go along with Gaia's will, humans might just endure as a species. If we refuse, the Earth will refuse us. In the long march of time, life on this planet will ultimately survive the current extinction event. The only real question is whether we want human beings to be a part of that recovery or not. Anarchy is order, government is civil war and capitalism is apocalypse. It is time to choose.

While there have been some seemingly progressive movements arise in response to the existential crisis we now face, notably Extinction Rebellion, a viable sense of emancipation is not going to happen under the thumb of those groups who pose as a radical while wearing a statist mask. So long as we remain committed to petitioning the state or working within its predetermined parameters, as is the domain of Marxist political ecology, we are simply spinning our wheels. What movements like Extinction Rebellion do then is actually make things significantly worse, because while people think they are rebelling and working to make a change, in fact they are only demonstrating a continuing faith in a leadership that has repeatedly proven itself not to care about our communities but rather in the capitalist bottom line. Despite honourable intentions, these groups continue to legitimize the idea that the state can be reasoned with and will eventually capitulate to the will of the public. But that has never been what states are all about. The state is an institution designed to concentrate power, not to redistribute it equitably. Extinction Rebellion and other Marxist movements like it have consequently set us up for certain failure and forestalled any possible revolution through a sort of pseudo-rebellion. The natural world as we know it today is under siege and humans may or may not survive the fallout of our own transgressions. If we do survive, it will be a massive reset on the political–social–economic system, and what remains will be fundamentally anarchist. In other words, in the aftermath of systemic civilizational collapse, we will see effectively small, tight-knit, hunter-gather groups organized around the principles of mutual aid. One way or another, the future is most definitely anarchist. The choice we are faced with today is whether we want to wilfully embrace such a trajectory to ensure that the violence of this inevitable transition is minimized or whether we will only get their kicking and screaming with an unintelligible loss of life.

STRUCTURE OF THE BOOK

The challenges we have to face call for new ways of organizing the landscapes of our lives and for resistance through everyday practices of space, community life and organization. This realization has drawn us to political ecology as offering a potential answer, but only when framed through the lens of an anarchist tradition that rids itself of the hierarchical trajectory of Marxian views that have heretofore dominated the field. The chapters collected here represent that desire for bringing political ecology into a new, more liberationist light that embraces anarchism, not as a singular ideology, but as a method of realizing a more horizontal balance between and amongst society and nature. The chapters collected in this volume are accordingly thematically and intellectually diverse, precisely because there are many anarchisms, and we have welcomed the plurality of positions that fit within a general anarchist register. What all of these chapters have in common is a desire to explore alternative modes of conceiving, living and organizing the landscapes of our everyday lives in ways that make life more liveable and connected for both human and non-human actors. As such they offer a kaleidoscopic vision that ranges from the global to the local, from the public to the immediate and more intimate, all interrogating both the rationale and the modalities behind our relationships to the environment in ways that strive for a more thoughtful approach to existence. Some reflect on how to foster more holistic, environmentally conscious and responsible ways of life while others make practical calls for action and resistance in the face of irresponsible behaviours, looming threats and imminent danger.

In chapter 1, Andrej Fideršek focuses on how a global human society organized around capitalist economic principles is faced with two significant issues: the rise of inequality and environmental destruction. These overarching systemic problems are a direct result of the linear economy embedded within capitalism. Fideršek then explores how a circular economy can be reclaimed by social ecology and what role de-growth must play in formulating a new economic system. The circular economy itself is in danger of being absorbed by the neoliberal capitalist ideology. Therefore, a new approach is examined with the aim of demonstrating that social ecology, with its focus on *first, second* and *free* nature, is the optimal framework within which the circular economy would be most effective. Attention is also devoted to the antagonism between economic growth spearheaded by the omnipresent forces of *the corporation* and its counterpart – *de-growth* based on local and decentralized grassroots movements with anarchist tendencies. The examination is conducted by focusing on how each system values affects the environmental, social and informational dimensions of our society. Two potential scenarios concerning economic transition are briefly postulated with the aim of preparing grounds for a continuous dialectical process. The chapter is concluded not as a manifesto but as a serious appeal to each individual as well as various communities around the world, emphasizing that the time is ripe for the creation of a new economic system: a system that is benign, as well as regenerative towards ecosystems, that leaves no one behind and that stimulates the inception of platforms for sharing knowledge freely and equally.

In chapter 2, Elizabeth Auclair shows how, against the economic, social and environmental issues that are facing our societies, alternative concepts and models have emerged in recent years, amongst which the two interrelated concepts of de-growth and the commons are gaining a wide audience. These concepts both contribute in establishing a theoretical and practical framework in order to counter the impact of endless growth, privatization and competition encapsulated in the neoliberal capitalistic model. Growing emphasis is currently set on the local level as a way to develop innovative patterns of governance, based on values of sharing, co-deciding and co-construction. In a context of hard competition between cities, a major challenge is notably to limit instrumentalizing heritage for mere territorial branding, tourism and economic matters. So, considering heritage as a commons supposes a significant shift, because it means reconsidering representations of heritage and inventing new management tools where inhabitants, alongside 'experts', decide which heritage elements are considered as fundamental for the population and must be preserved, and by what means. This chapter compares a series of place-based, people-centred experiences in the suburbs of the Paris agglomeration in order to analyse under what conditions heritage can be considered as a commons and to examine the relevance, but also the limits of this approach.

In chapter 3, Jérôme Pélenc, Anahita Grisoni, Julien Milanesi, Léa Sébastien and Manuel Cervera-Marzal focus on how mega infrastructure projects have become increasingly contested in Western Europe after the 2008 economic crisis. One of the most vivid manifestations of this contestation is the resistance movement against the 'unnecessary and imposed mega-projects'. The place-based struggles that belong to this movement do not only fight against the particular infrastructures that are to be built on their territories but against the world its represents. In this sense, they participate in the re-politicization of the environment. By bringing together elements from political ecology, radical democracy theory and anarchist geography, this chapter provides the first comprehensive analysis of the 'unnecessary and imposed mega-projects' resistance movement and highlights its relevance as both an 'object of study' and 'a subject of change' (social movement and transformative force) in the construction of an anarchist political ecology. It first explains how political ecologists conceptualize environmental de-politicization before giving an overview of the 'unnecessary and imposed mega-projects' resistance movement. Under the auspices of radical democracy, the authors build their theoretical framework by establishing a dialogue between Simon Springer's conception of public space and Oskar Negt's concept of oppositional public space. In the final section, they illustrate this framework by analysing the discourse of the 'unnecessary and imposed mega-projects' resistance movement through the lens of oppositional public space. Pelenc *et al.*

conclude by arguing that this movement creates an opportunity to re-politicize the environment, and thus an opportunity to develop an anarchist political ecology.

In chapter 4, Cassidy Thomas and Leonardo E. Figueiroa-Helland expose how with the entrenchment of the Anthropocene, the world's food systems have gradually shifted away from smallholder agriculture, locally controlled by indigenous and peasant communities, towards a globalized agro-industrial model characterized by state and corporate ownership, technocratic management, mechanized monocultures and the use of exuberant amounts of artificial chemical inputs. This on-going transformation has devastated both biological and cultural diversity. While biodiversity loss is often considered one of the gravest crises of the Anthropocene in its own right, its intimate connection to the erosion of cultural diversity must be acknowledged. This situation is because indigenous and smallholder lifeways often embody ancestrally rooted and locally adapted ecological knowledges that underpin autonomous livelihoods while simultaneously nurturing the health and agro/biodiversity of local ecosystems. As colonialism, modernization, capitalism and developmentalism have enclosed ecosystems and turned nature into resources in the service of anthropocentric industrial expansion, land-based indigenous and peasant communities have been dispossessed and displaced, along with their bioculturally adapted knowledge praxes. In their stead has come the expansion of a globalized industrial food system, whose technocratic monocultures erode both biological and cultural diversity. This chapter locates food sovereignty praxis in relation to anarchist theorizing and explains how the growing transnational food sovereignty movement challenges some of the key structures that underpin the hegemonic food system and the sociobiodiversity crisis it precipitates. Their arguments support the conclusion that decentralized local food systems informed by indigenous and agroecological knowledge are key to addressing the growing sociobiodiversity crisis.

In chapter 5, Martin Locret-Collet explores how urban green commons has recently emerged in academic and non-academic literature as holding a potentially powerful capacity to reshape the way we live in urban environments. Embodying a more participative, progressive type of citizenship and also echoing a certain alternative Zeitgeist, blending environmental awareness, a longing for truly democratic and participative movements, the development of the sharing economy as much as peer-to-peer networks, open-source software and the growing 'wikisation' of knowledge. A combination of common interests and physical spaces in cities, urban green commons and commoning initiatives acknowledge the criticality of an increased cultural and social diversity and have slowly started to reshape the geometries of power relationships and interdependences in cities. The growing lack of financial and managerial capacities from local authorities and public powers also favours their emergence, and urban green commons have re-developed vacant or disused spaces. By exploring anarchist conceptions of space, place and territory, this contribution highlights place-making as an active, on-going and perpetually challenged process, which eventually proves to be fundamentally at odds with the modernist, neoliberal arrangement of the city based on a functionally defined, consumer-oriented geography. Here, Urban Green Commons are presented as arrhythmic spaces that help develop diachronic environmental politics emancipated from electoral agendas and foster intergenerational justice through the transmission of place-based environmental knowledge and social values.

In the following chapter, Gerónimo Barrera presents a series of reflections around the meanings of an 'anarchist political ecology' framework. His approach departs from contemporary critical accounts on anarchism and moves to engage interrogations of 'ecology' and its conflictive genealogy considering Elisée Reclus' work. The first part of the chapter pushes to disturb and reflect on what an anarchist political ecology frame could do. The aim is not to argue for 'an anarchist political ecology' but to build on and with various voices to attend a more dynamic, heterogeneous and open-ended perspective through which understandings and practices of care, conservation and management of the environment are made. Gustav Landauer and Voltairine de Cleyre are the two figures the author follows, considering their contradictory, evolving and complex sets of ideas and practices, to reach what he names the 'darkness' of anarchists' landscapes. The second section then draws on his interest and previous work around ontologies and the pluriverse to discuss what a non-hierarchical/non-coercive frame could mean. Here landscape is a central concept, specifically the narratives that have been emerging around it as a form to understand human–non-human relations. The chapter problematizes 'landscape' as a notion and narrative to avoid predetermined definitions and proposes to travel across it and with it as part of the same reflection; certainly not to define nature or essential qualities of an 'anarchist landscape'.

In chapter 7, Gregory Knapp posits that if geographers have long seen Kropotkin and Reclus as pioneers, many anarchist thinkers who were not geographers have also engaged with geographical themes, including themes relevant to cultural and political ecology. In the mid twentieth-century United States, Kenneth Rexroth and Paul Goodman were significant discontents to modernist centralism and its ecological and cultural consequences during and after World War II, operating respectively out of west coast and east coast contexts. The east coast Black Mountain School and the west coast San Francisco Renaissance owed much to these anti-Stalinist figures who combined a concern for environment, urban design, poetry, Gestalt psychology, local creativity and global affairs. An examination of the life and work of Goodman and Rexroth helps in understanding the milieu which produced the initial generations of cultural and political ecologists and which still indirectly informs the work of young regional political ecologists and cultural geographers working at the periphery of the global economy. The identification of these early thematic connections is not just of antiquarian interest; the connections imply that the possibility exists of rooting cultural and political ecological work in American literary and intellectual history, as well as with currents in France, Britain and Germany. These writers responded to a perceived situation of environmental and cultural crisis which has become far more commonly shared. It may be time to re-read these writers and recognize their early membership in our interpretive communities. These men of letters would perhaps welcome current work but might be upset at the prestige accorded to academic and bureaucratic intellectual gatekeepers.

Chapter 8 is by Ryan Alan Sporer and Kevin Suemnicht, where through an investigation of the off-grid Earthship housing movement, they draws lessons that have positive implications for the nascent literature of anarchist political ecology. The authors argue that while mainstream political ecology has successfully criticized the liberal bourgeois foundations of environmentalism, it has not been able to move beyond the critique of the state to the question of whether the state itself is an appropriate or even viable vehicle for sustainable environmental practices – let alone environmental justice. Sporer and Suemnicht explore how the off-grid movement, in general, and Earthship building and dwelling, in particular, create avenues for people to partially escape the violence of the capitalist state and assemble more egalitarian forms of life. Through off-grid housing, people attempt to create convivial more-than-human relationships based upon anarchistic practices of mutual aid and autonomy. Lastly, there is an inherent limitation to off-grid housing as a politics as there is little to no broader mobilization or confrontation. Nevertheless, the Earthship movement stands as an example of how an emancipatory landscape can be built within an anarchist political ecology movement.

In chapter 9, Dan Fischer argues that mimicking the state's 'Green Scare' against environmental activists, many environmentalists internally repress their own movements' visions, strategies and tactics that might contribute to an eco-anarchist social transformation. Denouncing those who employ militant direct action tactics and advocate non-reformist solutions, the non-profit-industrial complex suppresses the very real ability of environmental movements to challenge world capitalism and build viable dual power institutions. Materialist and ideological explanations are necessary but not sufficient to account for this fear of wild nature and opposition to ecological radicalism. Much explanatory power can be found in the social psychological works of the libertarian Marxist Eric Fromm. Based on Fromm's contention that people living under conditions of incomplete freedom will desire their own oppression and develop a 'necrophilic' passion for destruction, this chapter argues that movements campaigning only half-heartedly for an ecological society will be unable to sincerely desire substantive green social change. Fromm's suggestions for fostering a biophilic or life-loving culture can be as useful to struggles for the liberation of non-human beings as it is for struggles of humans. In reaching an ecological society, collectively confronting psychological barriers may be as necessary as challenging material and ideological barriers. Using Fromm's framework, this chapter explores two symptoms of the internalized Green Scare. First, it looks at how mainstream environmental groups have adopted the state's discourse of 'eco-terrorism.' Second, it explores how these groups knowingly promote compromises that enable ecological catastrophe. Fischer concludes that an everyday resistance of human and non-human beings to capitalistic, extractivist, nihilistic ways is already taking place, all for a love of life which may well be the most important, revolutionary act of all.

Finally, Francisco J. Toro posits that de-growth strives to guarantee a set of political requirements to be implemented by means of a voluntary transition in all aspects of our everyday lives. In a nutshell, de-growth partisans are convinced that a monitored and guided de-growth has to be based on *bottom-up* strategies rather than the *top-down* practices which have characterized the policies for sustainability by both developed and developing countries, even following the dictation of trans-national companies and financial lobbies. Is this a call for an abolition of state and bureaucracy? On this point, there can be conflicting positions about preserving to a greater or lesser extent the political institutions linked to the capitalist state. Indeed, three fundamental critiques to the State have been identified: (a) as a repressive machine serving the economic status quo; (b) as an ideological machine serving the axiom of economic growth; and (c) as the main agent of productivism. This chapter analyses how important an anarchist approach might be in order to question the role that capitalist state and institutions have in environmental management, considering a scenario of economic contraction within a neoliberal ethos of nature–society relationship and how the anarchist utopia might help to materialize a landscape of post-statist de-growth, in which cooperation, the commons, food sovereignty and self-sufficiency ought to be the basic tenets.

INHABITING THE EARTH DIFFERENTLY

Doreen Massey reflected on landscape as a constant provocation that forces one to question the very notions of belonging, location, connection and nature (Massey 2006). It may be argued that landscapes, especially urban and anthropogenic ones, are also transgressions that are a constant push to interrogate oneself, to reconceive what is urban or natural, or more accurately, what is the city and what transcends its boundaries. Urban landscapes force us to transgress the traditional categories of natural and artificial, social and ecological, local and global, and because of the subtle prints left by connection and exchange with the wider world, they represent a constant push to question the idea of borders and frontiers. Deciphering any landscape thus transcends the usual boundaries imposed on our thinking. We could say that domesticated landscapes now comprise 'the majority of terrestrial space on Earth' (Coldings and Barthel 2013: 157), and be finished there, or we could look to the ways in which a 'wilderness' still exists. Our interpretive reading is key. Following Pickett and McDonnell (1993) and Pickett *et al.* (1997), Francis *et al.* (2012: 183) have argued that the study of urban ecosystems requires transdisciplinary work 'across the social/ecological divide'. Transgression consequently becomes constant and the call to re-think the relationship between 'the anthropic', 'the natural' and 'the urban' cannot be ignored, for, as Creswell (2004) states, landscapes are something we don't inhabit or occupy (like places), but something we look at. Indeed, it is in the interpretation of landscape that the provocation happens: we are presented with the deep interconnectedness of the natural and the social. More subtly perhaps this process is one of co-creation. By looking at landscapes, we shape the very idea we have of them, of the interactions between nature and society that take place there, and in doing so we begin to reshape these landscapes since 'nature' 'is produced via uneven patterns of spatial relations that emerge in the form of the landscapes of our lives, but also in the form of our ideas of these landscapes' (Prudham and Heynen

2011: 224). We are thus not only provoked by landscape but are simultaneously always shaping it by looking at it and trying to make sense of it. To be human is to constantly infuse landscape with cultural and social values and with our aspirations, hopes and concerns (Bratina Jurkovic 2014, Gabriel 2014).

To dream of a landscape of emancipation means freeing us from the chains of colonialism and the dominating impulse that this violent process involves. It means ending the extractive and exploitative practices that take our shared Earth for granted by accumulating resources in the interest of greed. But we also want to insist that an emancipatory landscape aligned to the liberation of natures and the undoing of human supremacy involves putting an end to the dualism of nature being positioned as somehow oppositional to humans, which renders it as something to be commandeered, conquered and controlled. Emancipation in this sense means the integration and reconnection of humanity within the landscapes, processes, flows and systems of the Earth. It is to reposition humans not as stewards serving a higher purpose, which is still indicative of an outsider status but rather as equal participants and beneficiaries of the beautiful and unfolding ballet of mutual aid, which is the lifeblood of this planet. While most of the chapters included here do not focus on landscape in the traditional academic sense of the term, they each contribute to the development of our thinking and practice of dwelling in the world differently, to the imagination of our potential forms of organization and to envisioning the geography of inhabiting the Earth in ways that are emancipatory for both human and non-human agents. We recognize that there are different ways to achieve this goal, and these chapters are reflective of the plurality of positions that can be taken towards a more emancipatory horizon. The point of this volume is not to offer a single explanation or blueprint of how we can realign the trajectory of our positions as humans, but to demonstrate that there are possibilities to be explored, and thus so too is there hope.

The landscapes of emancipation are ours to be shaped, collectively and through the principles of cooperation, reciprocity and mutual aid with and through the natural world, which after all, is also a human world. Such an interpretive view of landscape does not place it within the strictures of a confined academic practice but rather opens it up where 'landscape is seen as a holon: an assemblage of interrelated phenomena, both cultural and biophysical, that together form a complex whole' (Christensen *et al.* 2017). This definition is what we mean by landscape, and it lays the foundation for an emancipatory approach to understanding our connections to ecology. If landscape ecology 'is an interdisciplinary field of research and practice that deals with the mutual association between the spatial configuration and ecological functioning of landscapes, exploring and describing processes involved in the differentiation of spaces within landscapes, and the ecological significance of the patterns which are generated by such processes' (Christensen *et al.* 2017), then an anarchist political ecology insists on its politicization and prioritizes the virtues of mutual aid, voluntary association and cooperation in its realization. The relationship between humanity and the Earth upon which we dwell is one that is necessarily dialectical, resulting from the myriad ways in which mutual interaction between all of the Earth's inhabitants occurs. It is a dynamic, protean and unpredictable process of mutual determination that goes beyond notions of 'oneness', which implies a sense of static that we wish to avoid. As John Clark (1997: 32) suggests, 'it must be recognized that this interaction includes humanity's struggle with the rest of the natural world', which 'proceeds from conflict as much as from concord'. Inhabiting the Earth then is a delicate balance, an intricate dance that requires our astute attention and a willingness to practice so that we may improve.

But if we are to move and sway with the landscapes, we inhabit in ways that give rise to a more emancipatory framework for all living beings, we need to attune ourselves to the rhythms and melodies that are ubiquitous within the whole of existence. Why do we refuse this music of life and pretend we can't hear its melody? The vibrations of Gaia are ever present. When we listen carefully, she calls upon her orchestra to play for us. The wind blowing the leaves in the trees. The birds welcoming the morning sun. The water trickling over the rocks in a stream. The laughter of children on a warm summer afternoon. The distant howl of a coyote. The cicadas at sunset. The whisper of a bud as it bursts into flower. This is the rhythm of life. It is not a song, it is *the* song. But many of us have forgotten how to listen. Anarchist Political Ecology is about hearing this song. It is about learning how to listen again. To fall in love with the harmonies, to embrace the refrains, to understand the tempos, to recognize the phrasings and appreciate the articulations. When we remember that land (the dirt, the soil, the clay), landforms (the mountains, the rivers, the lakes) and land cover (the trees, the grass, the ice and snow) all have a cultural overlay of human interpretation and activity, landscape itself becomes a song. Within this music rests the seed of emancipation, for the melodies signify our deep and inseparable connection to the Earth. By acknowledging the unbreakable bond between the planet and ourselves, not as one of dominance or exploitation, but rather of symbiosis and interdependence, it allows us to hold the beauty of nature in reverence. Not as something separate from ourselves, but as an integral component of our being. Loving ourselves means loving the Earth, and loving the Earth is the only hope for a future that includes humans. We must begin to inhabit the Earth differently.

REFERENCES

Bertram, C. and Redhanz, K. 2015. Preferences for cultural urban ecosystem services: Comparing attitudes, perception, and use. *Ecosystem Services* 12, 187–199.

Bookchin, M. 1971. *Post-scarcity Anarchism*. Berkeley: Ramparts Press.

Bookchin, M. 1982. *The Ecology of Freedom: The Emergence and Dissolution of Hierarchy*. Palo Alto: Cheshire Books.

Bratina Jurkovic, N. 2014. Perception, experience and the use of public urban spaces by residents of urban neighbourhoods. *Urbani izziv* 25, 107–125.

Clark, J., 1997. The dialectical social geography of Elisée Reclus. *Philosophy and Geography* 1, 117–142.

Clark, J. P. 2012. Political ecology. In *Encyclopedia of Applied Ethics*, 2nd Ed., Vol. 3. San Diego: Academic Press, 505–516.

Clough, N. and Blumberg, R. 2012. Toward anarchist and autonomist Marxist geographies. *ACME: An International E-Journal for Critical Geographies* 11(3), 335–351.

Colding, J. and Barthel, S. 2013. The potential of urban green commons in the resilience building of cities. *Ecological Economics* 86, 156–166.

Creswell, T. 2004. *Place: A Short Introduction*. Oxford: Blackwell.

Christensen, A.A., Brandt, J. and Svenningsen, S. R. 2017. Landscape ecology. *International Encyclopedia of Geography*. Malden: Wiley.

Dallimer, M., Tang, Z., Bibby, P.R., Brindley, P., Gaston, K.J. and Davies, Z.G. 2011. Temporal changes in greenspace in a highly urbanized region. *Biology Letters* 7, 763–766.

Darwin, C. 2008. *On the Origin of Species*. New York, Oxford: Oxford University Press.

Death, C. ed. 2014. *Critical Environmental Politics*. New York: Routledge.

Dennis, M., James, P. 2016. User participation in urban green commons: exploring the links between access, voluntarism, biodiversity and wellbeing. *Urban Forestry and Urban Greening* 15, 22–31.

Eizenberg, E. 2012. Actually existing commons: three moments of space of community gardens in New York City. *Antipode* 44, 764–782.

Forsyth, T. 2008. Political ecology and the epistemology of social justice. *Geoforum* 39, 756–764.

Francis, R., Lorimer, J. and Raco, M. 2013. What is special about urban ecologies? *Transactions of the Institute of British Geographers* 38, 682–684.

Francis, R., Lorimer, J. and Raco, M. 2012. Urban ecosystems as 'natural' homes for biogeographical boundary crossings. *Transactions of the Institute of British Geographers* 37, 183–190.

Gabriel, N. 2014. Urban Political Ecology: Environmental imaginary, governance, and the non human. *Geography Compass* 8, 38–48.

Gaston, K. J., Avila-Jimenez, M. L. and Edmonson, J. L. 2013. Managing urban ecosystems for goods and services. *Journal of Applied Ecology* 50(4), 830–840.

Hardin, G. 1968. The tragedy of the commons. *Science,* New Series, 162(3859), 1243–1248.

Heynen, N. 2014. Urban Political Ecology 1: the urban century. *Progress in Human Geography* 38, 598–604.

Ince, A. 2012. In the shell of the old: Anarchist geographies of territorialisation. *Antipode* 44(5), 1645–1666.

Kaika, M. and Swyngedouw, E. 2012. Cities, nature and the political imaginary. *Architectural Design* 82, 22–27.

Keniger, L. E., Gaston, K. J., Irvine, K. N. and Fuller, R. A. 2013. What are the benefits of interacting with Nature? *International Journal of Environmental Research and Public Health.* 10, 913–935.

Lawhon, M., Ernstson, H. and Silver, J. 2014. Provincializing urban political ecology: towards a situated UPE through African urban studies. *Antipode* 16, 497–516.

Lefebvre, H. 2003. *The Urban Revolution*. Minneapolis: University of Minnesota Press.

Locret-Collet, M. 2017. *Commoning Our Futures? An Anarchist Urban Political Ecology*. University of Birmigham.

Lorimer, J. 2015. *Wildlife in the Anthropocene: Conservation after Nature*. Minneapolis: University of Minnesota Press.

MacNaghten, P. and Urry, J. 1998. *Contested Natures*. London: SAGE.

Massey, D. 2006. Landscape as provocation: reflections on moving mountains. *Journal of Material Culture* 11 (1–2), 33–48.

Millenium Ecosystem Assesment, 2005. https://www.millenniumassessment.org/.

Mishori, D. 2014. Reclaiming commons rights: resources, public ownership and the rights of the future generations. *Law and Ethics of Human Rights* 8, 335–366.

Murdoch, J. 2006. *Post-Structuralist Geography*. London: SAGE.

Ostrom, E. 1990. *Governing the Commons*. Cambridge: Cambridge University Press.

Pickett, S. T. A., Cadenasso, M. L., Grove, J. M., Boone C. G., Groffman, P. M., Irwin, E., Kaushal, S. S., Marshall, V., Mcgrath, B. P., Nilon, C. H., Pouyat, R. V., Szlavecz, K., Troy, A. and Warren, P. 2011. Urban ecological systems: scientific foundations and a decade of progress. *Journal of Environmental Management* 92, 331–362.

Prudham, S. and Heynen, N. 2011. Introduction: uneven development 25 years on: space, nature and the geographies of capitalism. *New Political Economy* 16, 223–232.

Redman, C. R., Grove, J. M. and Kuby, L. H. 2004. Integrating social science into the long-term ecological research (LTER) network: social dimensions of ecological change and ecological dimensions of social change. *Ecosystems* 7, 161–171.

Robbins, P. 2012. *Political Ecology: A Critical Introduction*. Malden: Wiley Blackwell.

Short, J. R. 2006. *Urban Theory: A Critical Assessment*. New York: Palgrave MacMillan.

Springer, S., Ince, A., Pickerill, J., Brown, G. and Barker, A. 2012. Reanimating anarchist geographies: a new burst of colour. *Antipode: A Radical Journal of Geography* 44(5), 1591–1604.

Springer, S. 2013. Anarchism and geography: a brief genealogy of anarchist geography. *Geography Compass* 7, 46–60.

Springer, S. 2016. *The Anarchist Roots of Geography: Toward Spatial Emancipation*. Minneapolis: University of Minnesota Press.

Sukopp, H. 2003. Flora and vegetation reflecting the urban history of Berlin. *Die Erde* 3, 295–316.

Vollan, B. and Ostrom, E. 2010. Cooperation and the commons. *Science* 330, 923–924.

Whatmore, S. and Thorne, L. 1998. Wild(er)ness: reconfiguring the geographies of wildlife. *Transactions of the Institute of British Geographers* 23, 435–454.

Whatmore, S. 1999. Geography's place in the life-science era? *Transactions of the Institute of British Geographers* 24, 259–260.

Whatmore, S. 2002. *Hybrid Geographies: Natures Cultures Spaces*. London: Sage.

Wu, J. 2014. Urban ecology and eustainability: the state of the science and future directions. *Landscape and Urban Planning* 125, 209–221.

Zimmer, A. 2010. Urban political ecology. *Erdkunde* 64, 343–354.

1

An Effective Approach to Circular Economy within the Domain of Social Ecology

Andrej Fideršek

All hitherto history of existing human society is a history of incremental environmental degradation, a struggle for fairer communities and a constant battle for the ownership of knowledge. Since the dawn of civilization, human beings in various social organizations have been impacting the natural world in an ever-increasing manner. Each consecutive industrial revolution greatly enhanced our capacity to manipulate matter and unlock the tremendous amounts of solar energy stored in fossil fuels. This proved to be a boon for human populations and economic activities increased. After the last 'oppressive' social structure (the Soviet Union) fell, prosperity was finally brought upon our planet, and capitalism won the battle for creating meaning in one's life. The end of history has been reached while the societies became wealthier, more developed and freer (Fukuyama 1992). However, the linear trajectory of progress does not withstand scrutiny in the context of social ecology. Once the effects of this rapid development from the eighteenth century onwards are analysed, and the ideological veil is removed, it is possible to determine that there are many flaws in the narrative of the Western industrial ideal of progress under capitalism. For with increasing industrialization came the inevitable increase of consumption of energy and resources (Klein 2014). Since this was under the domain of capitalism, it also brought the inevitable distribution of wealth towards the class of owners and simultaneous oppression of the working class as Piketty (2015) demonstrated. The level of inequality has now reached dizzying heights with four people hoarding more wealth than half of the world, according to an Oxfam report (2017). Furthermore, most consumption occurs in the global North where the top 10 per cent of earners consume more material than half of the global population (Oxfam 2015). Most of the global South not only has less material wealth, but they also suffer a disproportionate share of ecosystem collapse caused by the increasing linear consumption of material in the North. Therefore, it can be stipulated that environmental problems are rooted in social problems (Bookchin 2011), while the neo-liberal economic system treats nature as an externality. Our linear economies powered by dynamism and relentless growth are thus under threat of collapse, mainly due to heavy dependence on fossil fuels accompanied by reckless extraction of primary resources and subsequent disposal of vast mountains of harmful waste. This systemic combination has caused the collapse of many ecosystems and is the leading cause of the current changes observed in our climate. Alas, the situation is so bad that we are entering the period of 'long emergency' as described by Kunstler (2006). The oil supply is dwindling while the demand soars within the framework of global capitalist economies. The inevitable collapse of our linear economies will consequentially entail such global issues as mass starvation, extreme poverty and mass migrations accompanied by a general state of chaos. The collapse could be averted; however, people are locked within the dominant ideology by competition, fearful of losing possessions, blinded by the lights of mass consumption and coerced to play the capitalist game due to existing hierarchical relationships. In addition, humans lack senses to perceive long-term dangers, such as climate change as imminent threats (Goleman 2009). This retards our response to prevent the unimaginable suffering brought by climate change in the (near) future. These factors are disabling the creation of alternatives and mass movements outside the spectrum of consumerism. However, as Bookchin (1990) argues, these conditions should not prevent visionary thinking from emerging.

Admittedly, it is impossible to have technologically advanced human societies with zero impact on the surrounding ecosystems (Jensen 2006). Our spaceship Earth is vast and provides for everyone, with a caveat though. Our consumption must decrease drastically to return within the overshoot boundary of our planet, and the dream of infinite economic growth must perish. Personal change does not equate to social change (Jensen 2009). A long-lasting change can only be derived from a concerted effort of dedicated groups of individuals. Thus, to overcome the future challenges, we need a new universalism, an economic system that is universally and particularly applicable without damaging the vast diversity of human societies and ecosystems (Žižek 2017). An economic model based on ecology, humanities and open source knowledge. An avenue for such an exploration could as well be provided by the re-emerging concept of circular economy embedded within social ecology and underpinned by de-growth. Therefore, a three-pronged approach for tackling the environmental crisis and rampant inequality shall be examined in the following paragraphs.

SOCIAL ECOLOGY

Social ecology was engendered in academia by Mumford, Dubos and Bookchin (Morris 2017), while Kropotkin (1955) and Reclus (1905) first raised the issues that are now the core of social ecology: a communitarian society based on ecology, ethics and equity and supported by direct democracy enveloped in a confederate setup. It aims towards a transition from capitalism to a libertarian, socialist and ecological economic system. Its embodiment would be a post-scarcity world, free of hierarchies and attuned to natural boundaries. Such a system would foster cooperative and reciprocal relationships between diverse groups of people without impeding innate human desires, such as freedom and creativity. Nature would assume a much greater role in the economic system since all that is, stems from nature. Bookchin (1995) depicted 'first nature', the biological nature, as: 'cumulative evolution of ever-differentiating and increasingly complex life-forms with a vibrant and interactive inorganic world'. It is a dynamic force that exhibits progressive continuity of ever more complex and elaborate life-forms with an ability to conceptualize, communicate and understand information in symbolic terms. The extrapolation of awareness, sentience and systematization of knowledge are the basis for 'second nature', meaning human civilization. The capacity to work in concerted groups by systemically manipulating the environment with civilizational tools, such as technology and science, elevated us above the realm of purely first nature. Thus, natural evolution gave us the ability to alter first nature. However, second nature, a cultural, social and political 'human nature' enveloped and subjugated first nature. In the context of capitalism, this intertwined relationship is epitomized by Bookchin (1995) as: 'The domination of nature by man stems from the very real domination of human by human'. This point must be addressed thoroughly, because only when hierarchical relationships are discarded can we reach our true potential. People cooperate and, as Kropotkin (1892) argued, under the thin canopy of competition there lies a massive field of cooperation. Capitalists, of course, praise competition but ignore cooperation. The aim of social ecology henceforth is to develop new relationships between individuals within a community from which to ensue fecund, reciprocal and empathic societies whose primary objective is to satisfy the basic psychological, physiological and material needs of a given geographical population, regardless of class, identity, or gender. This should also involve a more equal distribution of power, via direct democratic assemblies and connections in global organizations underpinned by the same ground rules (Morris 2017). In addition, these approaches are more aligned with innate human motivations that are autonomy, mastery and purpose, as described by Pink (2009). It represents a world of play and not work, of cooperation and not competition and fostering healthy relationships with both each other and our habitat. However, second nature is an unfinished story. It is marred by class, state, race and gender divisions, as well as its over-excessive negative influence on the first nature. It is incomplete while its future in the biosphere entirely depends on transitioning into a new economic and social system. Bookchin (1995) calls this 'free nature': a conscious and ethical nature that would diminish suffering in both first and second nature; the tool for achieving this goal is knowledge. Knowledge is power and has in the past systematically been kept only for the elites to preserve their status. Alternatively, as Swartz (2008) postulated, 'Information is Power. But like all power, there are those who want to keep it for themselves'. Now that we have a decentralized information network, the internet, we can finally glimpse into a collaborative future of sharing and building upon the existing knowledge base. Examples such as Wikipedia, to which everyone can contribute; *The Stanford Encyclopedia of Philosophy*, which is expertly curated and freely available; and Scihub, the pirate journal website all prove the popularity of peer-to-peer information transfer (Oxenham 2016).

As there are three broad axioms – Nature, Knowledge and People – it is possible to determine that social ecology assumes a fractal approach to its organic development. The self-similar extrapolations of social ecology stem from seeing nature as inherent to our being, to foster symbiotic relationships between all people and to share knowledge freely and equally amongst all. This setup could bring us towards Bookchin's free nature (1995). However, this social theory needs a robust economic model as its foundation. Such a model could be found amongst various ecological, economic theories under the banner of the circular economy.

CIRCULAR ECONOMY

When thinking about new economic models, it is necessary to acknowledge cultural patterns within the dominant anthropogenic worldview as well as material needs of sustaining the global human population. We live on the verge of post-capitalism, where individuals are atomized despite advanced communicational technology and where robots are replacing human labour. There is also a vast discord between what is known and how it is acted upon (i.e., Climate change, Panama Papers, terror funding, etc.). Another important issue to acknowledge is that currently prosperity is perceived to be achievable only by growth through intensive extraction, consumption and waste of resources.

The biggest factors catalysing the collapse of capitalist industrial societies are unequal wealth distribution (Ahmed 2014) and consequent rising levels of inequality, as well as treating nature as an externality to our economic system, thus leaving a negative impact of human economic activities on the natural world (Roberts 2013). For guidance in the pursuit of new economic models, we can rely on the planetary boundaries derived by Rokstrom et al. the notion of planetary overshoot day and the doughnut model by Raworth (2017) that shows connections between the well-being of people and ecosystem health.

Despite the consequences of climate change and the consequently unavoidable adaptations to Western lifestyles, the future still offers hope. One of the reasons being renewed interest in the concept of circular economy. In the realm of thermodynamics, there are but two polar economic systems. They can be linear, circular, or various configurations of both, regardless of the dominant ideological assumptions (e.g., capitalism vs. communism). The distinction between the two is clear, with the focal point being *emergy* usage[1] as well as effectively keeping the materials within the material and biological loops. The linear economic model, however, has been the underlying base for the success of capitalism (Klein 2014). This has brought dire consequences, including biodiversity loss, ocean acidification, rampant releases of greenhouse gases and so on (Monbiot 2010; Lynas 2011). However, the circular economy (CE) is fundamentally different. It represents an economic system that is not ideologically driven but instead resource-based and needs-related – an economy of plenty, a post-scarcity economy that engenders fecund and healthy patterns of human development alongside natural boundaries. It utilizes various preventive approaches to waste from bottom up and can be defined as:

an alternative to a traditional linear economy (make, use, dispose) in which we keep resources in use for as long as possible, extract the maximum value from them whilst in use, then recover and regenerate products and materials at the end of each service life. (WRAP 2014)

CE has no one author. The idea and the existing principles were added and expanded by various contributors from diverse fields of science over the course of history, most prominently over the last fifty years:

- Boulding (1966) popularized the term 'Spaceship Earth' in academia,
- Stahel (1982) highlighted the concept of product life cycle (PLC),
- Pearce and Turner (1990) developed an economic model in which nature is not an externality,
- Greyson (2007) formed an instrument of insurance for product durability,
- Braungart et al. (2007) developed a cradle-to-cradle approach to product design,
- Ho (2013) connected circular thermodynamics and the CE and
- The Ellen MacArthur Foundation (2015) popularized CE, making it a mainstream concept.

Once all the various contributions are distilled, it is possible to say that the end goal of CE is to emulate natural systems (e.g., biosphere, forests, oceans, etc.) whose intrinsic characteristic is to maintain the flows of energy within the dynamic system boundaries, thus achieving zero-net entropy. Therefore, through the prism of circular thermodynamics, CE represents an economic activity that aims to minimize energy-dissipating flows and maximize non-dissipating cyclical flows throughout space and time (Ho 2013). The path towards the zero-net entropy ideal lies in the optimization of systems (e.g., production process, ownership, consumption) rather than components (e.g., product features). The optimization process entails non-linear thinking, emphasizing the circular nature of living systems and the application of biological characteristics to design a restorative industrial economy. Such an economy would seek reliance on renewable energy, eradicate waste through design and eliminate the use of toxic chemicals. The main principles can be further outlined as the prevention of virgin material extraction, the effective management of material flows (divided into biological and technical nutrients) and growth through regeneration (Ho 2013; Ellen MacArthur Foundation 2017). It is an iterative and organic model based on several principles that guide its future development.

The CE is an ideologically neutral economic model since its main function is to ensure that all the materials are managed effectively with an ideal zero material loss. However, it represents profound changes to our current models, starting with the production, consumption and ownership of products and services. Worldwide, that economy is largely linear. Matter and energy are wasted through the process of raw material extraction and all the subsequent processes leading to material waste at the end of the product life cycle (PLC). Regardless of the short-term economic gains through the linear process, the effects of this reckless consumption will be felt by the following generations in terms of material shortages,[2] climate change and habitat damage (Klein 2014). However, in the theory of the CE, no material is treated as waste. All the products, from food to electronics, are temporary assemblages of energy or *emergy* for short. This term describes all the various types and amounts of energy required in the procurement process of a given product (Goleman 2009; Roos 2014). The optimization process of *emergy* thus begins at the drawing board and entails simple, durable, reusable and recyclable design. One example of such a design is the cradle-to-cradle (C2C) approach, conceptualized by Braumgart et al. (2006). Some mainstream market examples include Frosch (cleaning products), Bauwerk (parquet), or SENS (e-recycling). In this mode of production, at the end of the PLC, the material is incorporated into new products or processed in 'refurbishment loops' to avoid waste. In addition, the optimal solution is that most finished products are sourced locally via micro-production facilities or the emerging fab-labs[3] (Ede 2017) supported by a flexible and responsive logistics network. Such design reduces the amount of transportation required as the user products are made in the vicinity of its end use. Once these products expire, they can be processed most effectively while the material remains in the local geographic area. Therefore, adhering to the principles of CE simultaneously reduces the need for overseas transport of raw materials and the mining of virgin material while ensuring that communities are materially wealthy.

In the context of consumption, the CE represents an idea that, as opposed to products, we need the service that these products provide, thus the shift from consumer to user, extended producer responsibility and price of products based on *emergy* and PLC (Jackson 2017). Such a transition is necessary to follow the material flow and eventually close the loop, thus making virgin material extraction unnecessary. Ideally, user products would be produced and circulated within a local community. Furthermore, the zero waste hierarchy highlights that the most effective method of waste and CO_2 reduction is to simply consume and produce less. Afterwards comes the maintenance, reuse and refurbishment of products, with recycling being the last resort before the worst option: landfill. Therefore, we need to create flexible webs that connect products with users in the most effective manner imaginable (Lehmann 2011). For example, an average car is used only 5–10 per cent during the time of ownership (Barter 2013). It is an immense waste, but most want to own one. Similar patterns are seen with other products such as washing machines, various electronics, cookware and tools. Sharing is thus the most effective option. Examples of this are already present in the form of car sharing or libraries for tools, appliances and seeds (Ede 2017). Such systems would extract the maximum value through PLC and limit new product purchases. To close the technical loop and for products to remain operational, maintenance will be required. Current examples of this are the expanding product repair and update economic sectors, sprouting globally and applied locally. These mostly grassroots movements are knitting communities closer by sharing and maintaining material wealth. Furthermore, addressing underlying systemic problems (mass consumption, extractivism, economic globalization, etc.) or 'precycling' as opposed to managing symptomatic impacts (corruption, pollution, resource wars, etc.) involves less complexity and less information, permitting a wider participation upon which a culture of cooperation, symbiosis and reciprocity with nature and between people becomes more plausible (O'Rorke 1988).

Although relatively unknown, the concept of the CE is gaining traction and more academic attention around the globe; it was even discussed in detail at the 2017 World Economic Forum in Davos. The benefits of CE implementation are plentiful as it stimulates local employment opportunities, reduces waste and energy consumption and drives greater resource productivity while addressing resource scarcity to deliver resilient local economies with a global outlook (Ellen Macarthur foundation 2017). Thus far, China is the only country in the world to have integrated the CE into law and their national development policy. This yielded thirty industrial eco-parks by 2012, in which the loop of resource flow is closed, and waste (by-products) becomes the resources for new products (Matthews and Tan 2011, 2016; Su et al. 2013). By 2013, strong governmental incentives improved resource intensity by 34.7 per cent and waste intensity by 46.5 per cent,[4] meaning that the resource consumption of raw material is decoupling from economic growth in relative terms. Accordingly, the treatment rate of pollution and waste increased in total by 74.6 per cent.[5] In the context of industrial parks, the state-managed approach seems to work, despite the technological and economic difficulties of connecting various companies and materials in the supply chain. However, economic growth remains imperative. Resource intensity fell by a third between 1990 and 2011, but overall resource consumption rose fivefold during the same period, thus negating the positive environmental aspects of maintaining materials in biological and technical loops (Matthews 2016). For this reason, the CE becomes a mirage in ecological thought (Narberhaus and von Mitschke-Collande 2017). Unlimited growth could hinder the potential of CE and put its effectiveness under question. Similar to the Khazzoom–Brookes postulate,[6] the CE could become a ledger for greater resource consumption in the context of capitalism (Monbiot 2009), counteracting its original purpose and turning it into a greenwashing agent of capitalism, or growth-dependent state socialism.

A similar notion entails changes in ownership which will occur during the transition towards the CE. Products or services and all the materials included could either be corporate owned or communally owned, with no right to repair (e.g., iPhone) or with encouragement for maintenance (e.g., Fairphone), created in light of planned obsolescence or made to last for generations. The question of ownership also pertains to means of production and intellectual capital. New technologies are quickly patented or licensed by corporations as they are obliged by law and ideology to maximize profits, often at all costs. This prevents widespread utilization and sharing information about cleaner technologies (Schnitzer and Ugliati 2007). A communal approach would be better suited as it focuses on the effective and fair use of technology to cover local needs. To update linear into circular economies, a sizeable investment in currently 'non-profitable' technologies[7] will be required. Obtaining regenerative technologies and processes by communal means has an advantage of direct oversight, allowing the effective and quick optimization of material flows. Therefore, the communal ownership of products and services could render corporate power obsolete, with the side effect being materially wealthier local communities and less strain applied on global ecosystems.

The CE applies warmth to the cold, rational economic thought as there is an emphasis on the interconnectedness of human beings and nature. For the system to remain functional, it is essential to acknowledge and synthesize variables, such as intellectual capital, state of natural capital and social capital into the decision-making processes of governments, municipalities and businesses (Su et al. 2013). The synthesis of these factors guides the development of the CE towards the zero-net entropy ideal. Similar to social ecology, it aims to establish economic processes that stem from the preservation of natural capital, the enhancement of social capital and the sharing of intellectual capital. The synthesized ideals of social ecology and the CE can thus be presented in a fractal-form: an algorithmic Turing-esque economy that is geographically iterative, self-similar and based on certain rules. It does not merely match supply and demand in equilibrium but recognizes the complex evolving economic processes with the aim of predicting the optimal material and *emergy* usage. Keeping in mind the closed system (planet Earth) within which we live and the fact that all our actions increase the entropy of this system, we can derive the following definition of the CE within social ecology:

> a geographically iterative economic process based on three axioms (Nature, People, Knowledge) whose outcome informs its continuous socioeconomic function and circular *emergy* utilization over spacetime.

In addition, three paramount questions must be answered to reach the ideal of this fractal-form economy:

- How will this process affect the local and global ecosystem?
- How will this process affect local and global populations?
- How will this process contribute to the common knowledge base?

Answering these requirements represents a blueprint with the potential to create an economy that is not ideologically driven but needs- and resource-related, while economic progress is decoupled from the profit growth assumption. Nature is meant to be regenerated, with rights installed to protect its beauty while people consume less, industries create less but science, arts and humanity thrive more. More economical and philosophic layers are required to provide a synthesis of the complex processes that create the social construct known as the economy; therefore, social ecology could act as a societal, moral and ethical compass, and the CE could present a guideline for new economic models, while de-growth could provide a new general direction of economic progress.

CORPORATION VS. DE-GROWTH

Human economic activities have ravaged the natural world. However, alongside the model of the CE, there is another alternative, the concept of de-growth. Economically speaking, there are two ways to implement CE, corporate (accumulation) or de-growth. Corporate also includes state socialist systems as the centralized decision-making and accumulation of wealth is the basic premise for achieving prosperity (Kallis 2017). Currently, the corporate mode is gaining more traction, with companies such as Coca-Cola, Apple, Ikea and so on showing high levels of interest. They aim to greenwash their intensive production processes and reliance on mass consumption by appearing to embrace the CE. However, de-growth is radically different as it addresses the core of the problem, overconsumption. It is aligned with the principles of social ecology and compatible with the CE. The two shall be contrasted with the main characteristics and consequences being examined.

DE-GROWTH

De-growth is an umbrella term for a set of principles that counteract the problems posed by overconsumption. Proponents of de-growth recognize the consumerist mind-set embedded in capitalist ideology as the greatest threat to planetary boundaries and Earth's carrying capacity. De-growth opposes the extractive, linear and productivist economies that dominated the development of civilization and became more rooted with each subsequent industrial revolution. Many critics oppose de-growth since they perceive it as a model that would lead to poverty, unemployment and a decrease of general well-being. However, this position only makes sense through the goggles of the flawed measure of GDP (Hickel 2017). De-growth aims to increase well-being, freedom and alleviate the human impact on ecosystems. This is achieved through 'non-consumptive' means, such as devoting more time to nature, family, culture, sharing work, consuming less and pursuing personal interests. In this model, the industrial output decreases whereas well-being increases (Kallis 2017). The ideal would be the 1970s levels of consumption when economies were still within the Earth overshoot day for a whole year.[8] De-growth is already seen in many communities that live within local means but are connected globally through the internet. Examples are transition towns or the Catalan Integral Cooperative (CIC), which loosely resemble a global village by utilizing bioregional conditions for their sustenance and improving well-being by accumulating knowledge sourced both locally and globally (Dafermos 2017).

The history of economic crises shows that reducing industrial output is the only reliable way to reduce CO_2 emissions and material extraction (Kallis 2017). The Khazzoom–Brookes postulate (1980) and Jevons paradox (1865) demonstrate that increasing energy or material efficiency only brings more energy and material demand (Kallis 2017). Recycling has similar connotations as the material becomes cheaper, but the quality is usually downgraded, and massive amounts of (fossil fuel) energy are needed for recycling. Why pursue energy efficiency and recycling if we can cut right to the root of the problem and reduce consumption as well as intertwined production processes. As Goleman (2009) highlighted, even a simple recycled glass jar consists of more than 600 interconnected industrial processes, all of them exerting a toll on ecosystems through reliance on fossil fuels to collect, transport, melt and reform the glass. The concept of CE is under similar threat as improved material flows could bring more demand and higher turnover of product use, in most part due to cheaper materials, improved distribution and production processes; coupled with greater affordability for consumers. Thus, individual products owned by individuals worldwide could accumulate, rendering the beneficial effects of prudent material use, useless. However, most products are not scarce but are made difficult to obtain due to marketing efforts manipulating market perceptions and industry collusion to keep prices artificially inflated (Anastasio 2018). Due to improvements in automation, we are about to reach zero-net costs of manufacturing. This will have dire consequences as labour could be replaced by robots, resulting in mass layoffs subsequently leading to a sharp decline in peoples' purchasing power (Rifkin 2014).

This presents a great opportunity to start discussing and implementing policies of de-growth, starting with redistribution and changing the perception revolving around scarcity. The accumulated wealth and material are abundant and could cover the needs of all inhabitants of this planet if redistributed and provided we live inside our means (Hickel 2017). Sharing products and maximizing their use through communal channels, such as libraries, would deprive none of their benefits. Without the ideology to produce more of the same but slightly different things (e.g., smartphones), and harmful practices, such as planned obsolescence, the virgin material extraction would cease to be. As a consequence, there would be less work, less transportation, less industrial output and less energy consumption, in general, but more play, leisure and communal endeavours. Scientific progress could in turn increase as more resources, and social capital could be devoted towards the pursuit of new horizons, while the repetition of production processes, intellectual property and narrow corporate research goals would no longer present a barrier to progress. It is time to stop devouring wealth on a mega-machine of extraction, production and pollution for the benefit of a few inhabitants. For once the priorities change, the accumulated material can be used for benign projects in science, arts, ecology, renewable energy and so on. An example is Costa Rica, whose less intensive industrial economy allowed the entire country to run solely on renewable energy for 300 days in 2017 (Embury-Dennis 2017). De-growth assumes that less consumption and environmental exploitations would diminish the Empire's need for colonization. Therefore, we could finally witness shrinking of the wealth difference between the global North and South.

De-growth provides answers to the three questions of an ecologically sound economy. Once the production and consumption decrease, it is possible to expect amelioration of ecosystems. Change of the industrial modus operandi could free people from mindless work and create a sense of community, care and belonging. The idle masses could then pursue their own interests and receive support for scientific endeavours thus broadening the horizon of communal knowledge.

De-growth answers the requirements of the CE within social ecology as the environmental pressure is reduced thanks to decreased production and consumption, while the positive effects to social capital can be seen in de-burdening the workforce and devoting more time to our inherently motivated activities.

CORPORATION

However, the biggest hurdle to achieving at least a modicum of sustainability is represented by the corporation. At first, the corporation was a benign creation by which the state granted a charter to several companies to act as one entity. It was utilized for big projects that one company or person could not handle. After businessmen realized how powerful their combined efforts could be, it became a permanent feature of human societies. Corporations are differently defined in different countries and by their core of operations (profit- or non-profit orientated). Their ownership structures also vary, ranging from stockholders of various sizes to complete private ownership (Bakan 2004). However, the big business corporation type is the one that exercises the most control over the market. This type shall be the subject of the analysis in the context of social ecology.

Too big to fail, too powerful to let go. The profit-orientated model of the corporation has become the tool of choice, deployed by capitalists to infinitely accumulate their wealth. Through revolving doors which intimately connect corporate profiteers to lawmakers, the corporation can also influence national and international laws (trade agreements). For this reason, various environmental protection laws, health and safety laws and laws limiting accumulation or exploitation of resources are quickly dismantled or difficult to implement. In contrast, laws enabling market liberalization, deregulation and privatization are fast-tracked, often without public approval. Furthermore, it is necessary to note that corporations as legal entities are obliged by law to pursue profit maximization as their primary goal (Bakan 2004). To put it in philosophical terms, neo-liberal ideology acts as a Lacanian 'big Other', enabling profit accumulation to be the sole legitimate goal of corporations, trumping other issues in spite of associated environmental and social harm (Žižek 2011). In addition, capitalism reinforces itself through crisis situations. In the contemporary globalized world, this affects every country to various extents, thus disabling long-term stability of the world's economy (Harvey 2010). Economic stabilization policies are thus prioritized over long-term investments into social safety nets, health care, education, public transport, circular economic models, or ecosystem regeneration. Moreover, relentless profit stimulation is not aligned with the innate human motivations of autonomy, mastery and purpose; as described by Pink (2009). Research into what drives us has consistently proven that the abovementioned three aspects motivate labour disproportionately more than monetary incentives.

The second systemic problem revolves around the notion of externalities. Nature and society alike are perceived as an externality in the neo-liberal model. In return, corporations bear no accountability for the social and environmental cost incurred during business operations. Furthermore, Boulding (1966) argues that the linear economic model, which we continue to follow, is patterned both by environmental impacts (pollution, waste generation) and by social impacts (exploitative, violent behaviour). In addition, unrestrained growth is embedded in the genetic makeup of the corporation, while failure to maximize the wealth of private shareholders leads to socialized austerity. This systemic configuration led not only to environmental degradation and broken local communities but also to economic imperialism, creating stark divisions between global North and South.

Corporations actively undermine environmental protection laws or simply disregard them. For example, a report by the Carbon Majors (2017) showed that just 100 corporations are responsible for 71 per cent of global emissions. One of the most notable recent environmental disasters was the 2011 BP Deepwater Horizon spill, which occurred due to cost-cutting and inadequate safety measures. The subsequent investigation revealed a wider pattern in an industry that is the main perpetrator of environmental problems.

These corporate wrongdoings would not be possible without liberated markets and global logistics networks, transporting immense amounts of cargo[9] from one corner of the planet to another only to be consumed and discarded thereafter. This not only contributes to fossil fuel use, waste issues and greenhouse gas emissions but also opens up a market for illegal activities due to the uncontrollable amounts of cargo being transported daily. Profit-driven objectives combined with apathy to natural capital leads to the mafia specializing in waste management. According to Saviano (2008), mafia clans offer a cheap way of disposing of toxic industrial waste (estimated at accumulated 14,000,000 tons in 2006), which ends up buried under ground, dumped in the sea or composted, thus building up in the food supply chain until unknowingly ingested by consumers. Another example of unaccounted waste is the extremely toxic e-waste site in Agbogbloshie permitted due to loopholes in international laws concerned with second-hand electronic equipment (the Guardian 2014). These examples are just a drop in the ocean of waste and damage produced by our globalized linear and capitalist economy.

Working conditions for labour in developing countries is arguably the most prominent subject of corporate globalization debates. Needless to say, cheap labour was one of the major catalysts of globalization. Due to the abovementioned tendency towards higher profits and exponential growth, corporations often pressure suppliers to deliver goods as cheap and fast as possible. This pressure combined with deregulated foreign economies and loose laws result in a wide array of issues symptomatic of current globalization conditions for the poor. The Rana Plaza disaster in 2013 claimed 1,138 lives due to buyers pressuring the management to proceed with the orders despite warning signs appearing on the factory building (Cleanclothes.org 2014). In 2014, workers from Apple's contractor formed a support group to raise the awareness of their poisoning with potent carcinogens (benzene and n-hexane) while producing gadgets (Who Pays Film 2014). In 2014, the *Guardian* uncovered that slave labour in Thailand is the backbone of prawn production, also sold by top four global retailers: Walmart, Carrefour, Costco and Tesco. Global profit-driven supply chains are a common cause of these and countless other similar tragedies. Furthermore, this mind-set also fails to recognize past mistakes and amend the harms inflicted on the local community. One of the most tragic examples is the Bhopal disaster of 1984. Due to gas leaks in the chemical plant owned by Union Carbide, more than half-a-million people were exposed and 25,000 have died to date as a direct consequence. Ownership was passed to chemical giant DuPont who has also failed to provide a compensation for one of the worst environmental and social disasters in history (Bhopal.org 2014). This exemplifies an indifferent approach to consequences of global corporate operations, which can be traced back to disregard of natural capital and zealous profit orientation. Globalization and corporate thirst for profit also affect workforce in developed countries. Such an example is the city of Detroit, whose population gradually declined from 2 million to 7,000,000, due to heavy reliance on automotive industry (Temple 2013). This sector was a subject of global oil spikes, off-shoring and planned obsolescence (Dannoritzer 2013). These factors damaged the local community in spite of its historical importance and showed that negative effects of corporate globalization could go two ways, correlating to the argument that capitalism solves its crisis through geographical redistribution of its effects. In addition, capitalism is able to constantly reinvent itself, most prominently seen in the number of 'bullshit jobs', rightly called so by Graeber (2016). These jobs[10] contribute little to society but help to expand the corporate influence and consequently devour natural resources, wealth and the time of people. Rampant cases of mental illnesses in the global North such as depression or anxiety (Schumaker 2016) are in part also caused by the meaninglessness of working in the corporate, growth-orientated mega-machine.

Another critical issue revolves around the concept of ownership and intellectual property. Giants such as Monsanto, Syngenta and DuPont-Pioneer currently own more than half of the commercial seed supply and even patent plant genetic codes, claiming them as their own (Genetic Literacy Project 2016). The unprecedented rise of lawsuits concerning intellectual property, extortionate prices of academic journals and difficulties in obtaining non-market-focused science grants suggest that capitalism undermines scientific progress on behalf of profit growth. Science, arts and culture are sacrificed on the altar of economic growth, while the means of free communication (i.e., the internet) are constantly targeted by corporations with an aim to monetize its services. Traditional mass media have long been a subject of corporate monopoly as just six corporations own most of the established U.S. media companies (Lutz 2012). They spew propaganda of consumerist ideology and deprive people of meaningful information (Jackson 2013). Corporations aim to shape our psychology to fully embrace the mass consumption of consumer goods, financial services and transport means, owned by a select few. For example, 54 per cent of financial assets in the United States are owned by only ten institutions, while fourteen corporations control our mobility by owning fifty-four major auto brands (Diaz 2014). Even more worrying is the study conducted by the Swiss Federal Institute of Technology (2011), which determined that 147 companies own and control 40 per cent of the wealth within the multinational commerce network.

The abovementioned underlying systemic processes and outcomes of the capitalist economy raise serious concerns about whether the CE could be implemented effectively within the growth-based capitalist domain. It is also in discord with the fractal-form economic outlook as the processes diverge from the fundamentals of ecological, scientific and humane development. The corporate ways of conduct do not represent a radical systemic change needed to avert the social and ecological crisis as argued by Žižek (2011). The corporation is the main enemy of de-growth and our odds of maintaining our ecosystems. Now, in the second decade of the twenty-first century, we are mainly faced with two options for taming the corporation.

Carrot

The carrot approach represents hope – the hope that capitalists would recognize errors of their ways and embrace the circular and socio-ecological vision of the economy. Ways to achieve social and environmental justice peacefully are numerous and have worked in the past, be it the racial justice movement spearheaded by Martin Luther King, Mandela and his ANC comrades or Norway's Labor party overthrowing the 1 per cent in 1935 (Lakey 2017). These movements changed the course of history. Environmental pressure groups, such as Greenpeace, Friends of the Earth and others, alongside indigenous communities and countless grassroots organizations, have also left a dent in the machinery of capitalism. The results were mostly translated into the creation of governmental environmental agencies, anti-pollution laws and Earth Day. Therefore, hypothetically, a concerted effort of various grassroots organizations around the world, coordinated by global institutions (i.e., the United Nations) and powerful individuals, could lead towards a peaceful transition towards CE and de-growth.

This approach assumes that 'captains of industry' would recognize the benefits of CE, while the people embrace the notion of de-growth into their personal lives. Organized grassroots anarchist movements would push lawmakers towards the implementation of ever-progressive laws, resulting in the final dissolution of the corporation. This, however, should be preceded by the corporation paying and fixing the mess they left on ecosystems (i.e., carbon taxes, price based on *emergy*, land use tax). Afterwards, the means of production, wealth and information would pass into communal hands. The principles of social ecology would be upheld, and over time and effort resulting in Bookchin's depiction of the free nature. The speed of de-growth would have to be staggering as well, with emissions cut by 8 to 10 per cent per year in the North to reach the goal of less than 2C warming by 2100 (Adrian E. Raftery 2017).

The transition is possible due to the wealth already being here. Buckminster Fuller (1969) estimated that we already have all the material excavated that is required for a highly technological civilization. In most parts, the sustainable technology and know-how that could aid de-growth are already here. Restraints on the economy in the form of carbon taxing, *emergy* pricing, or recycling insurance have also been tested alongside communal social organizations. We will need creative commons when it comes to information and geographical commons maintained by people for the people. A globally coordinated and locally enacted approach has the potential to create new economic processes required for the transition.

Stick

The stick approach is the opposite: a desperate measure for a hopeless situation, an outright violent revolution. Corporations have too much power, and they do not want to share it. Various carrot approaches have worked in the past but never put the final nail in the coffin of the capitalist mega-machine. Thus, it is in vain to expect that the capitalist will devolve their power and redistribute their wealth based on sound and scientific arguments. Unfortunately, the Marxist approach of violently seizing the means of production, redistributing wealth and collectivization is often seen as the only way of dealing with the crisis of neo-liberalism. The question that remains, however, is who would initiate and coordinate revolution? Will it be the state, a global institution, or various anarchist collectives? How will it pan out? Will it be globalized or localized, bloody or relatively peaceful? The question of the power vacuum also remains as the old institutions would crumble under the pressure of collective action. Would a global institution (i.e., UN) step in to prevent bullying by powerful individuals and remnants of the corporation? And how will the new rules be enforced on the local and global levels? These are unknown variables with many possible outcomes; however, any action is better than melancholically observing human civilization approaching its final collapse.

CONCLUSION

It is quite possible to say that currently we live at the brink of the sixth mass extinction, while the established world order is slowly losing its legitimacy. The Keynesian dream of social democracies has been forgotten while the neo-liberal capitalist doctrine is faltering under the weight of its own contradictions. Independence movements are gaining momentum and the geopolitical struggles are as alive as ever. The former is an indicator of the desire for self-determination. From Catalonia, Rojava, Scotland, Brexit and all the way to Palestine and the disarray seen in the United States of America, there is a tendency towards more control over local affairs, populism and taking power back, one way or another. All these developments, however, are overshadowed by the danger lurking amidst the consequences of climate change, the loss of genetic and functional biodiversity, and the degradation of soil amongst other environmental issues. These problems do not garner as much attention as social problems, such as reactionary responses to the refugee crisis and the consequential rise of far-right populists in the EU, for example. The reasons for our slow response to climate change can be found in the corporate desire to continue with relentless growth and ever-increasing virgin material extraction. In addition, we are witnessing the rise of artificial intelligence, cryptocurrencies, advances in quantum physics, sophisticated biotech tools (CRISPR), and the automation of industries. All along, the rich are getting richer, and the poor are getting poorer, while the ownership of technologies resides firmly in the corporations' grasp. As Žižek (2010) postulated, we truly live in the end times now. The reactionary forces are rising, and now is the time to counter them; otherwise, things might spiral out of control. We can either create a global village for all or broken cities for none. Therefore, the moment is ripe for a transition towards the CE within social ecology and guided by the principles of de-growth. If anything, humans have shown time and time again that we are resilient and can adapt to external changes of circumstances. When working in concert with the full array of information available we can achieve tremendous things. Cooperation is our greatest strength and, for implementing communal direct democratic assemblies, re-establishing commons enveloped in a confederate setup and implementing CE based on de-growth, we will have to cooperate and mobilize as never before. Free nature is an elusive concept; however, we can either reach for it and flourish in the future amongst the stars or perish as a failed sentient and conscious experiment of the evolution.

NOTES

1. Energy that is directly or indirectly used for procurement of products and services (Odum 2007).

2. The EU is almost completely reliant on imports of industrial materials with the likes of tantalum, phosphorus and natural rubber being entirely imported from overseas while having an "end-of-life recycling input rate" of less than 1 per cent (European Comission 2017).

3. Decentralized micro-production facilities with the aim of replacing mass production and economies of scale with optimised and localised computer-controlled tools, enabling mass customisation based on open source principles (Ede 2017).

4. Resource intensity is a measure of efficiency in terms of resource use (i.e., how many resources have been used for a production process) (John A. Matthews 2016).

5. Waste intensity (Waste generated per unit of GDP) indicates the relationship between waste generation and economic growth (John A. Matthews 2016).

6. Energy efficiency drives greater energy demand in the classical economic models.

7. Industrial processes that can de-polymerize, de-alloy, de-laminate, de-vulcanize, de-coat and generally regenerate our vast collection of materials stockpiled, buried in the landfills or floating in the ocean.

8. In 1970, the Earth overshoot day fell after January 1 1971, whereas in 2017 the overshoot day was reached on August 2 (Earth Overshoot Day 2017).

9. About 140,000 tonnes daily via air freight only (Iata.org 2014).

10. Financial services or telemarketing, corporate law, human resources and public relations (Graeber 2016).

REFERENCES

"Agbogbloshie: The World's Largest E-Waste Dump – In Pictures". 2014. *The Guardian*. http://www.theguardian.com/environment/gallery/2014/feb/27/agbogbloshie-worlds-largest-e-waste-dump-in-pictures.

"About The Stanford Encyclopedia of Philosophy". 2016. *Plato.Stanford.Edu*. https://plato.stanford.edu/about.html.

Ahmed, Nafeez. 2018. "Nasa-Funded Study: Industrial Civilisation Headed for 'Irreversible Collapse'? | Nafeez Ahmed". *The Guardian*. https://www.theguardian.com/environment/earth-insight/2014/mar/14/nasa-civilisation-irreversible-collapse-study-scientists.

Anastasio, Mauro. 2018. "Delivering Waste: Amazon Tells Employees to Destroy Brand New Goods". *META*. https://metamag.org/2018/06/14/delivering-waste-amazon-tells-employees-to-destroy-brand-new-goods/.

Bakan, Joel, Mark Achbar, and Jennifer Abbot. 2004. *The Corporation*. Video. https://www.youtube.com/watch?v=Y888wVY5hzw.

Barter, Paul. 2018. ""Cars Are Parked 95% of the Time". Let's Check!". *Reinventingparking.Org*. http://www.reinventingparking.org/2013/02/cars-are-parked-95-of-time-lets-check.html.

Bennett, Jeff W., D. W. Pearce, and R. K. Turner. 1991. "Economics of Natural Resources and the Environment". *American Journal of Agricultural Economics* 73 (1): 227. doi:10.2307/1242904.

Bookchin, Murray. 2018. "Murray Bookchin - The Meaning of Confederalism". *Inclusivedemocracy.Org*. https://www.inclusivedemocracy.org/dn/vol1/bookchin_confederalism.htm.

Bookchin, Murray. 2018. "Murray Bookchin: Ecological Problems Are Social Problems". *Climate & Capitalism*. http://climateandcapitalism.com/2011/03/25/murray-bookchin-what-is-social-ecology/.

Bookchin, Murray. 1995. *Philosophy of Social Ecology*. Montreal: Black Rose Books.

Boulding, Kenneth E. 1966. *The Economics of the Coming Spaceship Earth: Environmental Quality in a Growing Economy Resources for the Future*. Washington: Harper and Row.

Braungart, Michael, William McDonough, and Andrew Bollinger. 2007. "Cradle-To-Cradle Design: Creating Healthy Emissions – A Strategy for Eco-Effective Product and System Design". *Journal of Cleaner Production* 15 (13–14): 1337–1348. doi:10.1016/j.jclepro.2006.08.003.

Coghlan, Andy, and Debora MacKenzie. 2018. "Revealed – The Capitalist Network That Runs the World". *New Scientist*. https://www.newscientist.com/article/mg21228354-500-revealed-the-capitalist-network-that-runs-the-world/.

"Circular Economy 100 Directory". 2017. *Ellenmacarthurfoundation.Org*. https://www.ellenmacarthurfoundation.org/ce100/directory.

"Circular Economy System Diagram - Ellen Macarthur Foundation". 2016. *Ellenmacarthurfoundation.Org*. https://www.ellenmacarthurfoundation.org/circular-economy/interactive-diagram.

Dafermos, George. 2018. "The Catalan Integral Cooperative: An Organizational Study of a Post-Capitalist Cooperative - Commons Transition". *Commons Transition*. http://commonstransition.org/the-catalan-integral-cooperative-an-organizational-study-of-a-post-capitalist-cooperative/.

Dannoritzer, Cosima. 2010. *The Light Bulb Conspiracy*. Video. https://www.youtube.com/watch?v=l5Hlf6nLvV4.

"Do Monsanto and Big Ag Control Crop Research and World Food Supply? #GMOFAQ". 2018. *GMO FAQ*. https://gmo.geneticliteracyproject.org/FAQ/do-monsanto-and-big-ag-control-crop-research-and-world-food-supply/.

Diaz, Jesus. 2014. "Fascinating Graphics Show Who Owns All the Major Brands in the World". *Sploid.Gizmodo.Com*. https://sploid.gizmodo.com/fascinating-graphic-shows-who-owns-all-the-major-brands-1599537576.

Ede, Sharon. 2018. "The Real Circular Economy - Commons Transition". *Commons Transition*. http://commonstransition.org/the-real-circular-economy/.

Embury-Dennis, Tom. 2018. "Costa Rica Runs Entirely on Renewable Energy for 300 Days This Year". *The Independent*. http://www.independent.co.uk/news/world/americas/costa-rica-electricity-renewable-energy-300-days-2017-record-wind-hydro-solar-water-a8069111.html.

"Emergy". 2018. *A Prosperous Way Down*. Accessed May 29. http://prosperouswaydown.com/principles-of-self-organization/empower-basis/emergy/.

European Commission. 2017. "Communication From The Commission To The European Parliament, The Council, The European Economic And Social Committee And The Committee Of The Regions". Brussels: European Commission.

Fukuyama, Francis. 1992. *The End of History and the Last Man*. 1st ed. New York: Free Press.

Fuller, Richard Buckminster. 1969. *Utopia or Oblivion*. 1st ed. New York: Overlook.

Goleman, Daniel. 2010. *Ecological Intelligence*. 1st ed. New York: Broadway Books.

Graeber, David. 2018. "Why Capitalism Creates Pointless Jobs - Evonomics". *Evonomics*. http://evonomics.com/why-capitalism-creates-pointless-jobs-david-graeber/.

Greyson, James. 2007. "An Economic Instrument for Zero Waste, Economic Growth and Sustainability". *Journal of Cleaner Production* 15 (13–14): 1382–1390. doi:10.1016/j.jclepro.2006.07.019.

Griffin, Paul. 2017. "CDP Carbon Majors Report 2017". *The Carbon Majors Database*. CDP. https://b8f65cb373b1b7b15feb-c70d8ead6ced550b4d987d7c03fcdd1d.ssl.cf3.rackcdn.com/cms/reports/documents/000/002/327/original/Carbon-Majors-Report-2017.pdf?1499691240.

Hickel, Jason. 2017. "There'S Only One Way to Avoid Climate Catastrophe: 'De-Growing' Our Economy - Resilience". *Resilience*. http://www.resilience.org/stories/2017-10-20/theres-only-one-way-to-avoid-climate-catastrophe-de-growing-our-economy/.

Ho, Mae-Wan. 2013. "Circular Thermodynamics of Organisms and Sustainable Systems". *Systems* 1 (3): 30–49. doi:10.3390/systems1030030.

Hodal, Kate, Felicity Lawrence, and Chris Kelly. 2014. "Revealed: Asian Slave Labour Producing Prawns for Supermarkets in US, UK". *The Guardian*. https://www.theguardian.com/global-development/2014/jun/10/supermarket-prawns-thailand-produced-slave-labour.

IATA. 2013. "New Year'S Day 2014 Marks 100 Years of Commercial Aviation". http://www.iata.org/pressroom/pr/Pages/2013-12-30-01.aspx.

Jackson, Janine. 2013. "FAIR REPORT: 13Th Annual Fear & Favor Review". *FAIR*. https://fair.org/extra/fair-report-13th-annual-fear-favor-review/.

Jackson, Tim. 2017. *Prosperity Without Growth*. 2nd ed. Abingdon: Routledge.

Jensen, Derrick. 2006. *Endgame*. 1st ed. New York: Seven Stories Press.

Jensen, Derrick. 2009. "Forget Shorter Showers | Essays". *Derrickjensen.Org*. http://www.derrickjensen.org/2009/07/forget-shorter-showers/.

"Just 8 Men Own Same Wealth as Half the World | Oxfam International". 2017. *Oxfam. Org*. https://www.oxfam.org/en/pressroom/pressreleases/2017-01-16/just-8-men-own-same-wealth-half-world.

Kallis, Giorgos. 2017. *In Defense of Degrowth*. Ebook. 1st ed. Barcelona. https://indefenseofdegrowth.com/.

Klein, Naomi. 2014. *This Changes Everything*. 1st ed. London: Penguin Books Ltd.

Kropotkin, Peter. 1955. *Mutual Aid: A Factor of Evolution*. 50th ed. Boston: Extending Horizons Books.

Kropotkin, Petr Alekseevich, and Charles Weigl. 2008. *The Conquest of Bread*. Oakland, CA: AK Press.

Kunstler, James Howard. 2009. *The Long Emergency*. New York, NY: Grove Press.

Lakey, George. 2017. "How Swedes and Norwegians Broke the Power of the '1 Percent'". *Films For Action*. http://www.filmsforaction.org/articles/how-swedes-and-norwegians-broke-the-power-of-the-1-percent/.

Lehmann, Steffen. 2011. "Optimizing Urban Material Flows and Waste Streams in Urban Development Through Principles of Zero Waste and Sustainable Consumption". *Sustainability* 3 (1): 155–183. doi:10.3390/su3010155.

Lutz, Ashley. 2012. "These 6 Corporations Control 90% of the Media in America". *Business Insider*. http://www.businessinsider.com/these-6-corporations-control-90-of-the-media-in-america-2012-6?IR=T.

Lynas, Mark. 2012. *The God Species*. 1st ed. London: Fourth Estate.

Mathews, John A., and Hao Tan. 2011. "Progress Toward a Circular Economy in China". *Journal of Industrial Ecology* 15 (3): 435–457. doi:10.1111/j.1530-9290.2011.00332.x.

Mathews, John A., and Hao Tan. 2016. "Circular Economy: Lessons from China". *Nature* 531 (7595): 440–442. doi:10.1038/531440a.

McDonald, R. (2018). "Jevons paradox: When doing more with less isn't enough." [online] Grist. Available at: https://grist.org/energy-efficiency/2011-09-04-jevons-paradox-when-doing-more-with-less-isnt-enough/ [Accessed 7 Dec. 2017].

Meek, James. 2014. "Sale of the Century: The Privatisation Scam". *The Guardian*. http://www.theguardian.com/politics/2014/aug/22/sale-of-century-privatisation-scam.

Monbiot, George. 2010. *Vroče*. 1st ed. Ljubljana: Krtina.

Morris, Brian. 2017. *Pioneers of Ecological Humanism*. 1st ed. Montreal: Black Rose Books.

Narberhaus, Micha, and Josephine von Mitschke-Collande. 2017. "Circular Economy Isn't a Magical Fix for Our Environmental Woes". *The Guardian*. https://www.theguardian.com/sustainable-business/2017/jul/14/circular-economy-not-magical-fix-environmental-woes-global-corporations.

Oxenham, Simon. 2017. "Meet the Robin Hood of Science". *Big Think*. http://bigthink.com/neurobonkers/a-pirate-bay-for-science.

"Past Earth Overshoot Days". 2018. *Earth Overshoot Day*. http://www.overshootday.org/newsroom/past-earth-overshoot-days/.

"Pay Up!". 2018. *Clean Clothes Campaign*. http://www.cleanclothes.org/ranaplaza.

Piketty, Thomas. 2015. *Kapital V 21. Stoletju*. 1st ed. Ljubljana: Mladinska Knjiga.

Pink, Daniel H. 2009. *Drive: The Surprising Truth About What Motivates Us*. 1st ed. New York, NY: Riverhead Books.

Raftery, Adrian E., Alec Zimmer, Dargan M. W. Frierson, Richard Startz, and Peiran Liu. 2017. "Less Than 2 °C Warming By 2100 Unlikely". *Nature Climate Change* 7: 637–641. https://www.nature.com/articles/nclimate3352.

Raworth, Kate. 2017. "What on Earth Is The Doughnut?…". *Kate Raworth*. https://www.kateraworth.com/doughnut/.

Reclus, Elisee. 1905. *L'homme Et La Terre*. Paris: Librairie universelle.

Rifkin, Jeremy. 2014. "Capitalism Is Making Way for the Age of Free | Jeremy Rifkin". *The Guardian*. https://www.theguardian.com/commentisfree/2014/mar/31/capitalism-age-of-free-internet-of-things-economic-shift.

Rifkin, Jeremy. 1994. *The End of Work*. 1st ed. New York: Tarcher.

Roberts, David. 2013. "None of the World's Top Industries Would Be Profitable if They Paid for the Natural Capital They Use". *Grist*. https://grist.org/business-technology/none-of-the-worlds-top-industries-would-be-profitable-if-they-paid-for-the-natural-capital-they-use/.

Rockström, Johan, Will Steffen, Kevin Noone, Åsa Persson, F. Stuart Chapin, Eric F. Lambin, and Timothy M. Lenton et al. 2009. "A Safe Operating Space for Humanity". *Nature* 461 (7263): 472–475. doi:10.1038/461472a.

Roos, Göran. 2014. "Business Model Innovation to Create and Capture Resource Value in Future Circular Material Chains". *Resources* 3 (1): 248–274. doi:10.3390/resources3010248.

Rowson, J. (2018). Did Somebody say Khazzoom-Brookes postulate? - RSA. [online] Thersa.org. Available at: https://www.thersa.org/discover/publications-and-articles/rsa-blogs/2013/05/did-somebody-say-khazzoom-brookes-postulate [Accessed 7 Dec. 2017].

Saviano, Roberto. 2009. *Gomorra*. 1st ed. Barcelona: Debolsillo.

Schnitzer, Hans, and Sergio Ulgiati. 2007. "Less Bad Is Not Good Enough: Approaching Zero Emissions Techniques and Systems". *Journal Of Cleaner Production* 15 (13–14): 1185–1189. doi:10.1016/j.jclepro.2006.08.001.

Schumaker, John F. 2016. "The Demoralized Mind". *New Internationalist*. https://newint.org/columns/essays/2016/04/01/psycho-spiritual-crisis.

Stahel, Walter. 2017. "Product-Life Factor (Mitchell Prize Winning Paper 1982) | The Product-Life Institute". *Product-Life.Org*. http://www.product-life.org/en/major-publications/the-product-life-factor.

Su, Biwei, Almas Heshmati, Yong Geng, and Xiaoman Yu. 2013. "A Review of the Circular Economy in China: Moving from Rhetoric to Implementation". *Journal of Cleaner Production* 42: 215–227. doi:10.1016/j.jclepro.2012.11.020.

Swartz, Aaron. 2008. "Full Text of "Guerilla Open Access Manifesto"". *Archive.Org*. https://archive.org/stream/GuerillaOpenAccessManifesto/Goamjuly2008_djvu.txt.

Temple, Julien. 2010. "Detroit: The Last Days". *The Guardian*. https://www.theguardian.com/film/2010/mar/10/detroit-motor-city-urban-decline.

"The Circular Economy Concept - Regenerative Economy". 2018. *Ellenmacarthurfoundation.Org*. https://www.ellenmacarthurfoundation.org/circular-economy/overview/concept.

"Union Carbide's Disaster". 2018. *Bhopal.Org*. http://bhopal.org/what-happened/union-carbides-disaster/.

White, Heather. 2014. *Complicit Film*. Video. https://www.youtube.com/watch?v=ns-kJ5Podjw.

"World's Richest 10% Produce Half of Global Carbon Emissions, Says Oxfam". 2015. *The Guardian*. https://www.theguardian.com/environment/2015/dec/02/worlds-richest-10-produce-half-of-global-carbon-emissions-says-oxfam.

"WRAP And The Circular Economy | WRAP UK". 2014. *Wrap.Org.Uk*. http://www.wrap.org.uk/about-us/about/wrap-and-circular-economy.

Žižek, Slavoj. 2009. *First as Tragedy, Then as Farce*. 1st ed. London: Verso.

Žižek, Slavoj. 2011. *Living in the End Times*. 1st ed. London: Verso.

Žižek, Slavoj. 2017. "Only a New Universalism Can Save Us from the New World Order – Opinion – ABC Religion & Ethics (Australian Broadcasting Corporation)". *Abc.Net.Au*. http://www.abc.net.au/religion/articles/2017/05/11/4667236.htm.

2

Heritage as a 'Common'

Exploring Alternative Approaches for De-growth

Elizabeth Auclair

Against the economic, social and environmental crises that are facing our societies, alternative concepts and models have recently been emerging, or re-emerging. A wide scope of theories and analyses concern 'transition' towns and initiatives (Hopkins 2008), ways of living based on frugality, sobriety and moderation (Rabhi 2010), 'slow' movements (Aries 2010; Diestchy 2015), 'buen vivir' approaches in Bolivia and Ecuador (Acosta 2017), or 'convivialism' (Caillé et Chanial 2014). They are often correlated to social and political movements, fighting for cultural and human rights and protesting in various countries against the neo-liberal economy, such as Occupy, *Indignados*, Places, Global Justice, or *Nuit Debout* and the *Zadists* in France. The movement *Nuit Debout* which took place in the spring of 2016, first in Paris, on the famous *Place de la République* and then in other French towns, mobilized crowds of activists, protesting against a labour law project. The *Zadists*[1] are communities of anti capitalist and ecologist activists who occupy spaces, in different regions where large urban development projects are planned. They contest the relevance of these projects, considering them as expensive, useless and environmentally harmful. The most mediatized ZAD is the one close to the city of Nantes, where the project of a new airport has been mobilizing activists for several years.[2]

Amongst these theories and movements which interconnect in many ways, the overarching concept of de-growth seems to be gaining an increasing audience amongst social movements as well as scholar works (Abraham et al. 2011; D'Alisa et al. 2014; Paulson 2017) even though it remains quite controversial. The term de-growth is still frequently understood as merely decline and regression. Scientists however have been investigating for many years models for a society 'without growth', using explicitly or not the term de-growth (Georgescu-Roegen 1971, 1994;

Meadows et al. 1971; Rist 2009; Jackson 2009; Gadrey 2012). The beginnings of de-growth can be found in France in the early 2000, especially with the significant works of the economist Serge Latouche (Latouche 2004, 2006, 2007, 2011, 2012), and the organization in Paris in 2008 of the first International Conference on de-growth for ecological sustainability and social equity. A number of analyses show evidence that there cannot be infinite growth on a planet with limited physical, geological and natural resources. Facing the increase of social inequalities between countries and within countries, and the intensification of environmental problems, a sort of 'urgency' seems to give the concept of de-growth a new dynamism. This can be seen in the works conducted by the members of the emerging international social movement called 'De-growth in movement(s)'.[3] It leads to contest the ideology of 'higher, further, faster' based on endless growth (Burkhart and al 2016) and to propose other models against the process of privatization, profit and competition, encapsulated in the neo-liberal capitalistic model (Kempf 2009). Though the term de-growth appears somewhat provocative in times of massive unemployment, social exclusion and poverty, the concept can propose models which foster moderation and environmental preservation and promote values of social justice, local democracy and conviviality. These models however must undoubtedly adapt to various contexts and take into account the diversity of situations, in the North as in the South.

Moreover, a growing emphasis is set on the local level as a way to build new theoretical as well as practical alternative patterns (Auclair 2011). The inability of international bodies and Nations to take collective decisions concerning the urgent climatic or social matters – the Rio+20 Summit in 2012 was a major failure – explains the importance of the local level seen as a relevant way to explore new approaches. An increasing number of social movement activists – NGOs, association of citizens, groups of inhabitants – as well as actors working in local institutions, promote place-based, people-centred, bottom-up approaches, enhancing the values of localness and setting the citizens as key actors of the changes. Grassroots experiences flourish in many parts of the word, addressing shared gardens, seed banks, alternative currencies, renewable energies, recycling activities, etc. (Manier 2012; Frère et Jacquemain 2013; Hopkins 2014; Daniel 2014; Dupin 2014).

Within this context, the recent 'revival' of the concept of commons can be seen as a kind of catalyst of these different theories and movements (Gadrey 2013; Dardot and Laval 2014; Bollier 2014, Bollier and Helfrich 2012, 2015 ; Coriat 2015 ; Cornu et al. 2017). It federates activities mobilizing for the implementation of sustainable societies and struggles against privatization and commercialization processes linked to the neo-liberal model. The worldwide spreading concept of 'commons' appears as a consistent means for preserving fundamental resources, promoting emancipation and social wellbeing and enhancing collective responsibility and self-organization. This concept performs as a transformative pathway, set between private management and market-oriented strategies focusing on consumerism and economic growth, on one side and centralized top-down public administration, on the other side. It is based on values of sharing, co-deciding, co-constructing. First applied to natural resources (Ostrom 1990), then to knowledge and digital resources (Bauwens 2015, 2017; Le Crosnier 2015), the use of the concept is extending to many other elements such as landscapes (Hatzfeld 2006; Sgard 2010), urban spaces (Sohn et al., 2015), or territories (Magnaghi 2014).

In this chapter, we propose to continue our work on culture and heritage, considered as commons (Auclair 2014b, 2015b, 2017b; Auclair et al. 2017), and analyse how heritage seen as a 'common' can foster new models of governance and local initiatives of de-growth. Widely acknowledged as a fundamental dimension of every community, heritage appears as a contemporary issue. In a context of hard competition between cities and between territories, a major challenge is notably to limit intrumentalizing heritage for mere territorial branding, tourism and economic matters (Auclair 2017a). Defining heritage as a common, in this perspective, leads to a theoretical and practical shift since it supposes community-based governance, collective decisions and inhabitant's participation. This means reconsidering definitions of heritage – not only famous UNESCO's heritage and touristic sites but also every day, ordinary heritage – and inventing management tools, where inhabitants alongside the 'experts' decide what elements are considered as heritage and define together local actions and policies (Auclair and Fairclough 2015).

Our analysis is based on theoretical investigations and on a series of recent academic works concerning several projects conducted in France, in different cities located in the suburbs of Paris. The chapter consists of three parts: following this short introduction, the first part shows how the concept of commons is currently mobilized for seeking alternative models of territorial development. The second part discusses the capacity of new heritage approaches to foster emancipation and citizenship in changing cities. The third part examines the processes of co-construction of heritage policies; it is followed by a conclusion that proposes a framework for considering heritage as a common.

DEFINING ALTERNATIVE MODELS FOR URBAN AND RURAL TERRITORIES

The concept of commons is not recent, since it has existed in Europe for several centuries (approximately from the twentieth to the eighteenth century), and close to 2 billion people still use such collective self-organized systems for managing their daily resources, in many parts of the world, such as Africa, Australia, South America, India, etc. (Bollier 2014). The concept however has been dismissed for many years by 'main stream' economic theories, worshipping private ownership and open market policies as the only way for managing efficiently fundamental resources. Notably, Garett Hardin argued against the efficiency and success of the commons and gained a large audience with his article titled 'The tragedy of commons' (Hardin 1968).

Nonetheless, the economist Elinor Ostrom (1990) showed in her academic work that alternative models of governance, related to the concept of commons, were successfully used in many countries by small communities for the management of natural resources, that is, water, forestry, biodiversity, fish, seeds and agriculture resources. She stressed the relevance of these traditions for protecting essential resources and promoting wellbeing for the whole community. Her work highlighted a number of values and principles that shape a model for preserving and managing tangible and intangible resources. Rather unexpectedly, Elinor Ostrom was awarded in 2009 the Nobel Memorial Prize in economic sciences (often referred to as the Nobel Prize in economics) for her work on the commons, and this helped the concept to spread amongst academic fields and social movements. So the concept of commons currently appears as an appropriate pathway for social and cultural transformations. The aim is to resist to enclosure, privatization and exploitation of fundamental resources, such as natural resources but also knowledge, culture, tangible and intangible heritage.

According to Bollier (2014), three conditions are required for defining a common: first, a shared acknowledgement of the importance of a specific resource; second, the existence of a community concerned by the value of this resource; and third, a collective organization for managing and preserving this resource. So commons are the result of a social construction: they only exist when people – forming a community – decide together to take in charge a resource, which they consider fundamental, and when they define common rules and practices for a fair, sustainable and democratic use of them. Hence, commons are not just elements or objects that need to be protected; they suppose a process based on participation, transparency and equity. Against theories pointing individualistic attitudes of consumers pursuing their own interest, the concept of commons is based on the hypotheses that people are willing to get together, share and protect their resources – if they are given the chance. Hence, promoting the commons is not only an economic or legal matter (Parance et De Saint Victor 2014), it is above all a political issue: it can be considered as an objective for future policies, as a 'revolutionary model for the XXIst century' (Dardot et Laval 2014). Nevertheless, this rapid and wide use of the concept raises some misunderstandings and discussions around the 'accurate' meaning of the term commons, and there are semantic debates amongst experts on this subject. It is indeed a complex notion, since it is connected to other notions, which seem close but can induce different approaches and policies, such as common goods, public goods, public interest, common interest, etc. Some academics talk of the common goods while others prefer to use the term commons, and others the single term common.

Whilst the concept of commons is an object of theoretical investigation and debate, it leads to number of experiences throughout the world, directly linked to the concept or based on its main principles. Citizens and social networks are developing projects considering knowledge as a common, such as the 'Copy left' principle developed by Richard Stallman, and the growing movement related to open source, open data software, creative commons. Other activities concern exchanging, sharing and co-constructing knowledge, such as the participative cartography 'Mapjams', the FAC LAB's (Factory Laboratories) and the DIY (Do-It-Yourself) initiatives.

A series of projects aim at preserving natural resources and landscapes as commons, improving ways of living in cities, as well as in rural areas, and developing food activities with the participation of the citizens. Various experiences are emerging in France, as in other countries, even though the actors concerned do not always specifically use the term 'commons'. The French *AMAP* network[4] fosters direct relations between farmers and urban consumers, and consequently encourages traditional farming practices, good-quality and environment-friendly agriculture products. Citizens and farmers decide together to create local associations, they define the range and diversity of products to be proposed, they fix the practical organization and prices, and discuss the main farming principles. More than 2,000 *AMAP* have already been created, concerning 250,000 consumers, and the movement is still spreading.

The 'transition towns' and 'transition initiatives', which are developing rapidly in different parts of the world,[5] also appear as innovative experiences where inhabitants decide together to activate alternative values and principles for sustainable territories (Hopkins 2008, 2011, 2013 2014). The projects support democratic place-based, people-centred initiatives. France counts around 150 transition towns or initiatives. In Cergy-Pontoise, a town situated in the outskirts of Paris, a network of associations and citizens, created in 2014, organizes different events, film projections, debates and conferences. Various activities involve the inhabitants in order to encourage alternative and more sustainable ways of living. The project addresses various issues such as recycling (repairing activities), food and agriculture ('Incredible edible' actions), soft transport measures (cycling paths, car sharing) and hosts a local exchange trading system and a participatory habitat experience.

Moreover, in order to enhance the concept of commons, national and international networks[6] have carried out various initiatives. The network called *Réseau francophone des biens communs,* created in 2012 by the Association Vecam, organized in October 2013 the first Festival 'Cities as commons' (*Festival des Villes en bien communs*). It enabled the identification and promotion of activities taking place in France and in other countries throughout the world, such as changing urban wasteland into shared gardens, creating 'open street maps' with the inhabitants, and sharing knowledge, software and technologies. A second Festival called the 'The time of the commons' (*Le temps des communs*) was organized in October 2015, with 200 events in France and more than 50 events in the Paris region. The objective of these Festivals was to promote the concept of commons, to give more visibility to the collaborative initiatives and to show their power to deal with contemporary economic, social and environmental issues. A 'University of commons' was created in France, in 2017, by a group of persons and associations,[7] on the model of existing universities launched in Belgium, Holland, Italy and Argentina. It is hosted in a cultural centre in Paris.[8] Conferences and debates are organized once a month, in order to touch a wide audience, share knowledge in a participative process and publicize the concept of commons as a way to support territories and cities based on environmental awareness, justice and democracy.

FOSTERING EMANCIPATION AND
CITIZENSHIP IN CHANGING CITIES

Amongst the fundamental resources of our societies currently considered as commons, we focus here on urban heritage. Facing the increasing urbanization of the planet's population, the future of cities becomes central in the reflections and works concerning sustainable territories. David Harvey (2012) analyses urban commons in connection with the concept of 'the right to the city'. He considers that the notion of right to the city, developed by Henri Lefebvre (1967), is useful, insofar as it allows to examine the political and economic dimensions of current urban developments and to stress the impact of neo-liberal ideology on territorial transformations. Harvey reinterprets this notion of right to the city and raises several crucial questions: what kind of city are we dealing with today? A right for whom? For which social categories? How to avoid the privatization of the city? How to avoid the privative appropriation of space? If the city is a common good, who manages this common? For whose benefit?

In the context of globalization, increased mobility, multicultural cities and metropolization of territories, the questions of heritage, identity, memory and attachment are re-examined. Patrimonialization processes have become a major urban planning issue around the world, but also an issue of social and cultural mobilization and demand (Auclair et al. 2017). Amongst the questionings concerning the future of our societies, cultural desires, values and aspirations appear at the centre of many of them. What are our essential needs and expectations? Who is in charge of managing and preserving our cultural resources? Which resources inherited from our past will we be able to transmit onwards and in what condition and context? Heritage has become a fundamental issue, not only of preservation but of creation, adaptation and resilience to change (Auclair and Fairclough 2015).

The notion of heritage has undergone significant changes for the last decades. Progressively it is moving from merely a collection of objects to rescue and preserve, to place-based, people-centred processes, articulating key values of memory, identity and place. It affects at a fundamental level who we think we are, how we live, and how we make the future. This approach is indicated in several recent international texts, such as the 2000 European Landscape Convention and the 2005 Faro Convention on the Value of Cultural Heritage for Society, adopted by the Council of Europe, as well as the UNESCO's 2005 Convention on the protection and promotion of the diversity of cultural expressions, and the UNESCO's 2011 Recommendation on Historical Urban Landscape. All these texts insist on expanding the concept of heritage and developing inhabitants' participation. This means acknowledging the plurality of individual and collective identities and encouraging dialogue and exchange between generations, between neighbourhoods and between communities. This leads to an enhancement of social, economic and cultural resources that in turn can contribute to shaping territories and identities.

The Faro Convention appears as a key link between heritage and commons. Indeed, the convention gives a broad definition of cultural heritage, which comprises tangible/intangible elements, perceptual/physical objects, actions, performances, customs and behaviours, as well as natural elements, urban buildings and monuments. The Faro Convention sets people's values, aspirations and needs first and celebrates the diversity and plurality of their views and values. It explicitly mentions every day, ordinary heritage, living heritage as noteworthy categories and recommends the use of specific criteria capable of placing people in the core of heritage policies and projects. It also insists on increasing the role of citizens in defining, deciding and managing their cultural environment (Fairclough et al. 2014). Hence, the relation between the values and principles promoted by the Faro Convention and those enhanced by the concept of commons seems close. In the words of the Convention, 'everyone, alone or collectively, has the responsibility to respect the cultural heritage of others as much as their own heritage'. Responsibility is a key principle defined by Hans Jonas (1979), which is embedded in sustainable policies and practices. Jonas highlighted the responsibility we collectively share, regarding the present generations but also regarding future generations. Thus, responsibility towards cultural heritage is not the exclusive domain of experts or public authorities. It induces new governance strategies and tools and supposes democratic participation 'to involve everyone in society, in the on-going process of defining and managing cultural heritage' and to preserve heritage not for its own sake, but for explicit and broad social benefit (Fairclough et al. 2014).

Furthermore, the 2011 UNESCO Recommendation on Historic Urban Landscape (HUL) has adopted this discourse and aims to promote the integration and valorization of culture and heritage in urban development policies. Local policies should be based on the 'respect of the inherited values and traditions of different cultural contexts'. This means mapping 'the city's natural, cultural and human resources' and assessing the vulnerability of these elements according to sustainability criteria, such as socio-economic stress or climate change. Against the dangers, risks and problems which affect urban environments, tangible and intangible heritage is gradually viewed as 'a key resource in enhancing the liveability of urban areas', according to HUL's recommendation. The issue seems decisive because of the existing conflict between urban development and heritage preservation. As a paradox, either protecting heritage appears as an obstacle for urban projects, and is therefore no longer guaranteed, or on the contrary, heritage is considered as a valuable component and finds itself instrumentalized. In both cases, the choices seem determined by economic issues. Indeed, heritage valorization and cultural tourism are currently viewed merely as tools used by cities for economic development (Auclair 2017a). HUL encourages the inclusion of more partners in the decision taking and the involvement of inhabitants in the patrimonialization process. The intention is 'to reach consensus using participatory planning and stakeholders' consultation on what values to protect for transmission to future generations' and 'to establish the appropriate partnerships and local management frameworks for each of the identified projects (. . .)'. So the objective is to consider urban areas as 'common cultural heritage'.

National and local policies in France however are still often characterized by a rather narrow representation of heritage, founded on Malraux's cultural policy model, and a certain tardiness to implement participative procedures – France has not yet signed the Faro Convention. But despite this kind of reluctance of public authorities in France to adopt new heritage approaches, many projects conducted by cultural centres, associations and NGOs develop strategies enhancing ordinary heritage and promoting inhabitants' participation, notably in the Paris suburbs (Auclair 2014a, 2015a). Suburbs seam undeniably relevant spaces to study, as they reveal critical urban issues. They combine diverse processes of deindustrialization, urban sprawl, renovation and development projects, increased spatial fragmentation and social segregation, gentrification and impoverishment of certain urban areas. They also often suffer from both intern and extern perception problems and image issues (Auclair et Herzog 2015). In these territories, we nevertheless can observe new ways of defining heritage, which involve different categories of actors and induce alternatives practices. Frequently defined as 'ordinary', 'modest', suburban heritage refers to the territories of 'everyday life'.

These new representations of heritage are for example developed by the *Maison de banlieue et de l'architecture* (House of Suburbs and Architecture), located in the city of Athis Mons, and by the Val de Bièvre Eco-museum, in the city of Frênes, two institutions that we have studied (Auclair 2014a, 2015a). These two cultural institutions situated in the south of Paris belong to the network *Les Neufs de Transilie*. This informal network created in 2003 brings together about fifteen cultural institutions, whose objective is 'to offer a different and renewed look at the realities of the contrasted and complex Paris region'. The two structures in Frênes and Athis-Mons drive a questioning on 'what makes heritage for the inhabitants'; they reject the conventional definitions of heritage and contest the inherited relationships of domination between centre-periphery, elite-people, expert-inhabitants, etc. It is no longer the aesthetic, historical, or architectural dimensions that are put forward but 'what matters to the inhabitants', 'what they are attached to'.

The objective of the *Maison de Banlieue et de l'Architecture* is to develop research and increase knowledge concerning history, heritage, architecture and landscapes in the suburbs and to share this comprehension with the inhabitants and with outside visitors. By organizing exhibitions, visits and conferences, the ambition is to make people understand the city and its changes, increase the sense of belonging and feeling of attachment, and help the inhabitants act as citizens. The aim is also to promote social cohesion by increasing exchanges and relations between the different neighbourhoods and between the various communities of the city. Urban walks are regularly organized for groups, with the participation of various people invited to talk about specific topics. Some walks are organized in collaboration with the inhabitants who act as guides and give explanations about their own neighbourhood, an approach which flourishes today in many towns throughout the world.

The Val de Bièvres Eco-Museum develops a similar approach, based on the valorization of suburban heritage, with exhibitions, outdoor visits, pedagogical activities, etc. The aim of an eco-museum is primarily to enhance the tangible and intangible heritage of a territory and its population, and the participation of the inhabitants is one of its major principles. So the objective of this institution is to 'map' what is significant for the inhabitants themselves, by collecting histories, memories and objects, which form part of the population's heritage. However, heritage is not only considered as the past, it also relates to the contemporary issues of these urban areas. Inhabitants are invited to cooperate during the different stages of the process and particularly in collecting objects and stories. The principle is to let the population decide what should be transmitted to the following generations.

The activities organized by these cultural institutions reflect recent trends promoting new methodologies for sharing open spaces, landscapes, culture and heritage issues, and thereby increasing the role that inhabitants play in defining heritage. We can mention for example the multiplication of participatory inventories conducted by cities, cultural institutions, museums, but also by national or regional parks.[9] Involving the population gives the inhabitants keys to become actors of their own territories. These alternatives approaches, which are based on the concepts of empowerment (Baqué et al. 2013) and capabilities (Sen 1985; Nussbaum 2011), can contribute in defining heritage as a common.

CO-CONSTRUCTING HERITAGE POLICIES

Considering heritage as a common is not a recent idea, however, since for years academic works and national or international texts have mentioned the term common – or commons – when addressing heritage issues. The sociologist André Micoud for example considers explicitly heritage as a common good in his works (Micoud 1995). The French Ministry of culture refers to heritage as a 'common good of the Nation'. International texts and Conventions also use various terms and notions, which indirectly relate to the present concept of commons. Since UNESCO's 1972 *Convention* concerning the protection of cultural and natural *heritage*, the term World Heritage is regularly used. Facing the risks and dangers of globalization, the United Nations Development Program launched in 1999 the notion of 'global public goods'. This notion means public goods throughout the world, which are non-rival and non-exclusive, as opposed to public goods, which can exist just in one area. This notion is close to the concepts of common heritage of mankind or common heritage of humanity, frequently used. The global public goods relate to international law which indicates that defined territorial areas (e.g., the Antarctic) and elements of humanity's common cultural and natural heritage should be maintained for future generations and be protected from pure economic exploitation by private corporations. This relatively complex notion rises however several political, economic and legal issues (Lille 2008). All these different terms and notions cannot be strictly associated to the frame of values and democratic approaches of the commons, which are currently spreading.

More generally, many national or local policies still aim at defining and safeguarding major heritage elements, according to historical, architectural, or esthetical criteria. Moreover, the preservation and management of this type of heritage are still frequently based on top-down policies, with an increasing emphasis set on tourism development and market-oriented strategies. The challenge is therefore to define other criteria, based on what counts for people, what makes sense for the inhabitants. This leads to identifying what heritage means for people, what they value in their local environment. It means finding ways for designing, managing and preserving ordinary, everyday heritage. This new approach stresses the sensitive, affective dimensions of heritage. Many works led by geographers, sociologists and anthropologists since the 1990s developed what is now called critical heritage studies, devoted to new representations of heritage. They notably study 'what matters', 'what makes sense' for the inhabitants (Smith 2006; Watremez 2008; Veschambre 2008; Fabre 2013, 2016; Auclair et al. 2017). In his work on 'patrimonial emotions', Daniel Fabre (2013) emphasizes 'the strength of local attachments and emotional investments', as well as the importance of 'personal stories'. The ordinary, the familiar, the intimate are, for him, essential values to understand and analyse contemporary processes of heritage (Fabre 2016). We can also refer to the analyses of Laurajane Smith (2006), who considers that heritage is a complex process that includes acts of commemoration and memory, but also the construction of feelings of attachment and belonging. It participates in the construction of place, space and territory and promotes the understanding of the present. According to her, although heritage can mean different things to different people, heritage is a process that builds common cultural values and meaning. She considers heritage as a cultural practice, which implies the construction and organization of a set of values and representations. The authenticity rests on the meaning that the inhabitants give to heritage in their daily lives. This approach brings out other values for heritage, such as identity, experience, memory, sense of place, and highlights the importance of participatory approaches to contest 'authorized discourses, based on the Western national and elite class experiences (. . .)' (Smith 2006). Such new approaches are emerging in many cities throughout the world, and academic works are currently addressing these projects (Auclair et al. 2017).

The concept of commons appears to promote alternative approaches and foster the co-construction of urban heritage policies, mobilizing various stakeholders. A debate exists however between the advocates of the commons, addressing this co-construction and the choice of actors that should be involved. Some consider that commons should be positioned out of reach of public authorities and private interests and be completely taken in charge by the inhabitants themselves – with the support of associations and NGOs – while others are more favourable in experiencing new types of cooperation and collaboration with local governments. Some activists have even created political groups and parties, in Spain and in Italy for example, in order to highlight the concept of commons during the elections. Consequently, the candidature 'Barcelona in common' won the municipal elections in 2015,[10] and activists defending the commons entered the municipality in Madrid. Several Italian cities have also fixed rules and regulations in order to protect specific commons.

Despite the controversies concerning the place and role of public authorities in the management of the commons, it seems that dealing with heritage, in France, does in fact require involving state bodies and local governments, since public policies still appear decisive for culture and heritage matters. It supposes nonetheless clarifying the role of each actor in order to create governance procedures, giving power and responsibilities to the inhabitants. A number of changes are required for shifting from 'traditional' heritage policies to the recognition of heritage as a common, though many transformations are already discernible, and experiences are being launched in French cities.

In urban areas and notably in the suburbs, new actors are currently 'working' with the inhabitants with renewed intervention methods, combining architecture, urban planning, social and cultural actions. Multidisciplinary teams are forming, amongst which are architects, landscape architects, designers, artists, anthropologists, geographers, philosophers, etc. They intervene in the shape of collectives, associations and cooperatives. We can however note that these structures are sometimes relatively ephemeral and some have a short life span. Protesting against globalized and standardized urbanism processes, they seek new ways to found cities which are more human and friendly, less consuming and more ecological. These new forms of mobilization and engagement in the city have the shared purpose of being alongside local residents and influencing urban transformations. A survey conducted in the Paris region[11] identified fifty experiences articulating culture, heritage, environmental and planning issues, such as AAA (*Atelier d'Architecture Autogéré*), whose aim is 'to make the city more ecological and more democratic by developing a collective project of research and action concerning urban mutations, cultural and social practices and contemporary policies'.

To identify the aims pursued by these actors, the values they claim, and the participation methods they use, we can analyse the interventions developed in the Paris region by the collective called Cochenko that we studied in one of our works (Auclair 2013). Cochenko carried out several actions with the inhabitants, and in particular in the towns of Saint Denis and Stains situated in the Seine-Saint-Denis Departement (North of Paris). Most of the time, the actors do not explicitly claim a 'social' approach, even though the projects often concern marginalized populations living in poor neighbourhoods. The initiatives address urban areas confronted with various types of development projects, such as rehabilitation, demolition-reconstruction, changes in public spaces, or wastelands and 'forgotten', 'neglected' urban spaces. Cochenko intervenes mainly in public spaces to create what the actors calls 'zones of ordinary utopias', relying on modes of intervention which are 'playful and creative'. The objective is to involve residents in urban, architectural and heritage transformations and make them actors of the changes, while promoting a change of vision on the daily environment. The actions are based on tools related to arts, design, architecture, photography, geography. The inhabitants are invited to participate, using their living expertise in order 'to invent a creative and shared city'. The modes of participation of the population are expressly on the register of the co-construction. By the effective transformation of urban spaces, the inhabitants become subjects and no longer objects of urban development.

The inhabitants involved in these alternative projects are no longer considered as 'objects', 'audiences', or as the 'public' targeted by participative interventions but are fully recognized as citizens, carriers of knowledge and expertise. Thus, the projects invent new forms of association and collaboration with the inhabitants, based on reciprocity and self-management, and rely for this on discussion, exchange and dialogue, and collective intelligence. In contrast to architectural, urban and heritage projects that are often developed while ignoring the real needs and expectations of the inhabitants, these approaches seek instead to put people on the front of the stage. The goal is to shift from traditional tools of participation to a real co-construction and management of the living environment. The actors seek through creative processes to develop a more social and political participation (Auclair 2017a).

We observe currently the multiplication of this kind of trans-disciplinary projects, opening on collaborations between inhabitants and actors from various training and professional practices. The analysis of the interventions carried out by these new actors shows that they are generally based on a number of clearly stated values. The actors claim a very broad and transversal meaning of heritage and culture. Thus, projects often seek to break the boundaries between 'high' culture and 'popular' culture, between traditional heritage and new heritage approaches. Besides, the projects are often marked by a commitment to ecological approaches: they encourage local production to reduce the carbon footprint, recycling of objects and materials, reintroduction of nature in the city via shared gardens, which are designed and managed with permaculture processes, etc. These actors do not offer 'turnkey' solutions, and even if the projects feed on each other, the objective is to stick to the specificities of the territory and to invent each time, with the inhabitants, the project that seems most suited to their expectations and desires. It is therefore a question of truly experiencing place-based, people-centred, bottom-up approaches. Based on the analyses of Michel de Certeau (1990), they enhance 'everyday practices, the arts of doing and the ways of acting through which the ordinary man resists consumer society'.

These alternative approaches however do not always appear against public authorities but generate, on the contrary, new partnerships and collaborative processes. Indeed, the projects led by Cochenko, for example, marked by a strong territorial linkage, require political support, and therefore the involvement of local governments. In addition, in order to build adapted projects with the inhabitants, Cochenko's approach calls for the realization of assessments and studies that can only be developed through the establishment of partnerships with the various actors of the neighbourhood and the city.

So for many actors, it is not only a question of being on the side of the inhabitants during the transformations of the area, but through a re-appropriation of urban spaces by the population, and by the establishment of places of exchanges and debates, to try to recreate new forms of urbanity. In the current neo-liberal economic context, the challenge is to fight against the privatization of public space but also against the tendency to normalize and regulate the management of the public spaces. These alternatives approaches therefore illustrate the current mobilizations addressing the defence and recognition of the 'commons'.

CONCLUSION

In order to review the different values, principles and strategies, which characterize the alternative approaches for urban heritage policies, we propose a framework comprising three sections, closely intertwined, which expose the three conditions for defining a common, mentioned previously:

- considering heritage as a fundamental resource,
- acknowledging the community, concerned by this heritage, and
- co-constructing alternative governance strategies and participative tools.

Table 2.1 presents a theoretical framework for co-constructing alternative heritage policies. However, academic research addressing these issues raises several series of questions, which show that the turning point in heritage policies is still uncertain (Auclair et al. 2017). Which actors are really involved? How to mobilize inhabitants, beyond 'informed' people, composed of activists, academics, experts and associative members? Can we really speak of heritage co-construction? Are these processes really bottom-up or are they still 'descending'? Co-constructing heritage induces an 'intercultural' exchange, involving the delicate confrontation of practices, professional cultures, or disciplinary traditions and the questioning of inherited categories. But are researchers, professionals and specialists ready to "accept' and take into account the inhabitants' values and categories? Can they incorporate other discourses, skills, or forms of expertise into their practices? The famous 'collaborative turn' which is stated in many works appears still 'in progress'

Besides, other questions concern the impact of these processes on the territories. What kind of changes do these approaches actually bring to the cities? Patrimonialization processes can indeed be perceived as a means of taking into account everyday practices, valuing marginal territories, supporting social cohesion, integrating socially or spatially excluded minorities and fostering a sense of belonging to the community. But do the experiences of co-construction succeed in meeting these objectives of social justice and democracy and the desires of recognition and integration of the disadvantaged classes? In contemporary urban societies marked by the neo-liberal economic model, a major issue remains the fight against the risks and threats of privatization and commercialization of urban spaces. Do heritage co-construction processes manage to limit the restriction of public spaces and prevent prestigious and costly urban projects often desired and supported by local elected representatives?

The fundamental changes in the growth-oriented methods which seem urgent today can actually be viewed as cultural changes. It seems however that merely praising initiatives and alternative approaches conducted by grassroots social movements can include some risks, amongst which depoliticizing local action and encouraging forms of community individualism, protectionism and cultural isolation. So the current attention given to local social movements should not overshadow the need for a broad political vision. Strong political fights are still probably needed to ensure

Table 2.1   Heritage as a Common

Heritage as a fundamental resource	
Defining 'new' heritage	• ordinary, everyday, living heritage (and not only World Heritage sites, national heritage) • national, local and indigenous cultures • heritage as what counts, what makes sense for people • heritage for conviviality, well-being
A combination of elements	• tangible/ intangible heritage • biodiversity and natural heritage • simple and not only famous architecture and monuments • urban, industrial, rural sites, landscapes • history, memory, identity • traditions, languages, crafts, art and cultural practices
A community concerned by this heritage	
Multiple stakeholders	• inhabitants of a neighbourhood, a village, a town, a region • visitors, tourists • social movements, associations, NGOs • public authorities: local governments, state bodies • experts, cultural institutions, private partners
Objectives and values	• enhancing local identities and places of belonging • promoting cultural diversity and intercultural dialogue • supporting free access to culture and heritage • fostering human rights and cultural rights • promoting social inclusion, equity, fairness • setting heritage between past and future, • preserving and safeguarding heritage, but also transforming, adapting, experiencing
Alternative governance strategies and tools	
General principles	• place-based approaches • bottom-up initiatives • people-centred projects • transversal approaches for territorial development • articulation between short-term and long-term perspectives
Local democracy and citizenship	• supporting inhabitants' participation • fostering empowerment and capabilities • enhancing human dignity, emancipation, self-determination • promoting solidarity, collaboration, co-responsibility • co-constructing projects for defining and managing heritage

emancipation, self-determination and a good life for all and to foster sustainable territories.

NOTES

1. The term ZAD (*Zone d'aménagement différé*) officially means a pending development area. The activists have diverted the expression to name it as a zone to be defended (*Zone à*

défendre). Some people now use the term ZAL (*Zone des alternatives locales*) in order to experiment alternative local projects.

2. The French government announced in January 2018 the abandonment on the project, which raises many debates concerning financial issues of this decision.

3. De-growth in movement(s) : https://www.degrowth.info/en/dim/degrowth-in-movem ents/.

4. AMAP : *Association pour le maintien de l'agriculture paysanne.*

5. Rob Hopkins launched the first project in 2006 in Totnes (Great Britain); there are now approximately 2000 experiences conducted in 50 different countries.

6. Commons Strategies Group, P2P Foundation, Commons Institute, School of Commoning.

7. Open to various associations, social movements and academics concerned by the subject, the project is coordinated by Gilles Yovan and Cristina Bertelli from the association *Les périphéries nous parlent,* Frédéric de Beauvoir, the director of a cooperative cultural centre *Le 100,* and the economist Riccardo Petrella.

8. https://100ecs.fr/universite-du-bien-commun.

9. Several regional natural parks (PNR) in France have developed heritage inventories, such as the PNR de la Vallée de Chevreuse, le PNR du Ballon des Vosges, le PNR du Verdon, le PNR du Pilat and le PNR du Massif des Bauges.

10. The issues in Barcelona were to limit tourism massification, to guarantee the right to housing, and to remunicipalize fundamental services.

11. Livret de l'ARENE (Agence régionale pour l'environnement et les nouvelles énergies) « Culture et développement durable, Initiatives en Ile de France », published in 2011 by the Ile-de-France Region.

REFERENCES

Abraham, Y.M., Marion, L. and Philippe, H., eds., 2011, *Décroissance versus développement durable, ébats pour la suite du monde,* Montreal : Ecosociété.

Acosta, A., 2017, Rethinking the world from the perspective of Buen Vivir, https://www.deg rowth.info/en/dim/degrowth-in-movements/.

Aries, P. (dir) 2010, *Ralentir la ville…pour une ville solidaire,* Villeurbanne : Golias.

Auclair, E., 2011, Revenir vers les habitants, revenir sur les territoires, *Développement durable et territoires* 2, 2

Auclair, E., 2013, *La réappropriation de l'espace public, pour une ville créative et partagée, l'exemple des projets menés par le collectif Cochenko,* Paper presented for the Conference « Engagements et tensions autour de la rénovation urbaine », organised in Paris by the UMR LAVUE and Centre SUD.

Auclair, E. 2014a Paysages ordinaires de banlieue : reconnaissance et appropriation par les habitants, *Paysages urbains d'Ile de France,* Paris : Somogy éditions d'art.

Auclair, E., 2014b, *Culture, art and heritage as commons, a new paradigm for cultural policies ?* Paper presented for the session "Beyond the creative city : culture (policy) pathways towards sustainable urban development", International Conference on Cultural Policy Research, Hildesheim University (Germany).

Auclair, E., 2015a, Ordinary heritage, participation and social cohesion in the banlieues of Paris, Auclair, E. et Fairclough, G. (dir), *Theory and Practice in Heritage and Sustainability: Living between Past and Future",* London: Routledge.

Auclair, E., 2015b, *Heritage as a "common", a conventional idea or a new conceptual framework for sustainability?* Paper presented for the International Conference "Culture(s) in sustainable futures : theories, policies, practices", University of Jyväskylä, Helsinki.

Auclair, E, 2017a, Heritage and sustainability, Lopez Varela, S. (chief editor), *The SAS Encyclopedia of Archeological Sciences*, Wiley Blackwell.

Auclair, E., 2017b, *Heritage as a « common : a framework for degrowth and alternative local governance*, Paper presented for the session « Anarchist political ecology : theoretical horizons and empirical axes », Annual AAG Congress, Boston.

Auclair, E. and Fairclough, G., eds. 2015. *Theory and practice in heritage and sustainability: living between past and future*, London: Routledge.

Auclair, E. et Hertzog, A., 2015, Grands ensembles, cités ouvrières, logement social : patrimoines habités, patrimoines contestés, *Echogéo* (en ligne) 33/2015.

Auclair E., Hertozg A. et Poulot M-L. (dir), 2017, *De la participation à la co-construction des patrimoines, l'invention des communs?*, Paris, Éditions le Manuscrit.

Bauwens, M. et Vasilis Kostakis, 2017, *Manifeste pour une véritable économie collaborative. Vers une société des communs*, Paris : Editions Charles Leopold Meyer.

Bauwens, M. et Lievens, J., 2015, *Sauver le monde : vers une économie post-capitaliste avec le peer-to-peer* , Paris : Editions Les liens qui libèrent.

Baque, M.H., et Biewener, C., 2013, *L'empowerment, une pratique émancipatrice*, Paris : La Découverte.

Bollier, D., 2014, *La renaissance des communs*, Paris : Ed Charles Leopold Mayer.

Bollier, D. and Helfrich, S., 2012, *The wealth of the Commons, a world beyond market and state*, Levellers Press.

Bollier, D. and Helfrich S., 2015, *Patterns of communing*. Common Strategies group and Off the common books, Levellers Press.

Burkhart, C., Schmelzer, M., and Treu, N., 2016, Degrowth in Mouvement, strengthening alternatives and overcoming growth, competition and profit https://www.degrowth.info/en /dim/degrowth-in-movements/.

Caillé, A. et Chanial, P., 2014, *Du convivialisme comme volonté et comme espérance*, MAUSS, La Découverte.

Coriat, B. (dir), 2015, *Le retour des communs. La crise de l'idéologie propriétaire*, Les Liens qui libèrent.

Cornu, M., Orsi, F. and Rochefeld, J., 2017, *Dictionnaire des biens communs*, PUF.

D'Alisa, G., Demaria, F., Kallis, G. (eds), 2014, *Degrowth: a vocabulary for a new era*, New York, London: Routledge.

Daniel, E., 2014, *Le tour de France des alternatives*, Seuil.

De Certeau, M., 1990, *L'invention du quotidien. 1. Arts de faire*, Folio Essai.

Dupin, E., 2014, *Les défricheurs, Voyage dans la France qui innove vraiment*, La Découverte.

Dardot, P. and Laval, C., 2014, *Commun, essai sur la révolution au XXIe siècle*, Paris : La Découverte.

Diestchy, M., 2015, Tensions et compromis dans les valeurs spatiales du slow, *Carnets de géographes* n° 8.

Fabre D., 2013, *Emotions patrimoniales*, Paris, Edition de la Maison des Sciences de l'Homme.

Fabre D., 2016, « L'ordinaire, le familier, l'intime, loin du mouvement », in Hottin C. et Voisenat C. (dir), *Le moment patrimonial. Mutations contemporaines des métiers du patrimoine*, Paris, Editions de la Maison des Sciences de l'homme.

Fairclough, G., Dragicevic Sesic M., Rogac Mijatovic LJ., Auclair E. and Soini K., 2014, The Faro Convention, a new paradigm for socially- and culturally- sustainable heritage action? *Cultura (Skopje)* n° 5, vol IV.

Frère, B. et Jacquemain, M., 2013, *Résister au quotidien ?* Presses de la Fondation Nationale de Sciences Politiques.

Gadrey, J., 2012, *Adieu à la croissance, bien vivre dans un monde solidaire*, Les Petits Matins.

Gadrey, J., 2013, *Les biens communs : une notion au service des projets de l'économie sociale et solidaire*, Alternatives économiques.

Georgescu Roegen, N., 1971, *The entropy law and the economic process*, Harvard University Press.

Georgescu Roegen, N.,1994, *La décroissance*, Paris : Sang de la Terre.

Hardin Garett, 1968, The tragedy of the commons, *Science*, vol 162, issue 3859.

Harvey D., 2012, *Rebel cities. From the right to the city to the urban revolution*, London: Verso.

Hatzfeld, H., 2006, À la recherche d'un bien commun: la demande de paysage, *Les Cahiers de la Compagnie du Paysage*, n°2, Champ Vallon.

Hopkins, R., 2008, *The transition handbook. From Oil dependy to local resilience*, Green books.

Hopkins, R., 2011, *The Transition Companion : Making Your Community More Resilient in Uncertain Times,* Chelsea Green Publishing.

Hopkins, R., 2013, *The Power of Just Doing Stuff : How Local Action Can Change the World*, Green Books.

Hopkins, R. 2014. *Ils changent le monde, 1001 initiatives de transition écologique*, Seuil.

Illich, I.,1973, *La convivialité*, Seuil.

Jackson, T., 2009, *Prosperity without growth: economics for a finite planet*, London and New York: Earthscan/Routledge.

Jonas, H., 1979 (rééd. 1990), *Le principe responsabilité*, Paris: Flammarion, coll. Champs.

Kempf, H., 2009, *Pour sauver la planète, sortez du capitalism*, Seuil.

Latouche, S., 2004, *Survivre au développement, De la décolonisation de l'imaginaire économique à la construction d'une société alternative*, Mille et une nuits.

Latouche, S., 2006, *Le Pari de la décroissance*, Fayard.

Latouche, S., 2007, *Petit traité de la décroissance sereine*, Mille et une nuits.

Latouche, S., 2011, *Vers une société d'abondance frugale. Contresens et controverses sur la décroissance,* Mille et une nuits.

Latouche, S., 2012, *L'âge des limites*, Mille et une nuits.

Le Crosnier, H., 2015, *En communs . une introduction aux communs de la connaissance*, C. et F. Editions.

Lefebvre, H., 1967, *Le droit à la ville*, Paris, Economica, Antropos.

Lille, F., 2008, Que sont les biens publics mondiaux? *Politis* (hors série octobre novembre 2008 : Quelles solutions pour un autre monde?).

Magnaghi, A., 2014, *La biorégion urbaine, petit traité sur le territoire bien commun*, Etoropia, Rizhome.

Manier, B., 2012, *Un million de révolutions tranquilles, Comment les citoyens changent le monde*, Editions Les liens qui libèrent.

Meadows, D., Meadows, D., Randers, J., and Berhens W., 1972, *The limits to growth*, New York: Universe Books.

Micoud, A., 1995, Le bien commun du patrimoine, in *Patrimoine culturel, patrimoine naturel*, La Documentation française.

Nussbaum, M., 2011. *Creating capabilities. The human development approach,* Harvard University Press.

Ostrom, E., 1990, *Governing the Commons: the evolution of institutes for collective action*, Cambridge University Press.

Paulson, S , 2017, Degrowth: culture, power, change, *Journal of political ecology,* vol 24, n°1.

Pleyers, G. et Glasius, M., 2013, La résonance des « mouvements des places » : connexions, émotions, valeurs , *Socio,* 2 | 2013, 59–80.

Rabhi, P., 2010, *Vers la sobriété heureuse,* Actes sud.

Rist, G., 2009, *Développement, histoire d'une croyance occidentale,* Paris Presses de Sciences Po.

Sen, A., 1985, *Commodities and capabilities,* Amsterdam: North Holland.

Sgard, A., 2010. Le paysage dans l'action publique : du patrimoine au bien commun. *Développement durable et territoires volume 1, n°2.*

Smith L., 2006, *Uses of heritage,* Routledge.

Sohn, H. Kousoulas, S. and Bruyns G. (eds), 2015, Commoning as differentiated publicness. Emerging concepts of the urban and other material realities, *Footprint* vol 9.

Veschambre V., 2008, *Traces et mémoires urbaines. Enjeux sociaux de la patrimonialisation et de la démolition,* Rennes, PUR.

Watremez A., 2008, « Vivre le patrimoine urbain au quotidien : pour une approche de la patrimonialité », *Culture & musées* n° 11.

3

Local Resistance to Mega Infrastructure Projects as a Place of Emancipation

Land Use Conflicts, Radical Democracy and Oppositional Public Spaces

Jérôme Pélenc, Anahita Grisoni, Julien Milanesi,
Léa Sébastien and Manuel Cervera-Marzal

Since the 2008 crisis, mega infrastructure projects in western Europe, such as airports, high-speed trains, shopping malls, dams, mega-jails, nuclear waste treatment plants, landfills, highways and massive tourist facilities, have been increasingly contested. One of the most vivid manifestations of this contestation is the 'unnecessary and imposed mega-projects' resistance movement (Robert, 2014). This decentralized movement – Robert (2014) speaks of a rhizome of resistance – is composed of multiple, place-based struggles that have assembled a diversity of actors, for example, local inhabitants, farmers, local NGOs, ecological and anti-capitalist militants and activists, who are sometimes, but not always, associated with the illegal occupation of threatened land. Since 2010, the movement has met every year as part of a forum to contest 'unnecessary and imposed mega-projects', an expression that was created by the movement itself and that illustrates the common threads of the different struggles. These place-based struggles are not only against planned territorial infrastructures but against the world they represent. In this sense, they constitute the first stage of re-politicizing the environment.

By bringing together elements from political ecology, radical democracy theory and anarchist geography, this chapter provides the first comprehensive analysis of the 'unnecessary and imposed mega-projects' resistance movement and highlights its relevance as both an 'object of study' and 'a subject of change' (social movement and transformative force) in the construction of an anarchist political ecology. With regard to the methodological aspects, the chapter has been written by five researchers who have been involved in varying degrees and from various positions, that is, from activism to a more academic action research in various struggles against megaprojects in France, Italy and Belgium. A multiplicity of methods has been used, depending on the personal lines of research, ranging from participant observation, semi-structured interviews to the making of a documentary. Rather than present a particular case study or method, this chapter is therefore an attempt to offer an indepth analysis of the movement by combining the authors' personal experiences with a variety of academic and militant literature.

The chapter first explains how political ecologists conceptualize environmental de-politicization before giving an overview of the 'unnecessary and imposed mega-projects' resistance movement. Under the auspices of radical democracy, we then build our theoretical framework by establishing a dialogue between Simon Springer's conception of public space and Oskar Negt's concept of 'oppositional public space'. In the final section, we illustrate this framework by analysing the discourse of the 'unnecessary and imposed mega-projects' resistance movement through the lens of oppositional public space. We conclude by arguing that this movement creates an opportunity to re-politicize the environment, and thus an opportunity to develop an anarchist political ecology.

THE POST-POLITICAL SITUATION AND THE DE-POLITICIZATION OF THE ENVIRONMENT

At the end of the 1990s/beginning of the 2000s, several political philosophers, such as Chantal Mouffe (2005), Jacques Rancière (1999), Slavoj Žižek (1999), Colin Crouch (2004), started to speak of 'de-politicization', 'post-political' and 'post-democratic' with reference to the deterioration of our democracies. Kenis and Lievens (2014) explain that *depoliticization* happens when the exercise of hegemonic power and the antagonisms that result from it are covered up. It is the hegemony of neo-liberal discourse and politics that ignores alternatives and conceals conflict, division and power. The space of the political is being foreclosed when the predominant representations of society no longer recognize their contingency and become embedded in non-contestable, essentialist principles which may be technical (austerity), religious (divine laws), natural (ecological dictatorship), etc. What remains invisible in 'post-politics'[1] is the fact that a social order is fundamentally contingent and that embedding a social order always generates exclusions, and therefore antagonisms. As a consequence, any dissident voice which radically contests the dominant order is considered an 'enemy of democracy' to be eliminated or silenced. Japhy Wilson and Eric Swyngedouw (2014, p6 and 8), after a wide review of the literature on the topic, offer the following description of post-politics:

> a situation in which the political – understood as a space of contestation and agonistic engagement[2] – is increasingly colonised by politics – understood as technocratic mechanisms and consensual procedures that operate within an unquestioned framework of

representative democracy, free market economics, and cosmopolitan liberalism. In post-politics, political contradictions are reduced to policy problems to be managed by experts and legitimated through participatory processes in which the scope of possible outcomes is narrowly defined in advance.

On the contrary, it is the loss of the 'political' that undermines democracy, not the other way around. Indeed, according to Kenis and Lievens (2014, p533), 'the very condition of possibility of democracy is to make the political dimension of social relations and of our relation to "nature" visible, and to turn it into the object of debate and conflict'. The authors argue that neo-liberal environmental governance, as a manifestation of the post-political order, has tended to reduce sustainability issues to technical questions through the imposition of the techno-scientific and economic rationality and through state-controlled procedures of so-called 'participation'. Thus, eco-modernization and green economy discourses dominate. From this perspective, 'Questions of socio-ecological inequality, environmental destruction and its associated power relations are relegated to an issue of effective techno-scientific eco-management' (Swyngedouw and Kaika, 2014, p 468).

We now present two major reasons for the difficulty in politicizing the environment. Swyngedouw (2007, 2009 and 2010)[3] explains that environmental questions are easily depoliticized, because they lack a clearly identifiable subject of change. Consequently, the environment is externalized from the social and we observe an absurd formulation of the ecological crisis, such as climate change that leads to 'society versus CO_2,' while almost every human or non-human action (breathing) involves CO_2 as a by-product (Swyngedouw, 2013). According to Swyngedouw, this absence of an identifiable political agent is a major element that distinguishes 'environmentalism' from other social movements, such as feminism, the civil rights movement, or the labour movement, where the subject of oppression, struggle and change is easily identified: women, African-Americans, workers.

For Kenis and Lievens (2014, p540), a second reason behind the de-politicization of environmental issues is the lack of *specific objects of focus* in which we could embed environmental change: 'strictly speaking, every single social relation, practice, or event has an environmental impact'. Consequently, this has led to a fundamental question: where do we begin? And we have observed a strong fragmentation of environmental actions, that is, the fight against biodiversity loss, desertification, water/air pollution, waste, urban agriculture and the demand for food sovereignty.

After a wide review of the literature on environmental post-politics, Kenis and Lievens (2014) affirm that it seems to be easier to diagnose de-politicization than provide suggestions for overcoming it. The goal of this chapter however is to demonstrate that place-based struggles, and in particular resistance to unnecessary and imposed mega-projects, offers a wealth of political subjects and specific objects upon which a 'genuine' process of (re)politicization of environmental issues can be constructed.

THE 'UNNECESSARY AND IMPOSED MEGA-PROJECTS' RESISTANCE MOVEMENT

Brief History and Main Characteristics of the Movement

Although opposition to land use projects is not new, the originality of the 'unnecessary and imposed mega-projects' resistance movement has been to bring together different struggles against different types of projects across different territories in Europe under the same banner since 2010. Indeed, before the rise of this movement, territorial resistance was either geographically or thematically based, for example the anti-nuclear movement in France/Germany and the anti-road movement in the United Kingdom, etc.

The 'unnecessary and imposed mega-projects' (UIMP) resistance movement was initiated in 2010 during a demonstration against high-speed trains by more than 15,000 people assembled between Hendaye and Irun on the Franco-Spanish border. French, Spanish and Italian organizations were present. At the end of the demonstration, they signed a common declaration, the 'Charter of Hendaye', acknowledging that transportation problems are the same everywhere and hence any opposition should shift from a local to a European context. Now the movement meets every year at a specific site of resistance. On average around forty resistance movements are represented at the annual forum (for a detailed analysis of the participants and their origins, see Robert, 2014). In 2011, the movement met in Val di Susa in northern Italy near the Alps where there still is a strong opposition to a high-speed train project between Lyon (France) and Turin (Italy). It is one of the most emblematic cases of the UIMP movement which notably comprises the illegal occupation of a large part of the threatened valley (see Ariemma and Burnside-Lawry, 2016). The movement is known as NOTAV. The occupation has been inspired and fuelled by the long anarchist tradition in Italy and by the numerous anarchist social centers that exist all over the country. In 2012, the forum was held in Notre-Dames-Des-Landes near Nantes (western France) where there is considerable opposition to an airport project (for details see Robert, 2014) that would destroy 1,000 hectares of natural and agricultural land. This case is also emblematic, notably because of the illegal land occupation that started in 2009 after a Climate Action Camp. The occupation is referred to as a ZAD 'zone to defend', and it has inspired a myriad of other movements against mega-projects in France and Belgium; illegal occupation has been adopted as the modus operandi for concerted action.[4] The ZAD movement in Notre-Dames-Des-Landes regularly refers to the 1871 Paris Commune insurrection (see Mauvaise Troupe, 2016a, b). In March 2013, the movement gathered at the world social forum in Tunis where a new charter was adopted. In substance, the Tunis charter declares that the battle of the movement goes beyond transport infrastructure and local issues to resisting capitalism as a whole. In a sense, this movement is an attempt to effectively block capitalism on the ground: 'Mega projects permit the capitalist predator to increase its dominance on the planet generating irreversible damage to the environment and the populace'. During the summer of 2013, the annual forum was organized in Stuttgart (Germany) where there is a strong resistance to the construction of a new train station; the movement is known as Stuttgart 21. In 2014, the forum was organized in Rosia Montana, Romania, where there is a strong social movement against a gold mine mega-project. In 2015, the forum was organized in Bergnara Arsa (northern Italy) by the collective fighting against a high-speed train project, and the 2016 forum was held in Bayonne in the French Basque country where local people are known for having a culture of resistance and where there are currently several 'development' projects on the go, such as a new high-speed train and mining.

This brief description of the movement illustrates two things: the movement is a constellation of interrelated place-based struggles at a European level, so it is bound to specific places, but connected transnationally and horizontally (idea of the rhizome developed by Diane Robert, 2014). Second, as illustrated by the Tunis charter, it is a movement of resistance, not only against specific projects but also against the 'capitalist world that they represent'. Consequently, the 'unity' of the movement can be found in a shared interpretation of who the enemy is and a more or less shared vision of the desirable world they want to build rather than in an organizational structure. This corresponds reasonably well to an anarchist organization.

Finally, one other particularity of this movement is that it brings together different types of actors. Indeed, the movement is composed of activists who illegally occupy threatened land, but also of activists who just want to lend a hand or sympathize with the cause. Then there are the local inhabitants who are directly concerned by the impact of the projects, for example, the farmers in the case of Notre-Dame-Des-Landes. Last but not least is a constellation of local/regional and sometimes national NGOs that were either created specifically for the struggle or have lent their support to the resistance. As a result, we have been able to witness the creation of highly 'unlikely' popular anti-project coalitions. This diversity of actors entails a diversity of *modi operandi* which are more or less complementary, ranging from petitions, lobbying and meeting with elected representatives to street protests and legal action, and to direct illegal action and activism. This diversity of people and actions is a source of richness and at the same time a source of conflict, notably between locals and outsiders, legalists and illegalists, the 'established' and the newcomers, those who occupy and those who do not, etc. We will now explain the 'unnecessary and imposed' character in detail.

Unnecessary Mega-Projects

According to Robert (2014, p69), 'By calling the projects against which they fight "unnecessary", the rhizome of resistance against mega projects reintroduces the issue of class struggle between the few beneficiaries of construction and exploitation of mega projects and the vast majority of people who are ripped off'. Indeed, the question is: who are the real beneficiaries of these mega-projects? The Tunis charter proclaims: 'Useless and Imposed Mega Projects are instruments that guarantee exorbitant profits for large industrial and financial groups, civilians and military persons, who are no longer able to obtain the elevated rate of profit in the saturated global market'. This statement is corroborated by scholars (notably Hildyard, 2012) who have highlighted that mega infrastructure projects have been identified by the financial sphere as first-class assets. Indeed, after the 2008 financial crisis, some investors started looking for profitable and less risky investments. The construction of these projects and sometimes their management (the airport project in Norte-Dames-Des-Landes for example) are operated through public–private partnerships. This type of contract has demonstrated its advantages for private companies and its disadvantages for public bodies: in sum, profit for the private sector and losses for the public sector. It is often associated with the privatization of public infrastructure or services. One could hypothesize in similar vein to the urbanization model described by David Harvey (2012) that the development of new infrastructure (at least in industrialized countries which are already saturated with infrastructure) is a way to reinvest the over-accumulation of capital in order to make new profits. Some transnational companies, such as Macquarie (an Australian private equity fund), seem to specialize in this activity. Spanish anarchist Miguel Amoros (2015, p131) explains: 'the impact (on capital accumulation) of the decline in the rate of profit and the decline in the rate of value can be compensated by the destruction of territory, that is to say, by transforming it into a productive force: wind power, fracking, GMOs, landfill sites, infrastructure, etc.' Moreover, as highlighted by the Tunis charter, the cost-benefit analysis for these projects, including job creation, is always overestimated. In addition, these projects are often denounced for their vested interests (see Robert, 2014 in relation to Notre-Dames-Des-Landes and Val di Susa). Finally, as mentioned in the Tunis charter, these mega-projects are detrimental to local needs, the local population, the local economy and the local (and global) environment, whereas the movement, in its various place-based struggles, has constantly demonstrated the advantages of cheaper, less risky and more sustainable alternatives, notably the benefits over costs of improving existing infrastructure rather than creating new infrastructure. Indeed, all the inherent weaknesses of mega infrastructure projects have led Ben Flivberg (2005) to call them 'Machiavellian mega projects'.

Imposed Mega-Projects

In a post-political situation, the decision about these projects inevitably comes across as being imposed, simply because any radical contestation is not possible within our post-political institutions. Besides the fact that so-called 'participatory procedures' have been implemented in European countries, the decision regarding the public utility or general interest of the mega infrastructure project seems in most cases to be defined before the participatory process begins. The public debate/consultation process only invites criticism of technical characteristics; there is no possibility of questioning the utility or soundness of the project. Place-based struggles are the manifestation of the failure of 'participatory governance'. The Tunis charter states that mega-projects 'exclude the effective participation of the population in the decision-making process and deny them access to the means of communication'. Indeed, either the procedure restricts the participation to technical comments or the project promoters argue that the project complies with all legal procedures and has been validated by elected representatives, thus it is impossible to question its legitimacy. In the case of strong resistance, such as Notre-Dame-Des-Landes, central government representatives (the prefect) can overrule the contestation and sign the 'public utility' document authorizing expropriations.

In this context, any dissident voice which radically contests the dominant order is considered at best as illegitimate and simply ignored, or at worst, an enemy of democracy to be silenced or labelled as an eco-terrorist. To speak in Chantal Mouffe's (2005) terms, the possibility of an agonistic confrontation, between equal political adversaries, turns into antagonism between enemies. If disagreement cannot be expressed in the political realm, it leads to violence. Contrary to what they claim the current 'post-political' institutions, via their obsession with consensus, control and security, generate exclusion and therefore violence. The state hence turns its monopoly of legitimate violence on those movements it places outside the democratic community. The Tunis charter emphasizes 'the militarization and criminalization of opposition' with reference to the massive presence of military forces and excessively armed riot police during demonstrations and to their intervention in the different illegal land occupations (Robert, 2014). This has led to numerous serious injuries and to the death of a young activist, Rémi Fraisse, on 25th October 2014 at the ZAD against the Sivens dam (south of France). The exclusion from public space and deliberation has been strengthened by the exclusion from or lack of access to mainstream media and more largely to the public sphere.

To conclude, since the 2008 financial crisis and the austerity measures that have been implemented all over Europe, and since the arrival of an ever-increasing number of global ecological crises, mega-projects appear completely incoherent with the critical situation we face. They come across as being 'unnecessary' and 'imposed' on a subaltern population who alone bear the costs (financial cost of construction, debt, socio-environmental degradation, etc.). These projects are symptomatic of the social metabolism of neo-liberalism that results from accumulation by dispossession. In line with Armario and D'alisa (2012, p57), we argue that: 'these conflicts should be seen and analysed as an experiment in new forms of participation, which are reshaping the borders among politics, science and the self'.

RADICAL DEMOCRACY, OPPOSITIONAL PUBLIC SPACE AND PLACE-BASED STRUGGLES

In this section, we build a theoretical framework in order to deepen the analysis of the 'unnecessary and imposed mega-projects' resistance movement and assign it an important role in the construction of an anarchist political ecology.

Radical Democracy and Agonistic Public Space

The concept of radical democracy was introduced in the 2000s as a reaction to the post-political order which had been established after the implementation of liberal democracy under the neo-liberal paradigm. Chantal Mouffe (2005, 2013) and Jacques Rancières (1999, 2001, 2010) are two of the most prominent radical democracy thinkers. In contrast to a liberal conception where democracy is understood as a quest for consensus through deliberative (Habermas' public sphere) or aggregative (voting, cost-benefit analysis, economic rationality) methods, a radical conception states that conflict, dissent and disagreement constitute a truly political conception of democracy. From this perspective, democracy is not a regime composed of stable (and unquestionable) institutions that guarantee individual freedoms (as it is in the liberal conception) but as a *praxis* of continuous scrutiny of the established power and its institutions. This is a perpetual struggle against the institutionalization of domination. Consequently, such reasoning enables us to see the emergence of democracy (understood in its radical conception) as antithetical to the development of centralized institutions, and ultimately, antithetical to the state (Abensour, 2004). Thus, as highlighted by anarchist geographer Simon Springer (2010, p533), the radical conception[5] of democracy is really close to that of anarchy: 'Radical democracy represents a disturbance of the anti-political order of sovereignty itself, and is thus, in a word, anarchy'.

At the heart of radical democracy lies a particular conception of public space that represents a manifestation of the political.[6] In line with radical democracy thinkers, Springer develops a particularly interesting conception of the public space: 'I argue for a conceptualization of public space that emphasizes an anti-hegemonic, anti-sovereign current, thus offering an opportunity to surmount the technocratic elitism that characterizes neoliberal approaches to development and problematizes civil societies. [. . .] Public space is understood as the battlefield on which the conflicting interests of the rich and poor are set, as well as the object of contestation' (2010, p526). One of the major facets of his chapter is how he develops a strong critique of the Habermassian public sphere, which has no physicalness, notably by establishing a clear difference between a public sphere and a public space: 'In contrast, public space must be taken literally as a material space precisely because this dimension provides visibility to political action. [. . .] In this light, the struggle for democracy is inseparable from public space' (Springer, 2010, 538 and 541). This conception of public space echoes what the German philosopher Oskar Negt[7] refers to as 'oppositional public space'.

Introducing the Oppositional Public Space

Alexander von Neumann, who has translated and popularized the work of Negt in France, asks the following question: 'What happens when social groups that are kept away from public deliberation become active and speak out outside the recognized political space?' (2014, p6). The answer is that we witness the creation of what Oskar Negt (2007) calls an 'oppositional public space'. Negt elaborated his concept in response to Habermas' 'bourgeois public sphere'. According to Negt (2007, p27):

Historically, the Bourgeois have used public space to resolve their differences, iron out certain problems and defend their interests while simultaneously excluding or neutralizing whole swathes of society. This control has led to public space taking on the mantle of an 'illusory social synthesis'. And the social groups which have been excluded from public deliberation choose to act and speak out as members of uprisings and movements occurring in various locations and adhering to various structures such as clubs, committees and councils created and sustained outside of the bourgeois public sphere that feigns to represent all society.

In a more recent discourse held in a French university after the 2008 financial crisis, Negt (2009, p192) goes on to explain: 'The bourgeois public sphere has no connection with the various forms of direct struggle against the social crisis because this "official" public space freely repeats the language and symbolism of the established economic order. [. . .] Constructing a suitable public space is one of the decisive elements of organized resistance and alternative courses of action'. In contrast to Habermas' idealized, bourgeois public sphere – conceived as a forum for deliberation and democratic representation which seeks consensus between parties based on 'reason and rationality' – Oskar Negt highlights the need to build an oppositional public space, a plebeian space where urban revolts and street demonstrations, may find their place (Sagradini, 2009). This notion of oppositional public space reintegrates the conflictual character of the social into the analysis by making visible those who were previously unheard and invisible (Sangradini, 2009). As noted by Springer (2010, p532): 'Radical democracy occurs when those who the sovereign deems to not count insist on being counted, not within the existing order, but within a new anti-order, an anarchy'. So this concept appears to be the conception of public space that matches the theoretical requirements of radical democracy described above. Indeed, it provides radical democracy with a strong and coherent conception of public space that puts conflict at the heart of democracy.

The Actors Involved in Oppositional Public Spaces

Having briefly introduced the concept of oppositional public space, we will now examine the actors involved. Although Negt also named his concept 'proletarian public space', the working class or workers in a Marxist sense are not the only relevant actors in an oppositional public space. Indeed, according to Von Neumann (2014), it is the lived experience of non-recognition that confers the 'proletarian quality' to an oppositional public space rather than an abstract, predefined social group, such as the industrial working class. Idem, Von Neumann explains that Negt warns us about using a general concept such as citizen or civil society. Von Neumann specifies that rather than representing an ideological struggle between two predefined/predetermined classes, bourgeois and proletarian public spaces denote two different ways of envisaging the actors' social experience. The bourgeois public sphere denotes the individual experience of citizens through abstract, general categories, whereas the oppositional public space respects and articulates the particular experience of certain social groups and individuals, and hence resists abstraction, de-contextualization, etc. Christophe Baticle (2015), who adopted the concept of oppositional public space to analyse the political discourse of a particular social group – hunters – in France, arrived at the same conclusion. Despite the fact they economically belong to the working class, they were more inclined to fight for their 'hobby' than for their job because their identity, and thus their lived experience of non-recognition was associated with their hunting, culture and traditions rather than their jobs. In this respect, Roger Gould, in his classic discussion of the Paris Commune, reminds us that: 'What tied workers from different occupations together in the Commune were the tangible bonds they experienced as neighbors, not the abstract bonds of joint structural position in the capitalist mode of production' (1993, p751).[8] This reasoning highlights the importance of the role of a particular territory and particular places for the emergence of oppositional actors.

Oppositional Public Spaces and Territory

As mentioned earlier, Simon Springer (2010) has introduced a useful distinction between a public sphere[9] and a public space. He specifies: 'Action and speech require visibility because for democratic politics to occur, it is not enough for a group of private individuals to vote anonymously as in aggregative democracy. Instead, because belonging to any public requires at least minimal participation, individuals must physically come together and occupy a common space' (2010, p537). He later adds: 'Public space offers a spatial medium to the frustrations subalterns feel with regard to systems of archy, neoliberal or otherwise. It allows them to locate their anger in a material sense' (p553). Eric Swyngedouw's formulation of the political echoes Springer's conception: 'The political is theatrically staged and enacted in the act of transgressing the socio-spatial configuration such that simultaneously equality is performed and the 'wrong' (the inegalitarian practice inscribed in the police) exposed' (Swyngedouw, 2011, p9). We argue that struggling territories, conceptualized as oppositional public spaces, are places where individual experiences of frustration, anger, violence, domination, etc. can be expressed in a common space and thus acquire a collective character. According to Baticle (2015), what gathers the actors of an oppositional public together is a kind of 'sensory' solidarity. More specifically, class consciousness, which is now so cruelly missing in the minds of the dominated, must be activated through the socializing experience of a proletarian public space, and hence a transgression of the spatial order imposed by class relations (ibid.). From this perspective, the occupation of the contested territory is a response to the lived experience of the domination and the affirmation of the legitimacy of the right to claim an equal voice in decision-making. In regard to our object of interest, that is, the 'unnecessary and imposed mega-projects' resistance movement, we agree with Chambru (2014), who studied the French anti-nuclear movement, that we are witnessing the creation of a fragmented (inter)national oppositional public space embedded in each local contestation. This dynamic transforms the local into a proper political space where issues at stake can be contested and contradictory debates can emerge. The actors involved in these oppositional public spaces develop counter-hegemonic alliances that are constantly renegotiated but which converge to a certain extent to defend and promote the threatened territory.

Re-politicization and Emancipation

Having developed our reasoning during this section, we will now define what we understand by re-politicization and emancipation.

If we consider the definition of de-politicization as the removal of conflict and contradictory debate, then the explosion of oppositional public spaces can be seen as a process of re-politicization, that is, as a means of contestation outside the 'policed public' spaces controlled by the dominant order. According to Swyngedouw (2011, p7, 8):

> The emergence of the politicization is always specific, concrete, particular but stands as the metaphorical condensation of the universal. This procedure implies the production of new material and discursive spatialities within and through the existing spatialities of the police. [. . .] Such production operates through the (re-) appropriation of space, the production of new spatial qualities and new spatial relations, both materially and symbolically, and express what Castoriadis would call a radical imaginary at work.

At an individual level, re-politicization might simply be the participation of an individual in an oppositional public space, and more generally as the development of 'struggling' or 'rebel' individual and collective subjectivities.

Springer (2010, p525 and 554) formulates the following definition for emancipation: 'Emancipation, understood here, means perpetual contestation of the alienating effects of contemporary Neoliberalization [   ] Emancipation must accordingly be understood as an awakening, a (re)discovery of power that is deeply rooted in processes of mobilization and transformation'. To speak with Castoriadis, we should add that emancipation is an endless struggle against established power. According to Kenis and Lievens (2014), Slavoj Žižek (2008, 2009a) sees the re-politicization of environmental questions as a potential emancipatory struggle. Following Ranciere's conception of the political, we can say that by resisting the opponents of imposed projects cause a dissident voice to be heard, a voice which was previously inaudible. They act as if they had the same say as more powerful agents. By acting this way, they make a conflict visible, they develop a counter-hegemonic discourse, and they construct a truly contradictory debate. In sum, they create what Oskar Negt's names 'oppositional public space'. This 'oppositional public space' is emancipatory because it is the vivid manifestation of the claim by the dominated for political equality.

When Two Irreconcilable Visions of Society Collide Spatially

In this final section, we contend that the movement against mega-projects is the concrete manifestation of the emergence of a place-based European oppositional public space. We thus investigate the makeup of this oppositional public space. We argue that this resistance movement focuses on contested land use projects as a vehicle for criticizing capitalism and hence creates a dissensus that disrupts the de-politicizing order established by neo-liberal governments. More specifically, these contested spaces articulate the dissensus around four conflicting key points. On the one hand, by basing their argument on techno-science and economic rationality, the promoters of mega-projects (upholders of the dominant order) advocate ecological compensation, growth and acceleration, globalization and representative (expert) 'democracy'. On the other hand, by basing their arguments on the 'lived experience of the territory' and criticism of 'technological gigantism', the opponents of mega-projects advocate ecological conservation, de-growth and deceleration, re-localization and direct democracy.

Growth and Acceleration versus De-growth and Deceleration

Discussions on growth are not something new, but the advent of the 'unnecessary and imposed mega-projects' resistance movement has brought an extra dimension to the debate. First, the movement highlights the pernicious effects of the commitment to growth and its hidden, shameful facets. Our consumer society does not appear quite so wonderful near a landfill site or deep inside the burial chambers for radioactive waste at Bure. The idea of preying on natural resources becomes much less abstract when contemplating a quarry that has devoured the body of a mountain, and the true value of the semantic riches associated with green, ecological and sustainable growth becomes much harder to appreciate when contemplating the 'archetypal' construction of a motorway. The resistance movement has formed a discourse on the direct, tangible effects of growth on different territories. This discourse is necessarily anti-growth, and it derives from the field, or rather, the land experience.

Mega-projects continue regardless because they are borne forward by an imagined scenario whose gaze is riveted on the future, and therefore the possibility of a saturation point ever being reached is rejected. Has anyone realized yet that there are sufficient roads, airports, high-speed railway lines and supermarkets to meet the needs of the populace? Promoters insist that this infrastructure will eventually become 'crowded" and therefore inadequate. Protesting the use of public funds for such risks and gambles (reflecting the usual outcome, i.e., the privatization of profits and the socialization of losses) are at the very core of a rationale that, interestingly, has shifted the debate towards conflicting expectations of what the future might hold. The official view of this uncertainty is one of a slower but constant increase in the mobility of people and goods in the years to come. It is a vision of the future which is contested by those who consider that the degree of maturity of advanced economies in tandem with recurring ecological crises will lead to a decrease, or at the very least, a stagnation in mobility.

The imagined scenario of growth has sat and still sits alongside the imagined ideal of an unremitting rise in production, consumption and mobility, which has been countered by ecology movements ever since the 1960s. But what has changed is that this imagined scenario is no longer contested from a normative point of view but by the facts from the ground. Mobility, together with other variables, is no longer rising as planned and, even worse, the whole system seems to be grinding to a halt. Behind the errors that the state has made in terms of rising road traffic, etc. we can see that future economic growth has been largely overestimated: GDP in 2015 was 20 per cent below what was projected in 1995.[10]

The 'unnecessary and imposed mega-projects' resistance movement has openly questioned economic growth and shown the urgency of redefining an imagined scenario which is adapted to a new era of post-growth.

Globalization versus Re-localization

In the face of the growth crisis that industrialized countries have been experiencing over the last forty years,[11] the dominant economic discourse has been one of encouraging national economies to push deeper into the mire of liberal globalization, and this requires the construction of a certain kind of bigger, larger, vaster infrastructure which has gradually left territories competing with each other for a slice of the transnational market. The aim has been to find, for example, in emerging markets, an external 'lifeline' for faltering internal growth. Moreover, developing a territory means creating or supporting a modern, competitive sector located in rival cities (Faburel et Girault, 2016). Territorial competitiveness has therefore become a major justification by cities for implementing mega infrastructure projects.

Today's resistance movements are fighting against the pursuit of this type of logic. This is the second line of disagreement. The rejection of these projects has therefore rapidly become the rejection of globalization and the heightened pressure on local lives and local areas to be competitive. Hartmut Rosa's research on social acceleration, that is, 'the desynchronisation of socioeconomic development and political action' (Rosa 2012, p 313),[12] is reflected in the comments by a protestor against the South-west high-speed rail mega-project on the potential consequences of this reorganization of the world on social cohesion: 'It's going to mean that people can travel really quickly from one place to another, and it's going to mean that people are going to be completely isolated. The people they're with in their work are never going to be the people they're with in their community. And if you want my opinion, this model of society is doomed'. Moreover, criticizing these projects is also a way of drawing attention to the environmental impact of globalization and questioning the relevance of proliferating free trade agreements at an international level.

Having taken ownership of social, economic and environmental issues, protestors have often reached the conclusion that organized, harmonious, endogenous local development, based on the reintroduction of a localized production system, is the most appropriate model.

Ecological Compensation versus Ecological Conservation

The growth and globalization discourse surrounding mega-projects can no longer avoid the ecological sustainability of this development model being scrutinized. As a result, the ecological component, that is compensation measures, is now included from the outset. This is the third source of major disagreement between promoters and protesters: the perception of ecological issues.

This disagreement is based on the well-known conflict between compensation measures and conservation measures and between the weak conceptions and strong conceptions of the substitutability of natural capital for economic capital and vice versa. In the face of a discourse that recommends pursuing development projects balanced by compensation payments for any CO_2 emissions or damage caused to nature ('the avoid, reduce, compensate mantra gives the false impression that everything will turn out just fine')[18], protesters respond by emphasizing the severity of ecological crises and the need to stop, *a priori*, any further development.

Behind these various arguments looms the irreversibility of an ecological crisis that brooks no compromise. Compensation measures have been contested, because they do not reduce the overall destruction of natural areas. They do not stop the whole process, and for voluntary organizations, any loss of natural space is a permanent loss of its ecological uniqueness and heritage.

Mega-projects that cause CO_2 emissions are also strongly contested from the standpoint of irreversibility because they provoke climate change, which is extremely serious. In addition, international commitment to a reduction in greenhouse gases supposedly places a brake on these projects: such an ambition is incompatible with 'climaticide' mega-projects; therefore, these projects must be abandoned.

Technophilia and Faith in Technoscientific Progress versus Technocriticism

In addition to compensation measures, promoters of mega-projects employ technological optimism to counter the reversibility of ecological crises. As a manifestation of faith in progress (Mussot, 2017), this discourse rejects the notion of impossibility linked to the hypothetical failure of technology, for example, following the construction of new infrastructure, increased air and road traffic is compatible with a fourfold reduction in greenhouse gases due to the spread of electric transport systems. We can also observe this optimism in relation to risk, especially the hazard of nuclear risk. 'When all said and done, progress nowadays is not about building more and more. I think that's how people see it. Progress is using what we have and making an effort to preserve what there is to preserve'.

Resistance movements are against this sort of gambling against the risk of irreversible change. They advocate caution and point to the headlong rush (see Illitch, Ellul and Charbonneau) towards technological solutions for problems caused by other technology, for example, in the case of the high-speed rail: 'All this technophilia stuff is just a magic potion. We're part of a society where everything can be sorted out with technology. Who cares that we still haven't figured out what to do with nuclear waste? It's like it doesn't matter'. Protesters are pushing for solutions that reflect social innovation, and this sits well with their imagined economic scenario of a return to localized activities. For them, carpooling is significantly more preferable to a new ring road and electric cars.

The 'unnecessary and imposed mega-projects' resistance movement shatters the vision of technology and progress operating in harmony. Time-saving has always been one of the main arguments used by the promoters of mega infrastructure projects, and even today it represents the overwhelming contribution to the projected earnings calculated by the state when undertaking the socioeconomic analysis of a project. In the face of an imagined scenario where journey times and the conception of distance are reduced to an absolute minimum, protesters are there to raise the specter of adverse economic, ecological and social effects of this headlong rush and praise the benefits of slowing down.

To conclude this section, we think with Grisoni (2018) that looking at these multiple place-based struggles through the conflictual lens makes it possible to integrate them to a broader social and political landscape, thus avoiding the pitfall of isolating the 'environment' as a politically neutral domain. Thus, this contributes to the task of the 'politicization of nature' advocated, amongst others, by political ecology scholars. Like Armario and D'alisa (2012, p59), we believe that place-based struggles exemplify the failure of the de-politicization of environmental issues and offer an example of re-politicization from a local level upward:

> Instead everything science, technology, the market, spaces, and bodies has become political. Fighting for the politicization of the process and of the very objects in question, the metabolic relationships linking production and consumption with the environment and people's bodies is what is at stake. This, in turn, creates room for conflict and democratic participation.

In line with Grisoni (2018), we argue that this re-politicization can be understood as the creation of oppositional public spaces which compete with and sometime disrupt the policed public sphere. These oppositional public spaces are built by the activists around socio-ecological continuities to which they identify. This individual and collective identification is elaborated in a way that is not metaphorical but through the use of tangible material elements that compose the territory – a forest, a valley, a river, or even a wasteland, etc.

CONCLUSION

Set in opposition to each other are the 'public sphere', which comprises proponents of liberal democracy, elected representatives, major media outlets, that is the elite, and the 'oppositional public space', which comprises protesters. As Springer has noted, these oppositional public spaces, in contrast to 'public spheres', are defined by their physicalness: an oppositional public space is material; a public sphere is immaterial. It is also a 'perceived-lived' space formed by protesters as a response to the 'conceived', even 'preconceived', space of developers, planners and other decision-makers. The concept of oppositional public space therefore embraces the creation of counter-hegemony discourses grounded in alternative/disruptive practices to re-appropriate threatened land. It is about defending a space against an unnecessary and imposed future by using alternative, oppositional practices that crash the party of the dominant order and at the very least, disrupt this party as much as possible. These practices enable the contestation of the capitalist, authoritarian appropriation of a space and its re-appropriation as an autonomous, emancipatory space.

The argumentation developed throughout this chapter naturally brings us to embrace the statement made by Kenis and Lieven (2014, p541): 'if we want to re-politicise environmental issues, not only 'nature' but also every enmity and conflict should be "internalised" again'. Indeed, as identified more than thirty years ago by Murray Bookchin (1985), environmental crises are not crises of 'nature' but crises of society and how the latter relates to its 'natural' conditions. According to Bookchin (1985), environmental problems are embedded in hierarchical forms of power and social organizations associated with capitalist modes of production and consumption. The very notion of the domination of nature by human beings stems from the very real domination of human beings by other human beings. In other words, as argued by Kenis and Lieven (2014, p541): 'we should turn environmental crises into social ones'. Local environmental resistance directly confronts the com-modification of nature, and thus it is where the dominant socio-ecological order can be directly contested (Martinez et al., 2016). We believe that the 'unnecessary and imposed mega-projects' resistance movement participates in this 'social re-embedding' of environmental problems because it offers political subjects (popular coalitions that fight against the projects) and specific objects (threatened territories/places) upon which a 'genuine' process of (re)politicization of environmental issues can be built. However, Chambru (2015) reminds us that a more or less important section of any oppositional public space always ends up being institutionalized. Here lies the risk of scission in a movement between its radical and more reformist fringes.[14]

ACKNOWLEDGEMENT

We would like to warmly thank Rowland Hill for its crucial contribution in revising the language and editing this manuscript.

NOTES

1. See Wilson and Swyngedouw (2014) for a review on the post-political concept.

2. According to Swyngedouw (2014, p90): '*The Political is the contested public terrain where different imaginings of possible socio-ecological orders compete over the symbolic and material institutionalization of these visions [. . .] a terrain that makes visible and perceptible the heteroge-neous views and desires that cut through the social body [. . .]*'.

3. Cited by Kenis and Lievens (2014).

4. The most important ZADs in France are Sivens (resistance against a dam project), Roybon resistance against a massive tourist facility), Bure (resistance against nuclear waste disposal) and in Haren (north of Brussels), Belgium (resistance against a mega-jail project).

5. Ranciere's conception of democracy is closer to anarchy than Mouffe's conception, which still acknowledges the central role of the state and its institutions (like elections, etc.).

6. See the definition of 'the political' in section 1.

7. The work of Oskar Negt has remained relatively unknown outside Germany, for example, there exists only one book (co-authored with Alexander Kluge) translated into English in 1993 and nothing else. In France his work on "oppositional public space" was only translated in 2007.

8. Cited in Nicholls et al. (2013, p4–5).

9. According to Springer (2010, p538): 'Thus, because public space cannot be established in the abstract, newspapers, radio, television, and the Internet are part of the public sphere and not public space'.

10. Milanesi, Julien, Aux frontière du calcul. A quoi sert l'analyse économique dans la décision sur les grandes infrastructures de transport ?, Communication au Congrès de l'AFEP, Mulhouse, juillet 2016.

11. This is relative to the economic patterns of the 'glorious 30s'.

12. Cited by Faburel and Girault (2016).

13. Denise Cassou, South Gironde, a protester against the GPSO high speed rail mega-project.

14. See Berlan (2016), who analyzes the internal divisions of the resistance movement to the Sivens dam where a young activist, Rémi Fraisse, was killed by the police during the night of 25th October 2014.

REFERENCES

Abensour, M. (2004). La démocratie contre l'État Marx et le moment machiavélien. Paris: Le Félin.

Ariemma, L., & Burnside-Lawry, J. (2016). Transnational Resistance Networks: New Democratic Prospects? The Lyon-Turin Railway and No TAV Movement. In *Protest, Social Movements and Global Democracy Since 2011: New Perspectives* (pp. 137–165). Emerald Group Publishing Limited.

Armiero, M., & D'Alisa, G. (2012). Rights of resistance: the garbage struggles for environmental justice in Campania, Italy. *Capitalism Nature Socialism*, 23(4), 52–68.

Baticle, C. (2015). Un espace public oppositionnel contrarié? L'institutionnalisation partisane de la rébellion cynégétique en France. *Recherches sociologiques et anthropologiques*, 46(46–1), 183–203.

Berlan, A. (2016). Entre contestation et cogestion, les luttes territoriales face à l'État. *Ecologie & politique*, (2), 105–128.

Bookchin, M. (1982). *The ecology of freedom: The emergence and dissolution of hierarchy*. Palo Alto, CA: Cheshire Books.

Chambru, M. (2015). La critique du régime technopolitique des sciences par la mouvance antinucléaire: un éclairage sur le concept d'espace public oppositionnel. *Les enjeux de l'information et de la communication*, 3(16), 29–38.

Crouch, C. (2004). *Post-democracy* (p. 70). Cambridge: Polity.

Faburel, G et Girault, M (coord.) (2016). La fin des villes, reprise de la critique. Mécanismes et impensés de la métropolisation et de ses grandes régions., Carnets de la décroissance, Numéro 2, avril 2016.

Flyvbjerg, B. (2005). Machiavellian megaprojects. *Antipode, 37*(1), 18–22.

Gould, R. (1993). Trade cohesion, class unity, and urban insurrection: Artisanal activism in the Paris Commune. *The American Journal of Sociology, 98*(4): 72–754.

Grisoni, (2018). L'écologie contestataire contre le développement durable. Le mouvement NotAV sur l'espace public oppositionnel en Italie. In Transition écologique et durabilité, politiques et acteurs : Regards franco-allemands sur le changement socio-écologique, pp. 375–396.

Harvey, D. (2012). *Rebel cities: From the right to the city to the urban revolution.* Verso Books.

Hildyard, Ni. (2012). More than Bricks and Mortar. Infrastructure as Asset Class: A Critical Look at Private Equity Infrastructure Funds, [Online], The Corner House, available at: http://www.thecornerhouse.org.uk/resource/more-bricks-and-mortar.

Kenis, A., & Lievens, M. (2014). Searching for 'the political' in environmental politics. *Environmental Politics, 23*(4), 531–548.

Martinez-Alier, J., Temper, L., Del Bene, D., & Scheidel, A. (2016). Is there a global environmental justice movement? *The Journal of Peasant Studies, 43*(3), 731–755.

Mauvaise Troupe. (2016). *Defending the ZAD.* L'Éclat.

Mouffe, C. (2005). *On the political.* Abingdon; New York: Routledge.

Mouffe, C. (2013). *Agonistics: thinking the world politically.* London: Verso.

Mussot, P. (2017). *La religion industrielle.* Paris : Fayard.

Nicholls, W., Miller, B., & Beaumont, J. (2013). Conceptualizing the spatialities of social movements. *Spaces of Contention: Spatialities and Social Movements,* 1–23.

Negt, O. (2007). *L'espace public oppositionnel.* Payot.

Negt, O. L'espace public oppositionnel aujourd'hui. Multitudes 2009/4 (n° 39), p. 190–195.

Rancière, J. (1999). *Disagreement: politics and philosophy.* Minneapolis: University of Minnesota Press.

Rancières, J. (2001). Ten theses on politics'. *Theory and Event,* 5(3), 1–21.

Rancière, J. (2010). *Dissensus: On politics and aesthetics,* London: Continuum.

Robert, D. (2014). Social Movements opposing mega-projects; A rhizome of resistance to neoliberalism. Master thesis, KTH Stockholm. http://stophs2.org/wpcontent/uploads/2014/12/D-Robert-Social-movements-against-UIMP.compressed.pdf.

Rosa, H. (2012). Aliénation et accélération. Vers une théorie critique de la modernité tardive.

Sagradini, L. (2009). La plèbe entre dans la surface de jeu », Multitudes 2009/4 (n°39), p. 205–210.

Springer, S. (2010). Public space as emancipation: meditations on anarchism, radical democracy, neoliberalism and violence. *Antipode, 43*(2), 525–562.

Swyngedouw, E. (2007). Impossible "sustainability" and the postpolitical condition. In R. Krueger, and D. Gibbs (eds.) *The sustainable development paradox.* London: The Guilford Press.

Swyngedouw, E. (2009) The Antinomies of the post-political city. In search of a democratic politics of environmental production. *International Journal of Urban and Regional Research, 33*(3), 601–620.

Swyngedouw, E. (2010). Apocalypse forever? *Theory, Culture & Society, 27*(2–3), 213–232.

Swyngedouw, E. (2011). Interrogating post-democratization: Reclaiming egalitarian political spaces. *Political Geography, 30*(7), 370–380.

Swyngedouw, E. (2013). The non-political politics of climate change. *ACME: An International Journal for Critical Geographies, 12*(1), 1–8.

Swyngedouw, E. (2014). Depolitization (The Political). In G. D'Alisa, F. Demaria, G. Kallis (eds.), *Degrowth: A vocabulary for a new era* (pp. 90–93). Routledge.

Swyngedouw, E., & Kaika, M. (2014). Urban political ecology. Great promises, deadlock… and new beginnings? *Documents d'anàlisi geogràfica, 60*(3), 459–481.

Wilson, J., & Swyngedouw, E. (2014). Seeds of dystopia: Post-politics and the return of the political. *The Post-Political and its Discontents*, 1–22. In Wilson and Swynguedouw, *The Post-political and its discontents : spaces of depoliticisation and spectres of radical politics*, Edimbough Univ Press.

Žižek, S. (1999). *The Ticklish subject: The absent centre of political ontology*. London: Verso.

Žižek, S. (2008). Censorship Today: Violence, or Ecology as a New Opium for the Masses [online]. Available from: http://www.lacan.com/zizecology1.htm.

Žižek, S. (2009). *First as tragedy, then as farce*. London: Verso.

4

Agri(Cultural) Resistance

Food Sovereignty and Anarchism in Response to the Sociobiodiversity Crisis

Cassidy Thomas and Leonardo E. Figueroa-Helland

Food production represents one of humanity's most intimate interactions with the Earth. Through the production of food, the labours of humanity and Earth converge in powerful ways that help shape the composition of entire ecosystems and sustain populations of different species. Throughout human history, we have witnessed both the beautifully creative and nurturing potential of this relationship, but also its terrifyingly destructive capacities when manipulated for purposes other than sustainable sustenance. Many of the globe's food systems were once defined by ecologically sustainable subsistence agricultural systems carefully tailored to local ecosystems by indigenous and smallholder peasant farmers. Unfortunately, the diverse collection of local food practices that sustained this past reality has shifted into an increasingly consolidated globalized food system that is controlled by transnational corporations and states and characterized by technocratic managerialism, industrial machinery, monocropping and artificial inputs. These forces have expanded, starting with modernity's first enclosures in Europe and the onset of modern European colonialism, with its genocidal, ethnocidal and racist conquests of indigenous peoples and its dispossession of the commons through primitive accumulation and ecological imperialism (Federici 2004; Foster, Clark and York 2010). This process unleashed a crisis of cultural diversity resulting from an 'epistemicide' that sought to destroy and/or invalidate indigenous knowledges while imposing the 'coloniality' of an 'epistemological monoculture' that has sought to universalize a technoscientific 'Western rationality' based on an anthropocentric and patriarchal 'mastery of nature' (Adelman 2015, 16). This epistemicide has entailed the marginalization and/or loss of an invaluable range of knowledges, philosophies, worldviews, cosmologies and the lifeways and practices they underpinned. Such practices include ancestrally nurtured intimate interactions with local ecosystems via food production and commons-based socioecological organization (Figueroa-Helland, Thomas, and Aguilera 2018). In addition to the rupture of indigenous sociocultural systems, the evolution of food systems has been dramatically affected by the technological innovations and economic developments of the twentieth century – which featured the development of industrial agricultural machinery, genetic modification and accelerated use of various artificial inputs (fertilizers, herbicides, pesticides, insecticides, fungicides, etc.) (McMichael 2017).

While there is growing awareness of the biodiversity crisis and its dangers, there is less awareness of biodiversity's intimate link with cultural diversity, or 'sociobiodiversity' (Rengifo 2011). Highlighting this link, Toledo (2001) notes that the 'remarkable overlap between indigenous territories and the world's remaining areas of high biodiversity' is due to 'indigenous views, knowledge and practices in biodiversity conservation' (451); such knowledges/practices not only maintain but also restore, nurture and enrich biodiversity (Berkes 2012; Gadgil et al. 1993). With the displacement of indigenous and peasant peoples and the expansion of modern-industrial food systems (amongst other hegemonic systems), food practices informed by local ecological knowledges which preserve and even improve ecosystem health and biodiversity are being continually eroded. The destruction of the diversity of land-based cultures is thus a major driver of the biodiversity crisis. Hence, any strategy to defend biodiversity demands solidarity with indigenous and peasant struggles to advance an interlocking *biocultural axiom* wherein 'global biodiversity only will be . . . preserved by preserving diversity of cultures and vice-versa' (Toledo 2001: 451). Moreover, revolutionary praxis in an Anthropocene epoch of intersecting biocultural crises must challenge not just the industrial food system and the state–capital nexus supporting it but also the infrastructures of power underpinning this nexus, including anthropocentrism, Eurocentric coloniality, patriarchy and technoscientific rationalism (Figueroa-Helland and Lindgren 2016). The purpose of this chapter is to discuss the kind of theory–praxis that can underpin effective strategies of resistance capable of constructing and defending spaces for alternative lifeways (Gelderloos 2016) – against and beyond the hegemonic systems that undermine lands and livelihoods while triggering sociobiodiversity crises. We first discuss sociobiodiversity, its link to indigeneity and their interrelated crises. Then we address food sovereignty debates and their intersections with anarchist political ecologies. Finally, we discuss how food sovereignty praxis and anarchist political ecology can synergistically defend and amplify spaces of resistance against and beyond the sociobiodiversity crisis.

THE SOCIOBIODIVERSITY CRISIS VIA THE CONQUEST OF INDIGENEITY

Biodiversity loss, measured by the rate of extinction, is one of the looming spectres of the twenty-first century; '[t]he preindustrial annual rate, referred to as the "natural" or "background" rate of species loss, was .1–1 per million . . . [the] current rate is greater than 100 per million (100–1,000 times the preindustrial background rate)'

(Foster, Clark and York 2010, 15). Moreover, according to the UN, 75 per cent of the world's crop diversity was lost in the twenty-first century; today, '[just] twelve crops . . . supply 80% of the world's plant-based dietary energy. Just four crops – rice, wheat, potato and maize– supply nearly 60% of plant-derived calories and proteins' (Gonzalez 2011, 496). These trends are alarming, as biodiversity 'serves as an absorptive barrier, providing protection from, and thus resilience against, environmental perturbations' (Pilgrim and Pretty 2010, 2). While the increasing attention given to biodiversity loss is appropriate, mainstream discourse has been slow to connect it to sociocultural diversity loss (Escobar and Pardo 2008). Many mainstream analyses restrict themselves to the technicalities of modernist natural science, shying away from deeper critiques of the structural socioeconomic and cultural drivers of biodiversity loss or other environmental crises (Rockström et al. 2009). Some critical literatures underline the histories and structures of capitalism, industrialism and anthropocentrism as root causes; but even then, deeper political and ethical questions concerning the loss of cultural diversity are not directly addressed (Harrington 2016). To do so demands confronting the historical and on-going atrocities of conquest, colonization, racism, forced relocation, genocide, ethnocide and epistemicide levelled against indigenous, peasant and other marginalized populations globally (Cudworth and Hobden 2014; Gonzalez 2011; Nibert 2012). Furthermore, critical analyses must highlight that the knowledge–praxes of most land-based cultures has always been more attuned to the complexities of preserving and fostering agro/biodiversity than the civilizational hubris of those who have brought injustice upon them and imposed the technoscientific mastery of nature (Altieri and Nicholls 2012).

Any discussion of cultural diversity must address indigeneity; as indigenous peoples have been the victims of on-going projects of cultural homogenization since the onset of modern colonialism. Here, the term indigenous refers to 'communities, peoples, and nations [who have] a historical continuity with pre-invasion and pre-colonial societies that developed on their territories [and] who [continue] to consider themselves distinct from other sectors of the societies [currently occupying] those territories' (Cobo quoted by Pellcan 2009, 55). In addition to this pre-colonial/ pre-invasion component of indigeneity, we must recognize the intimate relationship between indigenous communities and their surrounding ecosystems – a fundamental tenant of indigenous identity radically different from the anthropocentrism and human/nature dichotomy prevalent within the Western tradition (Cajete 2000; Pierroti 2011; Stewart-Harawira 2011). The fact that indigenous peoples generally share an intimate relation to their land-bases does not diminish their cultural and epistemic diversity; contrarily, diverse indigenous cultures are reflective of the lush variety of Mother Earth's ecological and biological diversity precisely because each is built around ethical responsibilities uniquely tailored to nurture socioecological communities of human and non-human life, adapted to specific ecosystems. Yet despite this diversity, there are similarities across indigenous philosophies and lifeways globally (Grim ed. 2001) – as shown by the ecologically rooted spiritualties, cosmologies and practices of indigenous peoples across North America (e.g., Cajete 2000), Mesoamerica (e.g., Ford and Nigh 2015; Lenkersdorf 2004), South

America (e.g., Gonzales and Gonzalez 2010), Sub-Saharan Africa (e.g., Le Grange 2012), South Asia (e.g., Grim ed. 2001; Kapoor and Shizha 2010), Southeast Asia (e.g., Alcorn and Royo 2000; Joshi et al. 2004), Central and Northern Eurasia (e.g., Regdel et al. 2012; Sirina 2009) and Australasia and Polynesia (Grim ed. 2001; Pomaikai McGregor et al. 2003; Rose 2005). Hence,

> Although indigenous cultures are richly diverse, they tend to share the following prin-
> ciples: Indigenous peoples do *not* conceive themselves as separate from or superior to
> Mother Earth or the rest of the life-web . . . indigeneity understands itself as a life-form
> that is organically coextensive with, embedded in, and communally co-responsible for
> the cycles, forces, and relational networks that constitute Mother Earth and the encom-
> passing cosmos. Indigenous worldviews often conceive human society as an organ with
> specific functions inside a larger fully living geo-body; each of us is but a cell in Mother
> Earth's macro-organic metabolic cycles, and every element of our constitution is just one
> transient manifestation of cyclically flowing and continually transforming cosmic, spiri-
> tual, physical, and geo-bio-chemical energy. (Figueroa-Helland and Raghu 2017: 196)

Indigenous environmental philosophies, like *Suma Qamaña/Sumak Kasway* from South America, *Ukama/Ubuntu* from Sub-Saharan Africa and Ecological *Swaraj* from South Asia amongst others, have increasingly become known worldwide as 'earth wisdom for a world in crisis' (Kothari et al. 2014; Olsson 2009).

Indigenous interconnectedness with surrounding ecosystems proceeds from a non-anthropocentric understanding of community. It is the wellbeing of whole ecosystem commons that must be nurtured; and if humans fulfil their reciprocal socioecological responsibilities, the ecosystem provides sustenance in return. Thus, indigenous communities have long been attentive to how their actions shape and affect their surrounding ecosystem. Over generations, they have collected knowledge carefully suited to their unique biodiverse ecosystems (Fowler and Leposky 2011). These knowledges have informed cultural practices (including food production) and lifeways that support whole ecosystems. It is not then by chance that,

> a good deal of the biodiversity of the planet is present in territories inhabited by indig-
> enous peoples, for whom nature never was a natural resource, as the West understands
> this notion. For these peoples, nature cannot be disassociated from society, within the
> frame of cosmologies that divide and classify this world in ways . . . different from the
> one enshrined by modern, Western cosmology. Colonialism and . . . later . . . forms of
> subalternization . . . are associated with attempts to destroy these cosmologies and their
> worlds. (de Sousa Santos 2008, xiiv)

Indigenous worlds are enacted from the acknowledgement that humans inextricably co-participate with all species and entities in a web of mutual and communal respon-sibility that enables the reproduction of whole ecosystems. Indigenous knowledges thus embody ethically inflected responses to environmental and non-human stimuli. Far from simple or outdated, these knowledges are often superior to Western sci-ence in understanding and predicting local phenomena (Anderson 2011; Pierroti 2011; Thomson 2011). This is because they are characterized by a care and response orientation towards the non-human which fosters reciprocal adaptability; thus, non-human 'nature' and humans mutually shape and nurture each other, enabling cycles of socioecological reproduction and the generational transfer of common knowledge. Hence, humans and non-humans dynamically co-evolve, *together* – not as 'human society' living off an 'ecosystem' but rather as an integrated community of life.

While a modern bias presupposes that humanity's interactions with the natural environment are inherently negative or even conflictual, a consideration of non-modernist and non-Western human–environment interactions reveals that our modern reality results from intersecting hegemonic systems of domination and not from a supposedly innate human propensity to exploit or destroy nature. Humans, particularly non-Western, indigenous, and many peasant societies, have interacted with their local ecosystems sustainably throughout much of human history – and many continue to do so. Food production lies at this complex convergence of human sustenance, cultural reproduction, ecological integrity and the preservation of biodiversity. As agricultural practices (e.g., selective breeding, controlled burns, intercropping, etc.) have been one way that some humans have simultaneously sustained their cultures and reshaped – in many cases enhanced – ecosystem biodiversity (Howard 2010; Pilgrim and Pretty 2010). Local resources were, for centuries, what the agri-cultures of developing countries were built upon:

> local varieties and indigenous knowledge, which have nurtured biologically and geneti-cally diverse smallholder farms with . . . resilience that . . . help[s] adjust to . . . changing climates, pests, and diseases. The persistence of millions of agricultural hectares under ancient, traditional management [such as] raised fields, terraces, polycultures (with vari-ous crops . . . in the same field), agroforestry . . ., etc., document a successful indigenous agricultural strategy and comprises a tribute to the 'creativity' of traditional farmers . . . Indigenous technologies [and practices] . . . reflect a worldview and . . . understanding of our relationship to the natural world that is more realistic and . . . sustainable than . . . [the] Western European heritage. (Altieri quoted in Figueroa-Helland and Lindgren 2016, 456)

These distinct cultural knowledges that inform ecologically sustainable food practices – underpinning the preservation of biocultural diversity – are increasingly under threat of extinction. While the sociobiodiversity crisis is rooted in the deci-mation of indigenous peoples and the recursive primitive accumulation and alien-ation of their lands through colonialism, modernization and developmentalism, its aggravation is perpetuated through the hegemonic coloniality of Western modernist technoscience and its institutionalization into a globalized capital–state–academic–industrial complex that continues to marginalize alternative knowledges. Despite colonial atrocities, many indigenous, peasant and other marginalized cultures and knowledge systems have survived, but their lifeways continue to be threatened by the 'ecological imperialism' of the 'imperial mode of living' (Brand and Wissen 2012; Foster, Clark and York 2010).

Currently, a collection of entities – including transnational corporations, state governments, elite socioeconomic classes and international organizations like the

World Bank, WTO and IMF – are fuelling the sociobiodiversity crisis by facilitating accumulation through dispossession of indigenous and peasant lands via land grabs, megadevelopment projects, neoliberal restructuring and 'free trade' policies (Capra and Luisi 2014). The past three decades have witnessed an increase in food systems becoming globalized through neo-liberal policies that

> placed decision-making authority over food production and distribution in the hands of national states, and supranational and transnational organizations, promoting agricultural and food practices that did little to alleviate world hunger. The over-commodification of food after World War Two resulted in concentrating the decision-making power over food, land, and seeds in the hands of . . . a few, and developing policies that regulated food to meet the demands of the agribusiness industry. This neo-colonial process impoverished millions of peasants and Indigenous peoples by displacing them from the land, resulting in many of them being forced into wage labor to serve the global food economy. (Cote 2016, 7)

This shift entails a process of structural dispossession where power over food is shifted away from those producing it while sustaining agro/biodiverse ecosystems and towards those who extract profit by imposing a monocultural rationality based on the mastery of nature. Local communities of life, including their human and non-human members, are ruptured when the place-based knowledge–praxis which enables their socioecological reproduction are replaced by states and corporations who 'manage' them according to criteria of growth, scale, efficiency, comparative advantage and profit maximization. In some cases, indigenous and peasant peoples are allowed to remain in the area but are forced to abandon their socio-ecologically tailored food practices and assimilate into the globalized industrial food system characterized by expansive monocultures of resource-intensive cash/export crops, flex-crops, livestock (preceded by massive land-use change including deforestation), artificial inputs, fossil-fuelled industrial machinery and export-oriented specialization. The globalization of industrially farmed and epistemic monocultures thus erodes both biological and cultural diversity. The biocultural axiom demands action; food sovereignty movements coupled with anarchist praxes can be instrumental in the struggle.

FOOD SOVEREIGNTY AND ANARCHIST PRAXIS IN RESPONSE TO THE SOCIOBIODIVERSITY CRISIS

If we look at different agriculture/food systems through the demands of the biocultural axiom, clearly, some aggravate – while others can help overcome – the sociobiodiversity crisis. The modern-industrial mode of food production is underpinned by an intersection of hegemonic systems of power which include coloniality, capitalism, patriarchy and anthropocentrism, all of which aggravate social and environmental crises. The question therefore is what are the socio-political ideologies and frameworks that might help emancipate food production from the grips of these hegemonic systems? Part of the answer, we contend, lies with the global food sovereignty movement, whose activists around the world mobilize and sometimes risk their lives to defend land and livelihood. We argue, moreover, that anarchist thoughts and praxis can aid these emancipatory struggles.

We must premise our discussion with a caveat, namely, that it is *not* our purpose to co-opt the work of indigenous and peasant food sovereignty activists into a justification for the whole of anarchist ideology or praxis. The purpose, instead, is to further solidarity by showing how anarchist political ecologies can converge with food sovereignty discourse and praxis in specific ways that help advance global food sovereignty struggles. Food sovereignty coupled with certain anarchist critiques and approaches can enhance strategies to confront the sociobiodiversity crisis.

The term 'food sovereignty' surged in popularity following the 1996 World Food Conference, where *La Via Campesina (LVC)*, an exceptionally active international indigenous, peasant and women's rights movement, offered a definition that profoundly influenced transnational struggles. Their definition of food sovereignty underlined the need to secure the right of local communities to sustainably produce and consume culturally appropriate foods (Altieri and Toledo 2011; Andrée et al. 2014; Fernandez et al. 2013; Grey and Patel 2015; and McKay et al. 2014). This definition 'implies new social relations free of oppression and inequality between men and women, peoples, racial groups, social classes and generations' (Borras Jr., Franco and Suárez 2015, 600–601). LVC and many of its allies also embrace the role that food sovereignty must play in cultural reproduction, making the struggle about more than just food. Grey and Patel (2011) note,

> food sovereignty [expands] beyond the familiar bundle of rights that attach to production and consumption, since the resurrection of Indigenous traditional foods and food systems is inextricable from a . . . general Indigenous cultural, social, and political resurgence. (433)

The question is how and what can anarchism contribute to food sovereignty struggles? Part of the answer may lie within an *anarchist political ecology*. While *political ecology* broadly names an interdisciplinary field focusing on the interaction of politics, economics and the Earth's ecosystems, it can be best understood as the study of the complex relationship between nature and society (Robbins 2012). Explorations of how different socio-political structures and relationships impact ecosystems fall within the concerns of political ecology. The 'political' in political ecology also entails an engagement with power relations and inequities. Hence, in identifying the root causes of issues like biodiversity loss, cultural erosion and hunger, political ecology includes critical analyses geared towards enacting 'less coercive, less exploitative and more sustainable ways of doing things' (Robbins 2012: 20).

Anarchism is a political ideology that interrogates hierarchal power structures. From its early days, anarchist thought in Europe sought to challenge the mutually reinforcing hierarchies of the state and capitalism (e.g. Kropotkin 2002, 2012). Over time, such analyses extended to 'all political and social coercive institutions' and now strive for a world that no longer privileges the interests of a select few social groups

(Rocker 2004, 1). Today, an increasingly diversified anarchist school includes critical engagements with the socio-political institutions of patriarchy, racism, cisheteronormativity, coloniality, anthropocentrism, ableism, ageism and speciesism (Gelderloos 2014). Some of our own work (e.g., Figueroa-Helland and Lindgren 2016) – on which this chapter is premised – has been informed by the growing interdisciplinary approaches to political ecology and global studies that seek to engage these multiple intersecting systems of power and domination through a combination of complex systems analysis, ecofeminism, decolonial and indigenous theory and post-humanism with anarchist thought (e.g., Cudworth and Hobden 2010, 2013, 2014). Overall, an *anarchist political ecology* articulates critical engagements that seek to delegitimize, subvert and overcome any socio-political and economic hierarchies and coercive structures that continue to uphold different forms of domination amongst humans and in relation to non-human nature.

The food sovereignty framework can relate well to some of the contributions of anarchist political ecology. A broad survey of both fields reveals three key areas of convergence, especially linked to the sociobiodiversity crisis: First, both approaches critically interrogate the coercive and mutually reinforcing hierarchies of neo-liberal capitalism and the state; second, they both recognize the intersection between nature and culture; and third, both value decentralized relationships between relatively autonomous localities.

The food sovereignty movement has levelled damning criticisms against capitalism and the economic hierarchies maintained by neo-imperialist trade policies and international organizations. In fact, it was in large part the struggle against neo-liberal structural land reform policies and the Agreement on Agriculture (AoA) facilitated by the WTO in the 1990s that helped thrust LVC onto the international stage (Margulis, Mckeon and Borras Jr. 2013; McKay, Nehring and Walsh-Dilley 2014). Food sovereignty activists have also recognized the important roles of the World Bank and IMF in having 'supported the creation and implementation of rights and rules that set the stage for the global land grab' (Safransky and Wolford 2011, 4). Land grabbing entails,

> the large-scale acquisition through buying, leasing or otherwise accessing productively used or potentially arable farmland by investors, that are most commonly corporations operating with state support, to produce food and non-food crops, to either boost supply for domestic and/or world markets or obtain a favorable financial return on an investment. (Akram-Lodhi 2015, 233–234)

Anarchist thought and food sovereignty discourse converge in their critiques of capitalism. Many food sovereignty activists have also recognized the role of the state in maintaining international economic hierarchies. In fact, LVC changed their initial definition of food sovereignty, replacing the word *nations* with the word *peoples*. Presumably, this emphasizes the more localist and grassroots strategy of the food sovereignty mission (as opposed to national or state-wide) since state-codified rights often do not ensure the wellbeing of indigenous, peasant and other marginalized peoples; moreover, national governments often facilitate large- scale land acquisitions (Grey and Patel 2015; McKay, Nehring and Walsh-Dilley 2014).

The emphasis on the link between nature and culture and the role of biocultural complexity and diversity in sustaining communities of life is another point of convergence. Being that food production, especially via local food systems informed by indigenous and local ecological knowledge, is intimately tied to ecosystem health, food sovereignty activists are often resisting the sociobiodiversity crisis by nature of their communal land-based praxis. Murray Bookchin, a prominent anarchist theorist, also underlined the importance of biodiversity:

> What ecology has shown is that balance in nature is achieved by organic variation and complexity, not by homogeneity and simplification...Left to itself an ecosystem. . .tends spontaneously toward organic differentiation, greater variety of flora and fauna, and diversity in the number of prey and predators. (Bookchin 2004, 8)

Importantly though, and unlike many strands of Western environmentalist thought, Bookchin recognized that the human–nature relationship need not be reduced to a dichotomous discussion of two extremes. His intention here was not to suggest that interference by humans must be avoided but rather that,

> The need for a productive agriculture – itself a form of interference with nature – must always remain in the foreground of an ecological approach to food cultivation and forest management. No less important is the fact that man [sic] can often produce changes in an ecosystem that would vastly improve its ecological quality. But these efforts require insight and understanding, not the exercise of brute power and manipulation. (2004, 8)

This previous quote is particularly interesting, perhaps even ironic, given that Bookchin voiced some questionable opinions on indigenous spiritualties and traditions (which cannot be separated from indigenous knowledges and the lifeways they inform). Actually, it is countless examples of indigenous communities who have lived in harmony with their local ecosystems for millennia that support Bookchin's comments. Furthermore, Bookchin recognized the interdependence between biodiversity, an ecosystem's wellbeing, and that of human society. Notwithstanding the needed critical revision of Bookchin's gendered language, we still highlight his critique that '[t]he homogenization of ecosystems goes hand in hand with the homogenization of the social environment and the so-called individuals who people it' (2004, 211). Moreover, '[the] imbalances man [sic?] has produced in the natural world are caused by the imbalances he [sic?] has produced in the social world' (2004, 23). Furthermore, 'in the course of replacing . . . complex ecological relationships, on which all advanced living things depend, for more elementary relationships, man [sic?] is steadily restoring the biosphere to a stage which will be able to support only simpler forms of life' (2004, 28). Ironically, the masculine gendering of the culpable agent in these quotes may confirm ecofeminist accounts of the 'Manthropocene' crises; yet the question remains, which 'Man'? Capitalist Man, Sovereign Man, Eurocentric Man? (Harrington 2016).

In the face of these catastrophic ecological crises, Bookchin proposed an alternative based on the mutually reinforcing nature of biodiversity and cultural diversity. He argued that if the ecological community is ever achieved in practice,

> social life will yield a sensitive *development of human and natural diversity*. . .we will see a colorful *differentiation of human groups and ecosystems*, each developing its unique potentialities and exposing members of the community to a wide spectrum of economic, cultural and behavioral stimuli. (2004, 39, emphasis added)

He also underlined the role of food production in this process,

> the agriculturalist must become thoroughly familiar with the ecology of the land; he [sic] must acquire a new sensitivity to its needs and possibilities. This presupposes the reduction of agriculture to a human scale, the restoration of moderate-sized agricultural units, and the diversification of the agricultural situation; in short, it presupposes a decentralized, ecological system of food cultivation. (2004, 9)

Furthermore,

> Food cultivation, practiced in a truly ecological sense, presupposes . . . [familiarity] with all the features and subtleties of the terrain on which the crops are grown. He [sic] must have a thorough knowledge of the physiography of the land, its variegated soils – crop land, forest land, and pasture land – its mineral and organic content and its microclimate, and he must be engaged in a continuing study of the effects produced by new flora and fauna. (2004, 32)

Interestingly (perhaps ironically), many of the abovementioned socioecological modes of organization and food cultivation practices proposed by Bookchin have already been embodied by indigenous cultures both historically and in the present (see, e.g., Altieri and Nicholls 2012; Figueroa-Helland, Thomas and Perez 2018). Taking all this into consideration, there seems to be much that food sovereignty discourse and an anarchist political ecology – one influenced by Bookchin at least – have in common. Both highlight the importance of sociobiodiversity and can embed a biocultural axiom. They may even converge on some alternatives to the crisis. Yet, as we discuss later, there are important points of disagreement which can enable fruitful and constructive debates.

As a final point of agreement, food sovereignty embraces 'local autonomy, local markets, local production-consumption cycles and farmer-to-farmer networks that promote agroecological innovations and ideas' (Altieri and Toledo 2011, 607). This coincides with traditional anarchist and communal-libertarian emphases on the sovereignty of local communities, as opposed to their reliance and deferral to a strong centralized entity. Within classic European anarchist thought, Kropotkin (2002) proposed an 'interwoven network, composed of an infinite variety of groups and federations of all sizes and degrees, local, regional, national and international – temporary or. . .permanent – for all . . . purposes' (284); Rocker (2004) identified 'a federation of free communities . . . bound . . . by their common economic and social interests' as a key anarchist goal (1). More recently, Bookchin (2004) proposed a libertarian municipalism and current anarchist activists like Gelderloos (2014) affirm the value of confederal networks. Again, food sovereignty projects appear convergent with anarchist values. Moreover, the structure of the world's paramount food sovereignty organization, LVC, embraces a decentralized organizational strategy that lends much autonomy to local organizations.

While often referred to as a singular entity, LVC is actually a decentralized collection of 164 local organizations and movements in over 70 countries across five continents, acting in solidarity with one another on diverse issues (La Via Campesina). 'The movement is based on the decentralization of power between all of its regions. The international secretariat rotates according to the collective decision made every four years by the International Conference' (LVC website, 10/14/2017). Much of this decentralized rotational model of consensual decision-making is actually inspired by indigenous communality (Maldonado, Meyer and Chomsky 2010). In addition to their adherence to decentralized power structures, the flexible nature of LVC's food sovereignty definition is an intentional effort to allow for a diversity of movements, local politics and interests under one umbrella (Grey and Patel 2015).

SYNERGIES IN SPACES OF RESISTANCE

While the encompassing, yet also capillary nature of anthropocentrism, coloniality, patriarchy, capitalism and the state complicates the viability of 'total' revolution, revolutionary values have nonetheless persisted and often flourish more successfully in localized spaces of resistance that embody alternative lifeways (Gelderloos 2016). These spaces tap variegated opportunity structures, left open by the blind spots of capitalism, the state and other systems of power (Araujo 2016; Barrera de la Torre and Ince 2016; Brookfield 2005; Gelderloos 2010). Some spaces for resistance emerge due to the very processes of these systems – the 'spatial fix' (Harvey 2011) being one such process. 'Spatial fix' refers to capitalism's tendency to geographically expand or relocate to overcome barriers and limits to over-accumulation; this ever expansive nature of capitalism consistently incorporates new markets and resources to fuel its growth. Capitalism requires such fixes because it's driven by endless accumulation understood as 'economic growth'; Capra and Luisi (2014) clarify:

> We have created a global monetary and financial system that requires growth. Economic activities are driven by money entering the economy through loans, and the interest on these loans can only be paid if the economy continues to grow. (367)

The growth impulse is satisfied by the dispossession/alienation of land-based cultures and forced assimilation of people and land into the capitalist world system, which ruptures the intimate relationships of indigenous and peasant farmers with local ecosystems – contributing to the sociobiodiversity crisis. Yet capitalism, as it expands and shifts, tends to abandon overexploited areas and populations where it no longer sees value. For example, since the 1960s, Detroit has undergone deindustrialization

– with capital, businesses and wealthier (often white) populations vacating the city (Draus, Roddy and McDuffie 2012; White 2010). In capitalism's wake however, an urban agricultural resistance has been led by African-American Women. This community-based resistance has not only sought to provide local populations with sustainably produced and healthy food but has also reclaimed and revitalized Afro-centric histories and cultures (White 2010, 2012). This is just one example of how spaces for resistance based on grounded alternatives that nurture sociobiodiversity can open up.

The previously discussed convergences between food sovereignty and anarchist political ecology suggest space for healthy and nuanced debates with a view towards solidarities and collaborations. Such debates can foster synergies that further culti-vate and expand spaces of resistance. Considering the dire nature of the sociobiodi-versity crisis, it is vital that any ideological allies that can engage in mutual aid find and support each other. In places like Chiapas (Southern Mexico), this synergistic alliance has already formed with great success amongst the Zapatistas:

> Named after Mexican peasant revolutionary Zapata and espousing a mix of indig-enous, Marxist, and anarchist ideas, the Zapatistas formed an army guided by popular 'encuentros,' or gatherings, to fight back against neoliberal capitalism and the continu-ing forms of exploitation and genocide inflicted by the Mexican state. [They emerged to raise] communities up out of poverty following generations of colonialism, and to help counter the effects of military blockades and harassment . . . [T]he Zapatistas called for support. Thousands of volunteers and people with technical experience came from around the world to help the Zapatista communities build up their infrastructure, and thousands of others continue to support the Zapatistas by sending donations of money and equipment or buying fair-trade goods produced in the autonomous territory. (Gelderloos 2014, 166)

Similar synergies have emerged in the neighbouring Oaxaca state (Gelderloos 2016). We must build from these examples and explore how anarchist political ecologies and food sovereignty frameworks might continue to align elsewhere around the world.

There are nevertheless some differences between food sovereignty and anarchist approaches. For example, despite shared analyses of capitalism, economic hierarchy and the state, the complex and diverse strategies employed by LVC affiliate organiza-tions have not always been deeply critical of state apparatuses and international insti-tutions like the UN – though some have been. Alberto Gomez, a North-American LVC delegate adds nuance, explaining that occasionally, when LVC engages the UN or other international organizations, LVC delegates merely work to slow down the bureaucratic processes and ensure that nothing *counterproductive* gets accomplished. Nevertheless, Gomez still considers state policy changes worth working towards (Radio Mundo Real Interview 2010, 2013). Here it would be fruitful to engage in debates that incorporate anarchist critiques. Even then, strategic contexts vary depending on location, positionality and the balance of power between states and oppressed groups, including the comparative coercive disposition and capabilities of different states towards diverse populations. For marginalized peoples, resistance demands a diversity of strategies and tactics which, under different circumstances, may range from direct confrontation to strategic engagement with state actors. It is up to those involved to collectively decide how to engage profoundly unequal fields of power.

Still the role of the state system in propagating the sociobiodiversity crisis must be confronted. Besides the dominion of nature as 'territory', another integral feature of the nation-state building process is the homogenization of culture, education and the economy (Maldonado, Meyer, and Chomsky 2010). As Kropotkin (2002) notes, the state is an institution devised to uphold the interests of certain segments of society at the expense of others through legal, educational and punitive institutions; and hence, '[t]his power cannot become an instrument of emancipation' (193).

the State is a jealous god. It must preempt, absorb, and concentrate power as a nutritive principle of self-preservation . . . Like the market, the State knows no limits; it. . .easily become[s] a self-generating and self-expanding force for its own sake, the institutional form in which domination for the sake of domination acquires palpability. (Bookchin 2004, 199–200)

While it may be easier to imagine the end of the Earth than the end of capitalism, colonialism and the state, anarchist (*and* indigenous) values have continued to exist and can flourish in the smallest spaces of resistance (Araujo 2016; Barrera de la Torre and Ince 2016). It is vital that a grounded and sustainable resistance fills these spaces. LVC has already provided decentralized blueprints for such resistance. Bookchin (2015) similarly identified a decentralized confederation of local communities, voluntarily entering into agreement with one another via mutual goals and interests, as the most effective means for establishing a dual power that can eventually rival the state apparatus. Contrary to a world with the homogenizing and hierarchal forces of the state and capitalism, a world defined by the socio-political framework of *libertarian municipalism* allows for *ecocommunities* to adapt to their surrounding ecosystems according to their needs and nurture sociobiodiversity.

The second convergence point calls for anarchists to learn from food sovereignty activists. Unfortunately, despite concerted efforts by some anarchist theorists and activists, many adherents of the anarchist ideology, particularly those from a white, male and Western background, have not engaged in a critical self-analysis that illuminates the problematic futurities often present in some traditional anarchist literature. This includes Kropotkin and even Bookchin in some instances. *The Conquest of Bread*, often referenced as a foundational anarchist text, contains some ideas that reveal Kropotkin's visionary limits. Counter to the values advocated for throughout this discussion, which focus on acknowledging the interdependence of human societies with their ecosystems, Kropotkin promoted a future where agricultural machinery and engineering feats would 'emancipate [humanity] from the climate' (2012, 191). Such ideas are firmly within the technocratic, developmentalist, industrialist and anthropocentric currents of Western philosophy that underpin the sociobiodiversity crisis.

Additionally, Bookchin occasionally espoused views that emulated the condescending tone of many Western imperialists. For example, he once stated, 'As much as I admired many features of organic cultures, I never believed that we could or should introduce their naïve religious, mythic, or magical beliefs or their cosmologies into the present-day ecology movement' (Bookchin 2005, 16–17). While some might dismiss this statement as misplaced or ignorant but ultimately harmless, such thinking must be critically engaged within anarchist currents if they are ever to decolonize their praxis and open spaces for cultural diversity to thrive. If anarchism is truly committed to fighting *all* coercive and hierarchal socio-political structures, it must necessarily be decolonial. By dismissing certain components of indigenous societies as 'naive', 'mythic' and 'magical', Bookchin can be interpreted (regardless of intention) to condone the selective appropriation of indigenous knowledges and lifeways for the benefit of colonially and racially dominant groups (Shiva 2008). While indigenous cosmologies and struggles do not need the validation of anarchist theorists, the selective appropriation of indigenous worldviews and practices fails to challenge colonialities of power. This is dangerous and can be employed to reassert the claims of dominant societies to have the power to judge what parts of indigenous lives are worth defending and which are not. Bookchin's comments suggest that he didn't realize that what he deemed as 'primitive' and 'naïve' beliefs often contained the knowledges, cosmologies, worldviews and philosophies collected, recorded and transmitted through generations (Flórez 2008); these contain, in condensed and sophisticated forms, the ethical teachings that promote and reproduce sociobiodiversity. Additionally, the methods by which many indigenous societies recorded and transmitted these knowledges are vital to their dynamic nature, which allows such cultures and ecosystems to co-evolve.

The final convergence point between food sovereignty and anarchism can enable mutual learning. There is shared admiration for decentralized networks of relatively autonomous localities. Decentralization and flexibility has enabled the growth of the food sovereignty movement. Anarchist theorists have also discussed prefigurative politics – the belief that means and ends must be unified, which entails that one must act every day, through every decision, in ways that prefigure a certain future (Barrea de la Torre and Ince 2016): '[w]e must consciously create our own world' (Bookchin 2015, 3). Anarchists have long admired decentralized socio-political networks acting upon mutual and solidaristic interests (e.g., Bookchin, Kropotkin, Rocker, Gelderloos). Yet, amongst Western anarchists, such praxis has often remained limited to those explicitly identifying as anarchists, most likely due to the few working examples in the modern West of how such an organizational strategy can operate on a larger scale. Yet the decentralized structure of the on-going LVC movement can serve as an example. While other movements, like the Zapatistas and Kurdish Rojava, are commonly cited by anarchists as their values in practice, LVC provides a template for how such values can proliferate intercontinentally. Conversely, while the food sovereignty framework has developed a formidable resistance structure through LVC, anarchist theory can help enrich its strategies and tactics and expand their prefiguration of socio-political futures beyond capitalism and the state. While some segments of the food sovereignty movement have been critical of the state apparatus, even sometimes advocating for a future without it, oftentimes they begrudgingly accept it as an unfortunate reality. Here anarchism alongside decolonial indigenous struggles can propel food sovereignty towards transformative strategies beyond anthropocentrism, coloniality, patriarchy, capitalism *and* the state.

CONCLUSION

If we are to overcome the sociobiodiversity crisis, we must act now, with a clear understanding of the nature of this struggle and the commitment it requires. We must resist the fast-paced consumerist culture that neo-liberal capitalism has sought to normalize and globalize (Bookchin 2015). We must realize that true change may not feel or appear particularly rapid. As Gelderloos (2016, 214) notes,

> In order to overthrow the existing power structure, we not only need to get strong enough to threaten it – something that has happened relatively few times in the last twenty years; we need to get strong enough to survive the starvation capitalism will inflict on us and to overcome the brutality the state will unleash on us.

The sixth mass extinction creeping upon Mother Earth brings with it the haunting spectre of an unprecedented starvation coupled with the brutal spectre of (re) emergent (neo)fascisms. The reclamation of food systems and the revitalization of indigeneity will be vital to the biocultural reproductive capacities of the resistance, as well as the socioecological health of the communities of life on which it all ultimately depends. The frameworks of food sovereignty and an anarchist political ecology, coupled with intersectional and decolonial struggles, will be key to overcoming this epochal Anthropocene crisis.

REFERENCES

Adelman, Sam. 2015. "Epistemologies of Mastery." In Grear and Kotzé, eds., *Research Handbook on Human Rights and the Environment*. Northampton: Edward Elgar.

Akram-Lodhi, Haroon. 2015. "Land Grabs, The Agrarian Question and the Corporate Food Regime." *Canadian Food Studies* 2:233–241.

Alcorn, Janis, Antoinette Royo, eds. 2000. "Indigenous Social Movements and Ecological Resilience: Lessons from the Dayak of Indonesia." PeFoR Discussion Paper, Biodiversity Support Program, Washington, D.C.

Flórez, Margarita. 2008. "Can We Protect Traditional Knowledges." In B. de Sousa Santos, (ed.), *Another Knowledge is Possible*, 249–271. New York: Verso.

Altieri, Miguel and Clara Nicholls. 2012. "Agroecology and Scaling Up Food Sovereignty." *Sustainable Agriculture Reviews* 11: 1–29.

Altieri, Miguel and Victor Toledo. 2011. "The Agroecological Revolution in Latin America." *The Journal of Peasant Studies* 38: 587–612.

Anderson, E.N. 2011. "History of Ethnobiology." In Anderson, Pearsall, Hunn, and Turner, *Ethnobiology*, 1–14. New Jersey: John Wiley and Sons.

Anderson, M.K. 2005. *Tending the Wild: Native American Knowledge and the Management of California's Natural Resources.* Berkeley: University of California Press.

Anderson, M.K. and Michael Moratto. 1996. "Native American Land-Use Practices and Ecological Impacts." University of California, Centers for Water and Wildland Resources.

Andrée, Peter, Jeffrey Ayres, Michael Bosia, and Marie-Josée Massicotte. 2014. "Food Sovereignty and Globalization: Lines of Inquiry.", In Andrée, Ayres, Bosia, and Massicotte (eds.), *Globalization and Food Sovereignty*, 23–52. Toronto: University of Toronto Press.

Araujo, Erin. 2016. "What Do We Resist When We Resist the State." In Lopes de Souza, White, and Springer (eds.), *Theories of Resistance: Anarchism, Geography, and the Spirit of Revolt*, 79–100. London: Rowman and Littlefield.

Barrera de la Torre, Gerónimo and Anthony Ince. 2016. "Post-Statist Epistemology and the Future of Geographical Knowledge Production." In Lopes de Souza, White, and Springer (eds.), *Theories of Resistance: Anarchism, Geography, and the Spirit of Revolt*, 51–78. London: Rowman and Littlefield.

Berkes, Fikret. 2012. *Sacred Ecology*. New York: Routledge.

Bookchin, Murray. 2004. *Post-Scarcity Anarchism.* Oakland, CA: AK Press.

Bookchin, Murray. 2005. *The Ecology of Freedom: The Emergence and Dissolution of Hierarchy.* Oakland: AK Press.

Bookchin, Murray. 2015. *The Next Revolution: Popular Assemblies and the Promise of Direct Democracy.* New York: Verso.

Borras Jr., Saturnino, Jennifer Franco, and Sofia Suárez. 2015. "Land and Food Sovereignty." *Third World Quarterly* 36: 600–617.

Brand, Ulrich and Markus Wissen. 2012. "Global Environmental Politics and the Imperial Mode of Living." *Globalizations* 9(4): 547–560.

Brookfield, Stephen. 2004. *The Power of Critical Theory.* San Francisco: Josey-Bass.

Cajete, Gregory. 2000. *Native Science.* Santa Fe: Clear Light.

Capra, Fritjof, and Pier Luigi Luisi. 2014. *The Systems View of Life: A Unified Vision.* New York: Cambridge University Press.

Cote, Charlotte. 2016. "'Indigenizing' Food Sovereignty. Revitalizing Indigenous Food Practices and Ecological Knowledges in Canada and the United States." *Humanities* 5(57): 1–14.

Cudworth, Erika and Stephen Hobden. 2010. "Anarchy and Anarchism: Towards a Theory of Complex International Systems." *Millennium* 39(2): 399–416.

Cudworth, Erika and Stephen Hobden. 2013. "Complexity, Ecologism and Posthuman Politics." *Review of International Studies*: 1–22.

Cudworth, Erika and Stephen Hobden. 2014. "Civilization and the Domination of the Animal." *Millennium* 42(3): 746–766.

de Sousa Santos, Bouventura, João Nunes, and Maria Paula Meneses. 2008. "Introduction: Opening Up the Canon of Knowledge and Recognition of Difference." In B. de Sousa Santos (ed.), *Another Knowledge is Possible*, xix–lxii. New York: Verso.

Draus, Paul, Juliette Roddy, and Anthony McDuffie. 2012. "'We Don't Have No Neighbourhood': Advanced Marginality and Urban Agriculture in Detroit." *Urban Studies* 51: 2523–2538.

Escobar, Arturo, and Mauricio Pardo. 2008. "Social Movements and Biodiversity on the Pacific Coast of Colombia." In B. de Sousa Santos (ed.), *Another Knowledge is Possible*, 288–314. New York: Verso.

Federici, Silvia, 2004. *Caliban and the Witch*. New York: Autonomedia.

Fernandez, Margarita, Katherine Goodall, Meryl Olson, and Ernesto Méndez. 2013. "Agroecology and Alternative Agri-Food Movements in the United States: Toward a Sustainable Agri-Food System." *Agroecology and Sustainable Food Systems* 37: 115–126.

Figueroa-Helland, Leonardo and Tim Lindgren. 2016. "What Goes Around Comes Around: From the Coloniality of Power to the Crisis of Civilization." *Journal of World-Systems Research* 22: 430–462.

Figueroa-Helland, Leonardo, Cassidy Thomas and Abigail Perez Aguilera. 2018. "Decolonizing Food Systems: Food Sovereignty, Indigenous Revitalization & Agroecology as Counter-Hegemonic Movements." *Perspectives on Global Development and Technology* 18(1–2): 205–224.

Figueroa Helland, L. E. and P. Raghu. 2017. "Indigeneity Vs. 'Civilization': Indigenous Alternatives to The Planetary Rift in the World-System Ecology." In J Smith, M. Goodhart, P. Manning, and J. Markoff (eds.), *Social Movements and World System Transformation*. New York: Routledge.

Ford, Anabel and Ronald Nigh. 2015. *The Maya Forest Garden: Eight Millennia of Sustainable Cultivation of the Tropical Woodlands*. Walnut Creek, CA: Left Coast.

Foster, John B., Brett Clark, and Richard York. 2010. *The Ecological Rift: Capitalism's War on the Earth*. New York: Monthly Review.

Fowler, Catherine S. and Dana Lepofsky. 2011. "Traditional Resource and Environmental Management." In E.N. Anderson, Deborah Pearsall, Eugene Hunn, and Nancy Turner (eds.), *Ethnobiology*, 281–304. New Jersey: John Wiley and Sons.

Gadgil, Madhav, Fikret Berkes, and Carl Folke. 1993. "Indigenous Knowledge for Biodiversity Conservation." *Ambio* 22(2/30): 151–156.

Gelderloos, Peter. 2014. *Anarchy Works*. Active Distribution.

Gelderloos, Peter. 2016. *The Failure of Nonviolence*. Seattle: Left Bank.

Gomez, Alberto. 2010. "Thousands of People Take to the Streets in Cancun to Demand Real Solutions to Climate Change." Interview. Radio Mundo Real. http://radiomundoreal.fm/ Our-Voices?lang=es.

Gomez, Alberto. 2013. "Watchful and Ready for Struggle." Interview. Radio Mundo Real. http://radiomundoreal.fm/6865-watchful-and-ready-for-the?lang=es.

Gonzales, Tirso and Maria Gonzalez. 2010. "From Colonial Encounter to Decolonizing Encounters. Culture and Nature Seen from the Andean Cosmovision of Ever." In Sara Pilgrim and Jules Pretty (eds.), *Nature and Culture*. Washington, DC: Earthscan.

Gonzalez. Carmen G. 2011. "Climate Change, Food Security, and Agrobiodiversity." *Fordham Environmental Law Review* 22: 493–522.

Grey, Sam and Raj Patel. 2015. "Food Sovereignty as Decolonization: Some Contributions from Indigenous Movements to Food System and Development Politics." *Agriculture and Human Values* 32: 431–444.

Harrington, Cameron. 2016. "The Ends of the World: International Relations and the Anthropocene." *Millennium* 44(3): 478–498.

Harvey, David. 2014. "Seventeen Contradictions and The End of Capitalism." New York: Oxford University Press.

Howard, Patricia L. 2010. "Nature and Culture." In S. Pilgrim and J. Pretty (eds.), *Nature and Culture*, 163–164. Washington, DC: Earthscan.

Joshi, Laxman, Kusuma Wijaya, Martua Sirait, Elok Mulyoutami. 2004. "Indigenous Systems and Ecological Knowledge among Dayak People." ICRAF Southeast Asia Working Paper No.3.

Kapoor, Dip and Edward Shizha, eds. 2010. *Indigenous Knowledge and Learning in Asia/Pacific and Africa*. New York: Palgrave MacMillan.

Kothari, Ashish, Federico DeMaria, and Alberto Acosta. 2014. "Buen Vivir, Degrowth and Ecological Swaraj: Alternatives to sustainable development and the Green Economy." *Development* 57(3–4): 362–375.

Kropotkin, Peter. 2002. *Anarchsim: A Collection of Revolutionary Writings*. Roger N. Baldwin (ed.). New York: Dover Publications.

Kropotkin, Peter. 2012. *The Conquest of Bread*. St. Louis: Dialectics.

La Via Campesina. https://viacampesina.org/en/. Accessed October 2017.

Lenkersdorf, C. 2004. *Conceptos Tojolabales de Filosofía y del Altermundo*. Mexico, D.F.: Plaza y Valdés.

Le Grange, Lesley. 2012. "Ubuntu, Ukama, Environmentl and Moral Education." *Journal of Moral Education* 41(3): 329–340.

Maldonado, Benjamín, Lois Meyer, and Noam Chomsky. 2010. *New World of Indigenous Resistance*. San Francisco: City Lights.

Margulis, Matias. E., Nora M. McKeon, and Saturnino M. Borras Jr. 2013. "Land Grabbing and Global Governance: Critical Perspectives." *Globalizations* 10(1): 1–23.

McKay, Ben., Ryan Nehring, and Marygold Walsh-Dilley. 2014. "The 'State' of Food Sovereignty in Latin America." *The Journal of Peasant Studies* 41: 1175–1200.

McMichael, Phillip. 2017. *Development and Social Change*. London: Sage.

Nibert, David. "The Fire Next Time: The Coming Cost of Capitalism, Animal Oppression and Environmental Ruin." *Journal of Human Rights and the Environment* 3(1): 141–158.

Olsson, Stephen 2009. "Earth Wisdom: For a World in Crisis." In *Global Spirit*. Cultural and Educational Media. Film.

Pelican, Michaela. 2009. "Complexities of Indigeneity and Autochthony: An African Example." *American Ethnologist* 36: 52–65.

Pierotti, Raymond. 2011. "The World According to Is'a: Combining Empiricism and Spiritual Understanding in Indigenous Ways of Knowing." In E.N. Anderson et al. (eds.), *Ethnobiology*, 65–82. New Jersey: John Wiley and Sons.

Pilgrim, Sarah and Jules Pretty. 2010. "Nature and Culture: An Introduction." In S. Pilgrim and J. Pretty (eds.), *Nature and Culture*, 1–22. Washington, DC: Earthscan.

Pomaikal McGregor, Daviana, Paula Morelli, and Jon Matsuoka, et al. 2003. "An Ecological Model of Native Hawaiian Well-Being." *Pacific Health Dialog* 10(2): 106–128.

Regdel, D. Ch. Dugarzhav and P. Gunin. 2012. "Ecological Demands on Socioeconomic Development of Mongolia under Climate Aridization." *Arid Ecosystems* 2(1): 1–10.

Rengifo, Grimaldo, ed. 2011. *Small-Scale Agriculture in the Peruvian Andes*. Lima: PRATEC.

Robbins, Paul. 2012. *Political Ecology: Critical Introductions to Geography*. Chichester, UK: Wiley and Blackwell.

Rocker, Rudolf. 2004. *Anarcho-Syndicalism: Theory and Practice*. Oakland: AK Press.

Rockström, Johan, Will Steffen, Kevin Noone, et al., 2009. "A Safe Operating Space for Humanity." *Nature* 461: 472–475.

Rose, Deborah. 2005. "An Indigenous Philosophical Ecology." *The Australian Journal of Anthropology* 16(3): 294–305.

Safransky, Sara and Wendy Wolford. 2011. "Contemporary land Grabs and their Alternatives in the Americas." Paper presented at the International Conference on Global Land Grabbing, University of Sussex, 6–8 April 2011.

Shattuck, Annie, Christina Schiavoni, and Zoe Vangenlder. 2015. "Translating the Politics of Food Sovereignty." *Globalizations* 12(4): 421–433.

Shiva, Vandana. 2008. "Biodiversity, Intellectual Property Rights, and Globalization." In B. de Sousa Santos (ed.) *Another Knowledge is Possible*, 272–287. New York: Verso.

Sirina, A.A. 2009. "People Who Feel the Land: The Ecological Ethic of the Evenki and Eveny." *Anthropology and Archeology of Eurasia* 47(3): 9–37.

Stewart-Harawira, Makere. 2012. "Returning the Sacred: Indigenous Ontologies in Perilous Times." In Lewis Williams, Rose Roberts, and Alastair McIntosh (eds.), *Radical Human Ecology: Intercultural and Indigenous Approaches*, 73–90. Burlington: Ashgate.

Toledo, Victor. 2001. "Indigenous Peoples and Biodiversity." In Simon Levin et al. (eds.), *Encyclopedia of Biodiversity*. Cambridge: Academic Press.

Thomson, Bob. 2011. "Pachakuti: Indigenous Perspectives, Buen Vivir, Sumas Kawsay, and Degrowth." *Development* 54: 448–454.

White, Monica. 2010. "Shouldering Responsibility for the Delivery of Human Rights: A Case Study of the D-Town Famers of Detroit." *Race/Ethnicity: Multidisciplinary Global Contexts* 3(2): 189–211

White, Monica. 2011. "Sisters of the Soil: Urban Gardening as Resistance in Detroit." *Race/Ethnicity* 5: 13–28.

White, Richard, Simon Springer, and Marcelo Lopes de Souza. 2016. "Performing Anarchism, Practicing Freedom, and Pursuing Revolt." In R.J. White, S. Springer, and M. Lopes (eds.), *The Practice of Freedom: Anarchism, Geography, and the Spirit of Revolt*, 1–22. London, UK: Rowman and Littlefield.

5

Our Graves above the Timberline

Urban Green Commons, Intergenerational Justice and Diachronic Environmental Politics

Martin Locret-Collet

> *Our graves*
> *Above the timberline*
> *Our names chalked*
> *The pressure of wealth*
> *No longer found*
>
> *Let them inherit this fire now*
> *Lest they will forget that we were*
> *Ever here*
>
> — Katatonia, "Inheritance"

The Commons are nothing new, but they have recently resurfaced, especially in their urban incarnation. Indeed, Urban Green Commons have enjoyed a certain surge of popularity lately, both in academic writings and in mainstream media, reaching non-specialist audiences like never before. This emergence was greatly favoured by the general economic, social and political conjuncture: prolonged periods of economic austerity, the rise of ecological and environmental awareness and a growing contestation over the multiple ways in which neo-liberalism is regulating and constraining our lives have helped Urban Green Commons enthusiasts and advocates gather a receptive audience. The time seems ripe, too: the continued rise of urban dwelling and consequent stressful lives, an increased disconnection with the natural world, unprecedented levels of diversity in communities (the so-called 'superdiversity'), etc. have all undoubtedly created the conditions for this development.

This chapter aims to show how Urban Green Commons can be seen as an anarchist-minded endeavour, stemming from people's ability and will to organize the modalities of their life, in accordance or in defiance with the neo-liberal ordering of the city. In addition, I intend to demonstrate that a radical, openly anarchist approach to human geography has much to contribute to political ecology in terms of analysis and gives us an appropriate lens to study the social dimension of sustainability and the 'grounded' political ecology of green spaces.

In the anarchist spirit of change enacted through thoughts put in action, I will endeavour to blend both theory and praxis in this chapter, which is mainly based on the research I carried out for my doctoral dissertation. More importantly maybe, I will attempt to give a glimpse of the everyday lives of (extra)-ordinary people, and how these people slowly but surely change the world.

In this chapter, I contend that Urban Green Commons:

- Help us advance towards an explicitly anarchist political ecology. Political ecology shares deep roots with anarchist thought and an early political ecology can be traced in the works of famous anarchist and geography pioneers, like Peter Kropotkin and Élisée Reclus.
- Are the locus of diachronic environmental politics emancipated from electoral agendas, pointing at deep transformations within governance systems (following a Foucauldian idea of Government as the 'right disposition of things', an optimum arrangement).
- Can foster intergenerational justice through the transmission of place-based environmental knowledge and social values, an aspiration to continuity and change in values and practice.

I will first go through some theoretical considerations, exploring anarchist conceptions of space, place and territory to lay out the intellectual framework of this study. By presenting place-making as an active, on-going and perpetually challenged process – between citizens, public and private institutions, etc. – happening through associations based on politics of affinity, on contestation and confrontation, such a radical lens offer a much sought-after escape from the 'territorial trap' (Reid-Henry 2010) at city level, as well as from the Foucauldian notion of territory as a disciplining and controlling device only (Antonsich 2009).

I will then show how, through environmental awareness, knowledge and education, Urban Green Commons foster the transmission of place-based knowledge and an ethics of care for both environment and communities, values which prove to be fundamentally at odd with the modernist, neo-liberal arrangement of the city based on a functionally defined, consumer-oriented geography. I will illustrate with some case studies and examples from the fieldwork I led in Birmingham (UK), Amsterdam (NL) and Belfast (UK), to present Urban Green Commons as places setting in motion a novel and radical reconfiguration of power relationships and governance arrangements at local scale.

Finally, I shall introduce Urban Green Commons as arrhythmic spaces that help develop diachronic environmental politics emancipated from electoral agendas and foster intergenerational justice through the transmission of place-based environmental knowledge and social values, but also take into account the temporality and fundamental fleetingness of most human social and political activities and organizations.

TOWARDS AN ANARCHIST SPACE

In its most straightforward definition, a space is a fraction of the 'overall' space (i.e. the surface of the earth), it is a location on the map (*Oxford Dictionary of Geography*), while a place is a space with added human value, it is a space to which meaning has been conferred by one person or a group of persons. According to Mayhew, places are 'spatial moments [that] come into being and continue being made at the meeting points of history, representation and material practice' (2009, 382). It is worth noting that in this acceptation places retain a potential for evolution, they are not fixed nor defined forever. It is acknowledged that their limits have a certain plasticity, and places may have some immaterial qualities or dimensions to them: a place does not need to be exactly fitting within the space it occupies for the affect does not fit within the borders. By addressing places and spaces, we also necessarily have to face the problems of limitations, boundaries and enclosures. Between places and spaces is an intimate link resulting in a constant movement 'in which the linkages established in networks draw some locations together while at the same time pushing others further apart' (Massey and Jess 1995, 94–95), as bonds are established and dissolved, networks woven and torn apart.

A territory can be defined as the interaction between the social and the institutional based on 'aspirations to continuity, contiguity and boundedness' (Ince 2012, p.1648), to form a homogenous group of a sort, be it a neighbourhood, a local community, or a nation (Antonsich 2009). These social and institutional elements are both inter-related and co-constitutive, running through multiple processes of territorialization and re-territorialisation, and thus very often become blurred (Ince 2012).

In a radical, anarchist-minded conception of space, both place and territory are defined through unfinished, never-ending processes of territorialisation and re-territorialisation, and space is seen as fluid in permanent reconfiguration. This understanding constitutes a significant departure from the neo-liberal conception and ordering of the city in which the use of space is highly regulated, as much as the circulation between various places. Indeed, the reconfiguration of the urban realm that accelerated through the second half of the twentieth century has resulted in a deep transformation of the politics and culture of city living, especially for working and middle-class residents, and in the emergence of an always sharper line between public and private space (Karsten 2008, 2013). This reconfiguration has strengthened the boundedness of urban spaces, marking the progressive disappearance of mixed uses of spaces such as sidewalks and alleys where the private and the public frequently mingled (Karsten 2008). As a consequence, it has also established firmly in our urban imaginaries the idea that a space should have a clear definition or purpose: residential, commercial, recreational, etc. (Ferrell 2012). This decidedly capitalist arrangement has been enforced through regulation and policing, based on a distinction between the proper and improper uses of space, which proved especially constitutive for open public spaces that are now promoted as consumer spaces (Ince 2012, Ferrell 2012). More accurately maybe public space is now designed to act as a space of transition, facilitating the circulation between places of consumption and thus supporting this ultimate purpose by establishing some standard sets of rules to help harmonize the geography of the neo-liberal city, so as to avoid stagnation, discussion and the possible expression of unwanted opinion, attuning open public spaces to the rhythm and patterns of the post-industrial urban life (Edensor 2008, Short 2006). As Short puts it:

> Privately controlled places such as shopping malls have become hubs of a form of public life that is controlled and managed. The privatization of public space entails restricted access and a limited range of behaviour. [. . .] Behaviour is monitored. (2006, p.98)

More recently, this re-ordering of the urban world has also been coupled with a growing concern for security. This movement has resulted in the increased privatization, fencing and access restriction of public open spaces and, consequently, has greatly impacted the social and cultural life of cities by displacing or preventing opportunities of social gatherings (always potentially political) and unwanted manifestations of counter culture and sub-culture to either 'appropriate' or private spaces (Low 2005). This has reinforced the decline of unregulated open spaces and the marginalization or part silencing of their users (Mitchell 1995) for, as Ferrell puts it,

> Risk-based policing and consumer-based urban economies coalesce around a central consequence: intolerance toward open urban space and those who would occupy or traverse it inappropriately. (2012, p.1689)

Occupy and traverse are purposefully chosen words: in fact, it must be noted that the geography of the neo-liberal city is one of strong territorial fixity, where space is carefully compartmented and regulated but where people (and goods) are supposed to be in constant motion, following precisely scheduled and rhythmic fluxes (Mitchell 1995, Ferrell 2012, Edensor 2008). It is thus only regarded as 'proper use' to be static in functionally designated spaces, such as home, school, or the working place. Consequently, the quality of life is now largely treated as a commodity that would ultimately be the privilege of those who can afford it, economically and hence spatially. Conjoined with an increased demand for movement control and personal safety in the post 9/11 world, this trend has contributed to establish and legitimize strong practices of territorial appropriation, segregation and enclosure (Ferrell 2012, Low 1996, 2005).

A radical conception does not ignore the dichotomy between public and private space but sees beyond it in its delineation of the practices of territorialisation, with a prioritization of cooperation and a clear advocacy of prefigurative politics. Prefigurative politics captures the strategies developed by anarchists to embed the political principles (such as mutual aid, self-determination and solidarity) of a conceptual, utopian anarchist society into their present everyday organization, in the spirit of some early anarchists who undertook some 'propaganda by the deed' (Ince 2012, p.1652, Clough and Blumberg 2012). Following the idea that a social project has to be a spatial one, anarchist strategy and philosophy rest on the acknowledgement that society, much like space, is permanently in motion. Consequently, 'revolution' can be described as a never-ending process of development and spatial reconfiguration (Springer *et al.* 2012). Even though modern-day anarchists still call for moments of upheaval and rupture, changes that can be considered as revolutionary are actually perceived as happening over long periods of time, those periods being necessary for organizational and relational reconfigurations to take place (Ince 2012).

This process is always in motion, never complete and always forward looking, an everyday revolution of a sort, for Utopia is not to be achieved: it is an unattainable goal. But, as Ince puts it,

> in striving to achieve it, we can move towards revolution through the constant creation and adaptation of revolutionary practices and relations in everyday life. This acknowledgement radically transforms the spatialities (and temporalities) of revolutionary praxis, producing political spaces that are processual and in tension between the present and future; between the actual and the possible, it is in this tension that anarchism resides. (2012, p.1653)

Studying space through an anarchist lens offers much flexibility when it comes to boundaries and functions: territory and borders are entwined in social relationships and, beyond the borderlessness hypothesis, it rests on the establishment of fluid, often temporary networks of associations and co-operations (Clough and Blumberg 2012, Ince 2012). Here, place making is an active, on going and perpetually challenged process between multiple actors and stakeholders: citizens, public bodies, private institutions, which happens through various associations based on politics of affinity, on commonalities of interests, on temporary arrangements. Through an anarchist lens, the everyday practices of bordering and territorialisation are seen as happening through associations and cooperation while the use of space is primarily defined around common goals and purposes constitutive of citizenship, identities and subjectivities (seen here as vectors of emancipation and of a potentially more radically democratic urbanism) rather than around the imposition of a common set of rules or a public/private space dichotomy which seldomly reflects its usage anyway (Ferrell 2012, Ince 2012). Finally, bordering should be stripped off its negative, xenophobic connotation in this context: here bordering is seen as a constitutive activity of social beings who define their place in relations to other and inscribe their activities spatially.

I advocate here the use of a radical, anarchist conception of territory for a more grounded political ecology, in which territory can be seen as an emancipatory tool (one of co-operative projects and free associations) as much as a controlling, coercive one. Urban Green Commons are a perfect incarnation of potentially liberating and emancipating spaces in the way they come to be, are managed, and often evolve over time.

URBAN GREEN COMMONS

In their original incarnation, as common land in pre-industrial England, the Commons were actually divided into three categories: 'common' land, 'stinted' and 'waste', the latter being the only truly common land in the modern sense of open, public access to all comers (mostly for foraging, gathering wood, etc.), the access to the two formers being subject to some form of common rights or seasonal regulation. The point is, the focus was on use rather than property rights. It must not be forgotten that these 'original' Commons, as relating to a common land source of natural resources, providing much needed supply for the subsistence of peasants, low class and landless agriculture workers, were exclusively a rural phenomenon (Eizenberg 2012).

The notion that central parts of cities can host critical environmental resources for the use or the enjoyment of all citizens is far more recent. It mainly emerged with the hygienist and paternalist concerns that gave birth to the early park movement in the second half of the nineteenth century (Short 2006), advocating the need of factory workers for fresh air, exercise and the possibility to grow one's own supply of fresh fruits and vegetables, at a time where most urban dwellers had grown up in the countryside before moving to cities, looking for employment opportunities. Such concerns declined strongly in the second half of the twentieth century, especially in the 1980s, but have known a revival of late and been on the rise for the last twenty years or so.

Broadly defined, a green space is 'any area of land not covered by impermeable surface' (Gaston *et al.* 2013, p.3) whilst the green infrastructure is an interconnected network of green spaces (Gill *et al.* 2007) including remnant vegetation, parks and gardens, natural and semi-natural spaces, allotments and community gardens, civic spaces, cemeteries, sport facilities or green corridors. Most urban green spaces, such as neighbourhood parks, pocket parks, community gardens, allotments, spaces of urban agriculture can be considered as Urban Green Commons – in the way they are used and managed rather than on their being public or private, gated or open spaces.

Urban green spaces are also major providers of Ecosystem Services and Cultural Ecosystem Services in cities. Ecosystem Services (ES) are the regulating, provisioning and supporting benefits provided by ecosystems that are 'directly relevant or beneficial to human well-being' (Haase *et al.* 2014, p.414), while Cultural Ecosystem Services (CES) are the non-material benefits people derive from ES through spiritual enrichment, recreation, cognitive development, etc. (*Ibid.*). The benefits of ES and CES include climate change adaptation and mitigation, health and wellbeing, preservation of wildlife and habitat, economic growth and investment, social cohesion and the strengthening of communities. The Millennium Ecosystem Assessment (MEA, 2003) laid important foundations by asserting the importance of ES and explicitly stating that CES do exist, are connected to human health and well-being and, most importantly, cannot be outsourced and 'provide multi-dimensional linkages between people and the environment they live in' (Andersson *et al.* 2015, p.165). ES and CES make a huge impact on urban health and sustainability, and Urban Green Commons are often critical for the mitigation of pollution, the regulation of climate change related hazards, such as floods, and the preservation of biodiversity. They also help improving the physical and mental health of city dwellers and their general wellbeing by allowing people to get some fresh air, exercise, run, walk their dog, or by providing open access to sport pitches or children playgrounds. Urban Green Commons are places where Society and Environment are afforded the possibility to unite or at least learn to co-exist more symbiotically and peacefully.

The apparition of Urban Green Commons also marks a very interesting historical shift: moving away from the 'old' and exclusively rural Commons, they constitute the dominant form of common land, following the evolution of society as a whole, with a majority of citizens (and especially poorer citizens) now living in urban areas. Still, a caveat must be introduced here: in the Western World (which is the cultural context of my research), Urban Green Commons don't sustain livelihood but sustain the possibility to live a decent, interesting and worthy life, sometimes to complement resources. In short, this is what makes the difference between living and surviving in a city.

By their very nature, Urban Green Commons are arrhythmic spaces in today's urban world: they are profoundly disruptive places in the modern, neo-liberal city, whose clockwork functioning relies on a mechanical, functional division of space, meant to maximize productivity, with a constantly flowing circulation in between its various parts, and a very limited (and controlled) ability to stop for what is considered as non-productive and non-monitored activities.

TOWARDS ANARCHIST SPACES

Most Urban Green Commons stem from the same essential principle an anarchist approach to human geography does: people's essential ability and the will to organize their lives with or against the grain of the neo-liberal city, the grid that constrain the everyday life of citizens. For this reason, it seems especially relevant to look at Urban Green Commons through a radical, anarchist lens and, further, to assess why it makes sense to apply a radical framework to political ecology.

Indeed, if political ecology has deep roots within anarchist thoughts and anarchist geography they were somewhat left behind and obscured when it developed in the second half of the twentieth century, where most conceptual efforts expounded a Marxist, materialist, critical paradigm. This school of thought revived political ecology and, despite strong convergences in their common critic of capital and imperialism, it also somewhat understandably consciously ignored or left aside the initial critique of state and centralization and arguments for self-organization (Springer *et al.* 2012, Springer 2013).

A reconciliation of political ecology with its anarchist roots provides new perspectives that help advancing the field. Anarchist geography and political ecology have much in common and much to offer to each other, philosophically, theoretically and methodologically. Anarchist geography shares some deep connections with humanistic geography in the attention it pays to the study of place and to the understanding of 'how mere space becomes an intensely human place' (Tuan 1976, p.269), its commitment to fieldwork and long advocacy of the necessity to critically build on knowledge (Smith 1984). Both fields retain from post-structuralism the notion that the creation of meanings – and thus, of place, is an unfinished process that continuously evolves as contexts and relationships change and evolve (Murdoch 2006), but part with its anti-humanist concern that individuals are less important than the systems they belong to in this process. Finally, both contend that any social project is always necessarily a spatial project.

At the heart of anarchist geography is the tension between people's aspirations to self-organize their lives as individuals or collectives and the 'everyday matrices of power' that regulate and constrain their capacities of doing so (Springer *et al.* 2012, p.1593). This tension mainly lies in the opposition of the vertical layout of these matrices to the horizontal layout of people's social and spatial practices. It must be stated clearly that the power here mentioned is not necessarily illegitimate or perceived to be so, and the constraints mentioned are also to be found in democratic societies for this tension is inherent to all the political philosophies building upon the social contract. Using an anarchist approach to human geography, Ince (2012) has questioned the notion of territory as a tension between a social space and an institutional space, while Ferrel has elucidated the 'proper' and 'improper' uses of open public spaces in a consumer-oriented society (Ferrel 2012). These recent efforts to re-investigate classical subjects like space or territory have helped to cast a new light on the flows and regulations that shape contemporary life and spatial organization, both in and outside of the neo-liberal and consumerist developments. Anarchist geography appears as both a solid and original analytical scope for a political ecological study. Also, as Springer notes,

> on the more theoretical side of things, anarchism has much to contribute to enhancing geographical knowledge, where themes such as state theory and sovereignty; [. . .] urban design and aesthetics; activism and social justice; [. . .] belongings and the politics of place; [. . .] and the manifold implications of society-space relations all seem particularly well suited to a more overt infusion of anarchist ideas, where new research insights and agendas might productively arise. (Springer 2013, p.56)

Far from being a stretch, using an anarchist approach to do political ecology is much more about reconciling the field with some of its roots and show how such an approach is relevant and potentially intellectually proficient today, especially when we consider that, political ecology, moreover, explores these social and environmental changes with an understanding that there are better, less coercive, less exploitive, and more sustainable ways of doing things. (Robbins 2012, p.20)

Various forms of cooperation and direct action are essential to the emergence, protection, preservation, enhancement and overall development of Urban Green Commons. This emphasis on cooperation can be traced to the roots of both anarchist geography and political ecology. Indeed, the genealogy of political ecology is quite easily traced: two major intellectual figures of the nineteenth century, Russian Peter Kropotkin and French Elisée Reclus, are widely acknowledged as its founding fathers. Both were respected albeit unorthodox geographers who got into troubles with the scientific and political establishments of their time. Interestingly enough, the influence of their work somehow faded after their death, only to be re-investigated and celebrated from the 1970s onwards (Springer *et al.* 2012). Following Humboldt, Kropotkin and Reclus broke with the long and prevailing tradition of environmental determinism which stated that the physical condition of any territory determines the moral and physical traits of the humans inhabiting that land, as much as their social organization and activities. Mirroring Darwin and Wallace, they also broke with deeply ingrained imperialist views on race and social domination (Robbins 2012). Most of their intellectual departure, theoretical insurgency and resultant advances in the field can be attributed to their philosophical and political thinking as much as to their concern for social justice and early environmental advocacy. Both prominent anarchists, they rejected the concepts of centrality, the legitimacy of any kind of domination and from evolution theory they had retained the idea that, beyond a dire competition, a certain level of cooperation and symbiotic living is necessary for any species to thrive (Robbins 2012, Springer 2013). As Darwin wrote in the concluding remarks of *On the Origin of Species,*

> [. . .] these elaborately constructed forms, so different from each other, and dependent on each other in so complex a manner have all been produced by laws acting around us. (Darwin 2008, p.360)

Neither Kropotkin nor Reclus ever characterized their work as political ecology, the use of the term spread in the 1970s, but they most surely laid its foundations with their conception of interdependent human–environment interactions, extensive and rigorous fieldworks, and a decidedly non-centralist approach (Robbins 2012, Springer 2013).

PLACES TO LIVE IN THE CITY

The essential question I came to ask myself when researching for my PhD was the following: why do people get actively involved in the stewardship of Urban Green Commons decide to initiate a community garden or feel the need to have a public green space on their doorstep? Three main answers emerged from the fieldwork and interviews I led.

First and foremost, Nature is disruptive of the mechanic, industrial time of the clock, the time of the calendar. It is defiant of the modernist, functional ordering of space that leaves no room for wandering, loss, contestation, expression and creativity and as such, ecology (the 'natural' course of things). In the middle of the hustle and bustle of great cities, trees and flowers take their own time to grow, sometimes for the 'sole' apparent purpose of making urban life more liveable. This attracts a lot of people who feel like these spaces are little 'oases' in the middle of a concrete jungle. Urban green spaces afford the possibility to breathe, to break away from the pressure of urban living without actually leaving the city. This is especially true for the poorest urban dwellers who seldomly can afford to leave the city for the weekend, not to mention have a countryside house. Located on Priory Road in Edgbaston, Birmingham, Martineau Gardens is a therapeutic community garden and registered charity. Only two miles away from the city centre, it provides abundant wildlife, gardening and outdoor workshops for the whole family and, most importantly maybe, peaceful grounds and therapeutic activities for ailed and recovering patients from the nearby Priory Hospital.

Second, Urban Green Commons provide city dwellers living in diverse (and 'superdiverse' areas) with a common ground to build a community and have a different, more meaningful social life. Urban Green Commons are some of the places where the politics of affinity are at their strongest: people with very different cultural and social backgrounds, with different occupations, ages, etc. having a common interest for nature, are afforded the possibility to build something together through the opportunities that green spaces provide. There is a universal interest for nature, and people can get together and sometimes embark on a project even though they might struggle to communicate otherwise. In Oost Indische Groen, a community garden of Amsterdam's Indische Buurt, a poor and highly diverse area in the eastern borough of Amsterdam Oost, some local residents who volunteer can't even communicate verbally, they do not have any other common language than their love for and knowledge of nature, and some hand gestures, which proves enough to dig, plant, prune and then cook together. Located on a former car park on Albertbridge Road, an interface between traditionally deprived protestant and catholic communities in East Belfast, the Bridge Community Garden has become a popular play area for children and a meeting place for their parents since its inception in 2014. Originally developed as a collaboration between Business in the Community and the Queen's University Belfast (to conduct research and experiments on urban soundscapes), it is now also used by Sure Start, a government programme providing support services for parents and children living in disadvantaged areas.

Finally, the urge for urban dwellers to assemble and organize is often kick-started by an imminent threat to a green space which is a meaningful place for the local community: eco-conscious citizens and members of the local community then feel prompted to step up, get involved and defend this common resource. The space can be meaningful for a broad range of reasons, but generally it is first and foremost a consequent provider of Ecosystem Services and Cultural Ecosystem Services; and most of the time, the threat comes from either the need for available land for housing development or from a lack of financial capacity from local authorities to keep on maintaining them, sometimes from a morally ambivalent mix of both. In Bournville, Birmingham (UK), the Friends of Cotteridge Park started off in 1997 with a petition to protest the increasing cuts in park management funds and the planned withdrawal from local authorities, who then wanted to remove the last permanent member of staff. The Friends group was then created by local residents to carry out all maintenance activities that were not covered by the Birmingham City Council's contract with a private landscape company and add the human value to this historic park. After a little more than twenty years, now dozens of strong groups have become a reckoned local force, environmentally, socially, politically but also culturally with the annual organization of the CoCoMad festival, one of the biggest in the West Midlands.

EMERGING MODELS OF GOVERNANCE AND STEWARDSHIP

Urban Green Commons also cause a disruption of the political agendas: these places are out of synchronicity when it comes to the political governance of the city. Schematically, the situation can be reduced to a problem of conflicting temporalities, those of political governance versus those environmental stewardship. The imperatives of conservation, environmental governance and stewardship don't accommodate with the characteristic patterns of the political agendas and electoral cycles which, most of the time, are planned over four years at best. Green spaces and especially Urban Green Commons are therefore arrhythmic spaces and, symbolically, places of contestation in their very being. Going back to the Foucauldian definition of governance as 'the right disposition of things', Urban Green Commons demonstrate that the present disposition of things is mostly wrong but also progressively changing.

Today some new models of environmental stewardship and urban green spaces governance are emerging, encouraged by a lack of financial capacity from local authorities, deep changes in urban economies and labour, and a growing political and environmental awareness from citizens, with a strong emphasis on local, direct, grounded action. The Highbury Orchard Community sits in a corner of Highbury Park in King's Heath, Birmingham. A non-for-profit Community Interest Company it has strictly no ownership on the land it uses, nor has it any lease or any right of use of any kind. Its existence is solely due to the determination of its founders and managers, its importance for the local community and the benevolence of the park rangers who are dramatically understaffed and happy to let the volunteers occupy and share their stewardship and maintenance duties.

As stated by Colding and Barthel (2013, p.159), Urban Green Commons encompass a vast diversity of arrangements that rest on practical management rather than on ownership rights *per se*. Indeed, ownership rights may belong to a range of actors including the state, a regional, municipal or local authority, public and private owners. The importance of focussing on the material, socio-political process of commoning and on the resulting governance arrangements rather than on property rights is twofold: as previously mentioned, the notions of public, private, open and closed are generally misleading and reflect a legal matter of fact rather than the actual use and management situation. Second, most Urban Green Commons did not develop as commons: the process of commoning, the re-territorialisation of a place as a common, very often happens when the previous arrangement is failing. Cuts in funding and a lack of management and stewardship capacity appear to be the starting point of many initiatives that can be identified as commoning of urban green spaces and resources.

Ultimately, more flexibility in the use of green spaces amounts to a more perennial, sustainable stewardship. This might seem counter-intuitive at first but by allowing places to transform and evolve according to the needs, means and aspirations of communities, we make them far more resilient and able to endure. And these arrangements are increasingly and overwhelmingly recognized as a win-win situation, except maybe for real estate developers on the lookout for available land.

THE SOCIAL IMPACT OF URBAN GREEN COMMONS

Urban Green Commons are places of education and transmission for urban dwellers of all ages: environmental education for children and younger people through forest schools or play days, places for the acquisition of new skills, lifelong learning and transmission for adults through volunteering and workshops. In addition, there is an important turnover of the people involved over time, both volunteers and management, which provokes a circulation of information, a renewal of knowledge and a mixing of influences. When it comes to Urban Green Commons, both people and places have a strong and very innate tendency to network, to encourage cooperation and the communalization of knowledge and resources. It must not be forgotten that a lot of 'active commoners' are activists of a sort or are actively involved in alternative, de-growth and conservation movements.

My interviews have highlighted a vast array of reasons why people regularly visit Urban Green Commons or decide to get involved in their maintenance or management: from a concern for environment and climate change, an educational purpose to an interest in healthy eating and food growing processes or the desire for a richer sociability and a vibrant community life to an increasing awareness of the physical and mental health benefits provided by such places. This variety of interests and motives highlights not only the broad range of benefits that people derive from urban green and are progressively becoming aware of but also a dynamic change in their environmental imaginaries and perceptions through a ripple effect of a sort, acquiring environmental, social and political dimensions.

One could rightfully ask if the grass is always greener on Urban Green Commons' side of the fence and, as a matter of facts, some limitations must be acknowledged.

First, according to all my interviewees, Urban Green Commons face a recurring problem of leadership, both in terms of leadership capacity and continuity. When (if) the original leaders go, most places tend to be threatened: as in many such projects or initiatives, leadership is a real issue because there is a need for a real drive, for time to invest, for leadership capacities, as well as for a charismatic persona to rally and enthuse volunteers. In addition, an irreducible amount of expert knowledge is needed, both administratively and technically; otherwise most structures just end up disappearing because of poor management. The involvement of volunteers seems especially difficult to sustain too, and many interviewees confessed their struggle to retain their volunteers beyond a core, stable number of dedicated members. Finally, if Urban Green Commons can help breaking segregation in some areas, they may also reinforce it in some other. This is a double-edged sword, especially in gentrified or gentrifying neighbourhoods where they facilitate the functioning of some communities but can isolate some others.

Urban Green Commons foster more resilient and better functioning communities, with a better integration of diversity and a more symbiotic relationship between society and environment. Coming back to the introductory quote, that's what we should be remember by, not by cities that are concrete graves, monuments to the pursuit of wealth that tower above the timberline but impoverish and ultimately jeopardize the lives of future generations.

CONCLUSION

Urban Green Commons shed some light on the importance of the moment and the momentary: these spaces are all a point in place and time, a reference, a temporary centre of gravity in the life of many people and communities. Urban Green Commons are both a locus and a catalyst, hence the necessity of political ecological works that pay attention to 'the momentary and the commonplace' (Gabriel 2014, p.42), to highlight the ambiguity, ambivalence, indecision and opportunities born from these interactions. Those allow the emergence of new dimensions of life through the connections between autonomous subjects and their environment. This also echoes a conception of space and society as flexible arrangements undergoing constant reconfigurations and ties in with an anarchist vision of people organizing and re-organizing the modalities of their lives both with and against the grain of the everyday matrices of power, depending on how those constrain or liberate their lives.

Urban Green Commons help foster environmental awareness and knowledge through education and the transmission of both place-based knowledge and of an ethics of care both for the environment but also for the community. Through this perspective, it becomes possible to envision the formation of the individual subject not as the product of the disciplining, uniformizing power held by the state but as a result of the productive forms of praxes that breed power and knowledge, while governance is understood as the exertion of control not through laws but through what Foucauld referred to as the right disposition of things,

> the processes of interaction and decision-making among the actors involved in a collective problem that lead to the creation, reinforcement, or reproduction of social norms and institutions. (Gabriel 2014, p.42)

This proposition, I argue, must be developed by suggesting that these processes don't necessarily favour a decentralized form of autocratic governance (Swyngedouw 2005) but can result in potentially liberating and empowering practices.

Indeed, a plurality of emerging urban realms can be identified by paying attention to the multiple, divergent social and spatial practices of urban citizens for,

> Here, governance is not examined by tracing the circuits of power through which citizens are controlled, dominated, or oppressed by the state and related institutions, nor is it treated as a force that operates unidirectionally to inculcate citizens as self-monitoring subjects of economic regimes that foist responsibility and risk onto the poor and working classes in the service of the interests of the elite. (Gabriel 2014, p.42)

REFERENCES

Antonsisch, M. 2009. On Territory, the Nation-State and the Crisis of the Hyphen. *Progress in Human Geography,* 33, 789–806.

Andersson, E., Tengö, M., McPhearson, T., Kremer, P. 2015. Cultural Ecosystem Services as a Getaway for Improving Urban Sustainability. *Ecosystem Services,* 12, 165–168.

Blumberg, R. & Clough, N. 2012. Toward Anarchist and Autonomous Marxist Geographies. *ACME,* 11, 335–351.

Chatterton, P. 2008. Using Geography to Teach Freedom and Defiance: Lessons in Social Change from 'Autonomous Geographies'. *Journal of Geography in Higher Education,* 32, 419–440.

Clark, G. & Clark, A. 2001. Common Rights to Land in England 1475-1839. *The Journal of Economic History,* 61, 1009–1036.

Clark, J. P. 2012. Political Ecology. *Encyclopedia of Applied Ethics,* London, Elsevier.

Colding, J. & Bartel, S. 2013. The Potential of Urban Green Commons in the Resilience Building of Cities. *Ecological Economics,* 86, 156–166.

Cresswell, T. 2004. *Place: A Short Introduction,* Oxford, Blackwell.

Darwin, C. 2008. *On the Origin of Species,* New York, Oxford, Oxford University Press.

Death, C. 2014. *Critical Environmental Politics,* New York, Routledge.

Edensor, T. 2010. *Geographies of Rhythm: Nature, Place, Mobilities and Bodies,* Farnham, Ashgate.

Eizenberg, E. 2012. Actually Existing Commons: Three Moments of Space of Community Gardens in New York City. *Antipode,* 44, 764–782.

Eizenberg, E. & lon-Mozes, T. 2016, The Emergence of Urban Agriculture as Part of New Urban Governance Constellations: Allotments and Farm Gardens in Israeli Cities, *Proceeding of Growing in Cities Conference, September 2016, Basel.*

Ferrel, J. 2012. Anarchy, Geography and Drift. *Antipode,* 44, 1687–1704.

Gabriel, N. 2014. Urban Political Ecology: Environmental Imaginary, Governance, and the Non-Human. *Geography Compass,* 8, 38–48.

Gaston, K. J., Avila-Jimenez, M. L. & Edmonson, J. L. 2013. Managing Urban Ecosystems for Goods and Services. *Journal of Applied Ecology,* 1–11.

Gill, S. E., Handley, J. F., Ennos, A. R. & Pauleit, S. 2007. Adapting Cities for Climate Change: The Role of the Green Infrastructure. *Built Environment,* 33, 115–133.

Haase, D., Frantzeskaki, N., Elmqvist, T. 2014. Ecosystem Services in Urban Landscapes: Practical Applications and Governance Implications. *Ambio* 43(4), 407–412.

Ince, A. 2012. In the Shell of the Old: Anarchist Geographies of Territorialisation. *Antipode,* 44, 1645–1666.

Ince, A. 2014. The Shape of Geography to Come. *Dialogues in Human Geography,* 4, 276.

Karsten, L. 2008. The Upgrading of the Sidewalk: from Traditional Working-Class Colonisation to the Squatting Practices of Urban Middle-Class Families. *Urban Design International,* 13, 61–66.

Low, S., Taplin, D. & Scheld, S. 2005. *Rethinking Urban Parks: Public Space and Cultural Diversity,* Austin, TX, USA, University of Texas Press.

Low, S. M. 1996. The Anthropology of Cities: Imagining and Theorizing the City. *Annual Review of Anthropology,* 25, 383–409.

Massey, D., Jess, P. 1995. *A Place in the World?: Places, Cultures and Globalization,* Oxford, Oxford University Press.

Millenium Ecosystem Assesment, 2003. https://www.millenniumassessment.org/.

Mitchell, D. 1995. The End of Public Space? People's Park, Definitions of the Public, and Democracy. *Annals of the Association of American Geographers,* 85, 108–133.

Ostrom E. 1990. *Governing the Commons,* Cambridge, Cambridge University Press.

Reid-Henry, S. 2010. The Territorial Trap Fifteen Years On. *Geopolitics,* 15, 752–756.

Robbins, P. 2012. *Political Ecology: A Critical Introduction,* Wiley-Blackwell.

Short, J. R. 2006. *Urban Theory: A Critical Assessment,* New York, Palgrave MacMillan.

Smith, S. J. 1984. Practicing Humanistic Geography. *Annals of the Association of American Geographers,* 74, 353–374.

Springer, S. 2013. Anarchism and Geography: A Brief Genealogy of Anarchist Geography. *Geography Compass,* 7, 46–60.

Springer, S., Ince, A., Pickerill, J., Brown, G. & Barker, A. J. 2012. Reanimating Anarchist Geographies: A New Burst of Colour. *Antipode,* 44, 1591–1604.

Swyngedouw, E. 2004. Scaled Geographies: Nature, Place and the Politics of Scale (Chapter 7). Scale and Geographic Inquiry: Nature, Society and Method, 2004. Oxford, Blackwell Publishing Ltd, 129–153.

Swyngedouw,, E. 2005. Governance Innovation and the Citizen: The Janus Face of Governance-beyond-the-State. *Urban Studies,* 42, 1991–2006.

Tuan, Y.-F. 1976. Humanistic Geography. *Annals of the Association of American Geographers,* 66, 266–276.

Tuan, Y.-F. 2011. *Space and Place: The Perspective of Experience,* Minneapolis, University of Minnesota Press.

6

An Anarchist Landscape?

Rethinking Landscape and 'Other' Geographies

Gerónimo Barrera de la Torre

For me, writing about Anarchist Political Ecology generates questions about the contours of what can be defined as such and what insights it can bring to the fore. It pushes me right away to think of how political ecology is un-anarchistic, which can arguably be traced to its origins in the 1970s with the combination of ecology and Marxist political economy frameworks. I, on the contrary, do not argue in this intervention for 'an anarchist political ecology'. I do not consider anarchism as self-evident and clear, but problematic. In doing this, I intend not to detach or become estranged, conversely, drawing on an anarchist framework, I argue for a plurality of possibilities, for change and diversity. As problematic, I aim to keep alive the messiness, the complexity and heterogeneity and shed light to murkiness. The intention is neither to consider anarchism as an axiom nor to become guardians or upholders of any given proposal. Exploring this contradictory setting, I expect to grasp intricacies, to keep open the possibilities and be mindful against doctrinal or unquestionable representation of anarchism. I do not presume this intervention will resolve these paradoxes, quite the opposite I use it to challenge, and following Koch (2011: 63), to explore the 'the conceptual limits of anarchism with the aim of revising, renewing and even radicalizing its implication'.

Ecological balance, harmony between human and non-humans and claims for an ecological revolution in the face of ecological catastrophes permeate several anarchist ecological discourses. How easily ecology or nature becomes self-evident! We have lost our responsibility and connection to the environment, to 'nature', something that reminds us our history of alienation and the coming of hierarchical–coercive relations. Strands of eco-anarchism as bioregionalism or social ecology can be criticized by their desire to adhere to universalistic green principles and Western

115

democratic procedures (Davidson, 2009). The particular case of social ecology clearly expresses a fundamental, inherent harmony through the assumption of evolution as a 'directional processes' (Davidson, 2009). To derive the principles of a social ecology from 'natural ecology' clearly poses the question of what are these ecological lineaments that have to be followed and if there is only one way to understand them? (Davidson, 2009). This framework, this style of thinking invites us to return to a teleological understanding; A programmatic idea of ecological revolution where ultimately causalities neglect the intricacies – the plurality of possibilities. Tensions aroused between the universal principles necessary to underpin an evolutionary account and a transcendental notion of harmony with self-determination and diversity. Nevertheless, such approaches do not necessarily 'fail' to give ideas on how to perform confederate municipal organization, as Rojava's example has demonstrated (Knapp, Flach and Ayboga, 2016). My point here is to stress the currently accepted teleological, dualistic and programmatic idea that many of our writings maintain in dealing with notions of ecological care. My take on this problem through this intervention is brief, it does not proclaim anything novel but aims to build on and with many other voices that remind us to go beyond our limits and to attend to the more dynamic, heterogeneous and open-ended processes through which environmental understanding and practices of care, conservation and management are made.

Facing a new phase of neo-liberalism entrenched in creating resilient communities and privileging the spontaneity of markets, ecological concerns have acquired renewed significance for this project of reproducibility. In this sense, political ecology 'as a constellation of ideas and approaches' allows to challenge notions and problematize what environment means and to whom (Watts, 2015 and Escobar, 2004). To interrogate not only the materiality of capital, the State appropriation and use of environment elements but also the conflictive and contradictory construction of knowledges about it: how and why some environmental discourses and practices become dominant and how diverse groups make sense of them, and at the same time build alternatives (Watts, 2015). Through the broad scope of political ecology, my intervention centres on the situated approach that this framework offers to reflect on the hierarchies and structures of domination that prevail in the performance of certain knowledges and the power relations that inhabit them (Barrera-Bassols, 2003). Needless to say, this entails a critique of modern construction of knowledges, but as I will examine later, my goal is to avoid reinstating a dichotomic distinction and univocality between Western and non-Western 'knowledges' or conception of nature. Truth, reason, objectivity and transcendence are at the heart of this intervention, as part not only of Western colonial projects but also of any other project that embraces such dominant discourses.

Landscape has been a central concept for geographical inquiry and has acquired multifarious meanings. In general, landscape has been circumscribed as a functional category, where changes occur, but different from territory and processes of territorialization as arenas of power–spatial relations. For me, both concepts are interrelated and inform each other, yet for this chapter, I will emphasize landscape exploring other possible ways of understanding it, but above all to disturb dominant and exclusionary notions to point to its limitations. Territory (Ince, 2012), region, or scale (Springer, 2016) have been examined and re-thought through anarchist frameworks by several authors. When thinking about anarchist landscapes, one of the main studies that comes to mind is Breitbart's (1989) work around the tenets of an anarchist landscape and the experience in Spain examined by Garcia-Ramon (1989). However, landscape has not received the same attention in recent years, and I suggest here to consider it to reflect critically on human–non-human relations. The endeavour here is to problematize 'landscape' as notion and narrative, to avoid pre-determined definitions. To travel across it and with it as part of the same reflection. Certainly not to ask what is or defines an 'anarchist landscape'.

As Neumann (2011) examines, landscape has been a relevant concept in political ecology especially as a conceptual tool to analyse 'socioecological transformation, investigations into the contested meanings of nature, and interrogations of colonial narratives' (2011: 844). In this context, landscapes have been defined as material results of forms of managing territories, but also as representation, containing symbolic meanings of nature. Landscape as contested natures and as struggles over its meanings combines with the materiality of human livelihoods (Neumann, 2011: 845). What interests me here is to highlight the productive political ecological critique towards landscape as concept and its theoretical tenets over the last several decades. This breaks away from previous notions in landscape studies, opens the possibility to integrate a critique on representational approaches through everyday experiences and daily practices together with dynamical understandings of power expressions that have material consequences over human and non-human lives. 'Politicization' of landscapes is clearly one of the critical endeavours of such approach, but also how they work to produce meaning and as performance in themselves (Neumann, 2011).

Through this intervention, landscape becomes an excuse to reflect on and interrogate the plurality of possibilities to question why an anarchist political ecology and to problematize landscape narratives from anarchists' purview. The anarchist frameworks that help me mediate and rapidly cross intricate topographies and topologies draw on an eclectic selection of sources. With the understanding that 'classical' and post-anarchist differentiation explore important conflictive assumptions of the variegate readings, it remains problematic as reiteration of dichotomic distinction. To navigate such tensions here I engage such ideas as new and renewed at the same time, in order to not reiterate such differences and at the same time appeal to extend their own limits. A vortical image of discursive renovation, encounters; of becoming *anarchisms*. As Jun (2011: 231) asserts, 'the so-called "classical anarchists" had already discovered several of the insights attributed to post-structuralists more than a century before the latter appeared on the scene' (2011: 231). Although discovery is not the word that portrays for me the complexity and historicity of these thoughts, the presence and continuity allow to engage efforts towards decolonization of anarchisms. Gustav Landauer and Voltairine de Cleyre are the two figures from which I depart in this journey. From their particular perspectives, that clearly do not escape a contradictory and complex evolving set of ideas and practices, I intend to reach the 'darkness' of anarchists' landscapes. With this first line of thought, I will traverse across contemporary critical accounts on anarchism and move to engage interrogations of 'ecology' and its conflictive genealogy considering Elisée Reclus' work. The first part of the chapter then pushes to disturb and reflect on what an anarchist political ecology frame means. A second section draws on my interest and previous work around ontologies and the pluriverse in relation to what a non-hierarchical/non-coercive frame could meant. Here landscape is the central concept, as well as the narratives that have been emerging around it as a form to understand human–non-human relations. I also draw on my experiences working with indigenous people and peasant communities in Oaxaca, Mexico, around their own understanding of their landscapes. The intricated topography and topologies remain as a trajectory, not answers, to what anarchist political ecologies are and how they are performed. To reflect on the question 'who knows what is best for the world as a whole?' (Escobar 2004: 54), the 'murky' landscape's proposed reply: 'clearly anarchists not'. Not to claim the latter is a novel approach, as already Rudolf Rocker recalled P.J. Proudhon words: 'A truly free man is never at all sure if what he claims is really fair' (Meza, 2015: 206).

THE ANARCHIST HORIZON, THE ANARCHIST DIFFERENCE

What are the possible contours of an anarchist political ecology? And what is the place of landscapes in such a framework? Does this endeavour lead us to ask how to unlearn the 'archist' ways of producing, making-sense and understanding landscapes? This first section reflects on these contours. Above all, before engaging with the productive conversation between political ecology and landscape approaches, I am interested in dwelling on definitions and advocacies for the 'Idea'. I would not claim any special position that gives this reflection any exceptionality, rather I expect to put some questions into consideration. Concerns that I think are necessary to have in mind while proposing renewed approaches to environmental problems from a non-hierarchical perspective.

Difference is what produces these tensions, boundaries that I contend requires our attention. Naming a certain political ecology approach as anarchistic opens the possibility to further critical engagement with, for example, State appropriation and exploitation of human and non-human. The long history of landscape transformation built on hierarchical forms that have defined exploitative and inequitable environment management. Nevertheless, it also opens contradictory and variegated ways to understand such landscapes, establishes priorities for its use and produces particular knowledges. It also opens gaps to differentiate the 'libertarian' approach from the one of the 'others'. As we can advance critical inquiries that appear precluded by other approaches, ours forgets its own limits. Differences placed to define what ought to be 'x' or 'y' ideal world, what would define a just and better society, whose landscape will reflect that underlying reality that has been negated, set ambivalent meanings. Anarchy as horizon, open-ended and continually unfolding, draws protean landscapes (Springer, 2016). But such horizon is in turn observed from different points of view, from different worlds that understand that horizon otherwise. Since its own existence, the libertarian perspective has been struggling with its own definition, its own difference(s). As on the 'inside', we found a great diversity and contradictions, on the 'outside', it has been condemned by its 'Europeanness' or as a Western invention that is locked up in its own worldview. For some years now, discussions around these aspects have incorporated post-structuralist critics and decolonial engagements. Here I explore such tensions not to determine if so-called 'classical' anarchists were or not 'modern'. My intention is not to advocate for radical alterities (i.e. Bessire and Bond, 2014). Instead, I consider necessary to explore such distinctions as a point of departure to argue on the meaning of what I am naming 'murky' landscapes in the next section.

A problematic distinction has been set to define a 'different' anarchism. Extensive pieces have been written around an alleged 'classical anarchist tradition' and a post-anarchist, a dualist and reductionist posture that I found problematic and have no intention of reiterating (Feretti, 2017). Many such discussions are confined to discrediting a certain supposed 'tradition' and limited to who already propose certain idea or who are the original upholders of the radical thinking. Essentialism, rationality, universalism, etc., function as the doctrinal corpus to judge who is or not 'modern', who is or not 'anarchist'. What do we gain by setting such static differences? Such boundaries that paralyse a broadly heterogeneous and contingent assemblage of people from many different backgrounds. Even worst, as Aragorn! (2009) criticizes, our idea (and critics) of this 'classical' anarchism is based mostly on 'iconic' figures, around the great thinkers (usually white men). Beyond reductionist critiques that portray anarchism as a positivist, Cartesian, modern project that is obsolete, irrelevant, or outmoded (Morris, 2015); I found productive to rethink and push the same limits of what has been said about anarchism. Instead of looking for static definitions, something that I think we need to maintain is the appreciation for an ever-changing, continually unfolding life. Horizons that embrace multiplicity acknowledging the people's 'capacity to be different, to change, move transform, create' (Jun, 2011: 242). A close reading of anarchist thought reveals, as already many have noted, complicated and conflicted subjects that, in their own life navigate their difficult oceans, sometimes projecting an image of themselves that please us and other times ones that may disgust us. But, it appears that what has been augmented in our reading of anarchism has tended to essentialize it. As Ferretti (2017: 893) eloquently put it, 'anarchist geographers used the intellectual tools available in their day to build a completely different "discourse", criticizing the ways in which science and knowledge were constructed'.

A relevant example here is the use of 'ecology' as a concept and its genealogy. Particularly, if we consider the work of Elisee Reclus, as studied by Pelletier (2013, 2015); an anarchist geographer that has been considered one of the 'pioneers in the development of an ecological worldview' (Morris, 2015: 180). Even though, he resisted the use of the same word 'ecology', choosing another neologism of that time 'mésologie' as a better way to express, from a non-hierarchical framework, the way he perceived and understood human–non-human relationships. At present, ecology appears a self-evident notion to make sense of landscapes dynamics, but as any other concept, it has a genealogy and the anarchist critique subverted it in the very moment of its inception in mainstream science. The latter does not mean that we must get rid of 'ecology' as an *a priori* authoritarian concept, but it serves an example of the critiques that anarchists open towards forms of understanding the world. Also, to signal the conflictive paths in which ideas transited and were appropriated in different moments by anarchists. In any way, it is something to have in mind while thinking what means an 'anarchist' political ecology frame. Between 1866 and 1907, several definitions of ecology were proposed by Ernst Haeckel. Throughout its voluminous work, Reclus evade this concept and criticized Haeckel approach at two levels: (1) he rejects ecological hierarchization of natural elements and phenomena as a self-evident way to understand 'natural' interactions and (2) the links established between social-Darwinism and the naturalization through science of inequalities and hierarchies. These scientific and ideological-political tenets on which such a view was developing supposed enough motivation for Reclus to avoid the use of the term (Pelletier, 2013: 323–337). Still, in the case of Spanish anarchists in the last decades of the nineteenth century, Haeckel's work was relevant in discussion around evolutionism, the meaning of nature and its dynamics. Cited and dismissed, this approach even produced a collaboration between the German biologist and Ferrer Guardia in a project related to education (Girón, 1996). Even though Haeckel's ideas about inequality and some of its interpretation of evolution were rejected, this example is evidence of the complex journey of ideas. As well, push us to continue asking what we are conveying through 'ecology' while naming the interconnection in 'natural communities' and how we can rapidly naturalize certain conceptions that may constitute a 'deeply colonial and oppressive practice'.[1] One key issue for anarchist political ecology in my view is to interrogate such concept, from other realities and worldviews as well.

The question here is not if anarchists followed an 'essentialist view of the human subject', if they defined the human person as 'having a fixed, immutable, benign metaphysical essence or that they articulated a Cartesian conception of human subjectivity' (Morris, 2015: 178). They surely in certain moment use that kind of language or discourse to convey a specific idea. But they also conveyed a pretty different perspective and struggle 'inside' anarchism to uphold a non-dogmatic and dominating perspective. The struggle against domination started inside the same anarchism. Against patriarchy, racism, colonialism, sexism, etc. And it is in that struggles that I found represented the possibilities to (un)learn and push further its limits. To extend the horizons, to question why we are so eager to find the solution in an 'Idea'. Are we not crystalizing and maintaining domination, circumscribing knowledges, or delimiting modes of subjectivation (Jun, 2011) through such search for an answer? Attempting 'to answer permanently what is temporary at best' (Aragorn!, 2009: 18). The only thing that appears solid, the only lighthouse that remains reliable appears to be the never-ending caution against domination and coercive power.

Solidarity has been one of the key features that anarchists intend to cultivate. A scarce resource in its history, it gets even more difficult to grow when reaching other ways of thinking and seeing the world. The latter settles a problem that penetrates the same definition of what is anarchism and what it intends to convey. As some have reiterated in the last few years, a whole family of anti-authoritarian perspectives has emerged at different times and places (Ramnath, 2011). Different voices remind us the baggage of anarchism as a Western 'invention', and although that is problematic in itself, I want to highlight that it has consequences on what reality is portrayed. The 'priorities', as Aragon! (2009) puts it, are different, the way the world is conceived differs. Which is not to say that – that differences represent insurmountable chasm, but fluid and changeable contours. I would argue here then that distinctions of non-European/European anarchisms end up reifying and presenting static and narrow notions of what it means to be indigenous or European. As Ferretti puts it 'anarchism does not match any simplistic definition of "modernity" and "anti-modernity", "humanism" and "naturalism"' (2017: 908). And it would be a mistake to think that other ideas, projects perspectives match simplistic definitions as well. Again, it is not the aim here to define an anti-modernist or critical stance against Enlightenment from anarchism, but to rehearse the complex and conflictive ways in which variegated understandings of anti-authoritarian worlds emerge. We need, following Aragon!'s critique, to expect dealing with those outside our own understanding of reality. If not, we are just expecting 'reality to conform to [our] subjective understanding of it' (Aragorn!, 2009: 23). Moreover, 'the form that anarchist criticism has taken about events in the world is more useful in shaping an understanding of what real anarchists believes than what the world is. As long as the *arbiters of anarchism* continue to be the wielders of the Most Appropriate Critique, then anarchism will continue to be an isolated sect far removed from any particularly anarchistic event that happen in the world' (Aragorn!, 2009: 24).

I argue here that decolonizing anarchism may be supported through de-centering anarchism from its 'Europeanness', but also to be aware at the same time of its heterogeneity and complexity. Essentializing anarchism, placing canons in stark distinction is far from allowing a critical advancement towards rethinking non-hierarchical approaches. The search for radical alterities that supposedly differentiates other worlds from *the* 'modernity' re-instates static distinctions. Instead, denying one or the other, as if novelty or originality in politics represented the mark of triumph, is not what I think could allow here to continue extending the limits of our horizons. Anarchisms have been critical of metanarratives, have been aware of the ideological nature of knowledge and the way knowledge has been produced. It has also been a form to define a certain reality and certain society-environment 'problems', defining appropriate forms of human and non-human relations. Nevertheless, this anti-hierarchical family supports a significant corpus of self-reflexive and critical experience. In its own tenets, advocates for platforms of conversation and dialogue to search multiple answers for the multiple and not-yet-to-known 'socio-environmental' questions. Becoming anarchisms unfolding through conflictive frames. I draw on such murkiness following lines of thought to question and reflect on 'anarchist' landscapes.

DARKENED LANDSCAPES

Landscape has multifarious meanings, incorporating even contradictory under-standings. But, in multiple occasions, its origin has been linked to elite discursive construction as well as symbolic vistas from those 'detached' from land (Neumann, 2011: 847); those who can see from above, that manage and control land. Europe has been the place of its origin, for some, and this conceptual monopoly also has led to a definition of certain ways to think what we define as landscape. Westerners 'see' and 'think' landscapes, the others have 'worlds' (Berque, 2009). Although such differentiation entails radical alterities and narrowed definitions of modern-Western thought (and worlds), it is productive to debate how we can produce notions that are far from just tracing boundaries but that can help to construct solidarities. Based on my experience working with indigenous and peasant communities in Mexico, I am here exploring what seems to be a path for unlearning and listening carefully. I explore the horizons that I visualize to rethink continually around landscapes and the possibilities that a non-hierarchical critic could offer to open spaces in which to gather. Here then I problematize the same conception of landscape moving towards a formulation that acknowledges the diversity of spatial–temporal human experi-ences and their human–non-human relations.

An anarchist landscape could be positively defined as the materialization of anarchism in place, as the transformation and even creation of totally new spatial organization that respond to, or are organized on, mutual aid, equality and social justice.[2] Such landscapes reflect different priorities than those present at the moment under authoritarian organizations. This material outcome of anarchist performance, that is always contingent, is not what interests me here but to dwell on its meanings. What we are saying when naming or tracing the contours of an 'anarchist' landscape. Observing the way landscapes are understood and known, to highlight the hierar-chies that prevail in the performance of certain knowledges and the power relations that inhabit them (Barrera-Bassols, 2003). My interest here is not to give an answer but to introduce some thoughts to navigate these tensions and to counteract the violence (epistemic, ontological, etc.) in the production of knowledge and meaning around landscapes. Here is where I think an anarchist framework could shed light over certain aspects to think differently and sustain an approach that builds solidari-ties towards the co-production of knowledges in a horizontal way; and at the same time, following my previous discussion, to decentralize and work outside the limits of that framework. An ethnogeographic approach, as Blaut (1979) proposed, to reflect on *our own* conception and thoughts around landscapes.

My take on landscape in the context of this intervention draws on my experiences and reflections that resulted from my work with Chatino people, in Oaxaca, Mexico (Barrera, 2017). I worked with several male members of Chatino communities to better understand how they comprehend and make sense of their environment, or what we would define as 'their landscape'. Clearly, as some of the people with whom I worked let me know, the Chatino world expresses itself differently from the 'Spanish' world, for the first life, or **Cha**-a **lyu**-i, means the world, the whole life, the life itself. And this world has its own ways to know and understand that life. Or as Tomás Cruz, chatino thinker murdered in 1989 because of his participation in self-determination fights and conservation of forest against paper enterprises, puts it: 'School is the first place where we are taught that our truth is erroneous, and that our knowledges are ridiculous before "science" (. . .) our rituals, behavior and wisdom, are now conceived as irrational, superstitious, absurd and false. The truth is now the Western truth, and not Chatino truth, even though this truth has allowed us to live for centuries' (Cruz, 1989: 23–24). Tomás Cruz was interested in Kropotkin, Ricardo Flores Magon and Pierre Clastres writings. He published several articles where he manifests his own particular sense of what Chatino self-determination and fighting against government and capitalism oppression should be. But not only the external agents that were destroying the Chatino culture but as part of on-going process that emerged within his own community.

This experience leads me to a linguistic and geographical examination of how the Chatino world is conceived and what could be a 'chatino geography'; a question that I resolved following other works on landscape and linguistics (Wilcock, Brierley and Howitt, 2013 and Mark et al., 2011) proposing an 'ontology of chatino landscape'. With all the above said, an ontology of Chatino landscape could appear as an alternate, contrasting worldview that is easily definable as an entity subjected to ethnocide by Western/modern/capitalist projects. But far from that, what I expected to transmit is worlds in continuous change that depend on the position of those with whom I worked. Becoming Chatino's worlds that unfold in a complex assemblage are not static worldviews. My discussion focused on the production of knowledges, its legitimation and the establishment of regimes of truth about what is a landscape. In this regard, and considering that 'landscape', as concept, does not exist in the Chatino conception, it seems necessary to me to rethink landscape through other worldviews and ways of seeing, acting and experiencing it. An ontology as a *translation* represents a form to expand 'landscape' horizons outside the same 'territories' of its own genesis.

In describing anarchistic horizons, landscapes become murky. The clearance of harmonious symbiosis with Earth elements, the balance taking apart environmental degradation turn chimeric as our imagination imposes concreteness from an abstract basis. Is this beautiful dream becoming compulsory for those outside? Difficult to observe if we are becoming upholders of a given system, if our contingent knowledge takes the character of facts. Gustave Landauer searched for such interstices and cracks, challenging and seeking for new possibilities to emerge. Not to say that he always took such an approach; his particular experience allows him to descry a multiplicity of horizons. Also, not to consider him as a model, nor an exceptional example, but as one that opened a door to acknowledge such complexity. And as one that decried the stagnation and immobility that plagued his contemporary fellows. For him, 'the anarchists have always been far too fond of systems and attached to rigid, narrow concepts' (Landauer, [1901] 2010: 91). Voltairine de Cleyre equally saw in change, in continuous transformation what defined the possibilities of anarchism. Keeping it eclectic and open, outside of the application of abstract principles that governed people's life, remained one of her preoccupations. She called against those who act as guardians of the anarchist 'tradition' (de Cleyre, 2005: 87), to remind that what she was following would not require specific systems and methods. Both anarchists represent here possibilities to rethink notions of landscape, however I would not, as they surely would not have wanted, follow their ideas as principles. Their perspective is taken here as an alternative, but not as original or as holders of truly radical thinking.

Following such alternatives, such endeavours, to approach landscapes differently departs from the main concern that dominant landscape representations oppress or neglect diversity. Defining anarchism as the only justifiable political stance or the ultimate politico-ethical horizon for radical democracy recurs in metanarratives and teleological markers (Kosh, 2011). Our protean and murky landscapes would not claim any ultimate horizon, just the opposite; their function is to remind us of the complicated, unstable and contingent context in which they are renewed every time. Thus, 'what most anarchists like to present to us as an ideal society – Landauer ([1901]2010: 89) criticizes – is too often merely rational and stuck in *our current reality* to serve as a guiding light for anything that could or should ever be in the future'. The landscapes we convey here are detached from their usual representation as outcome of 'another form' to administer things. De Cleyre pushes us to think anarchy as it has to do 'almost entirely with the relation of men [sic] in their *thoughts* and *feelings*, and not with the positive organization of production and distribution' (2005: 73); pushing us also outside of the masculine notion of exhaustive knowledge for the organization of life. Two aspects become central to my reflection on landscapes in the last part of this intervention: time and the pluriverse.

More than one century ago, Gustave Landauer ([1903] 2015: 34) published his reflections about Fritz Mauther book *Contributions to a Critique of Language*. Reacting to the linguist's sceptical philosophy, he asserted that: 'In the place of an explanation of a unique and absolute world (. . .) there are images of the world that, in their diversity, can come together side by side, images that are not the world 'in itself', but the world for us'. Language became a central part of the critique towards positivist, objective, rational renderings of the world. From Landauer, we get a sense of weariness around the problematic assumptions in which anarchism and socialism, in general, started to establish. I translate such anxieties as a problematization of the character of 'fact' that such proposals for organizing life were acquiring. My take on his reflections is the continual resistance towards transcendental definitions and teleological definition of a progress that will finally generate those landscapes of harmony and justice:

> We have long enough misunderstood socialism as a vague, general ideology, a magic wand that opens all doors and solves all problems. We should know by now that everything out in the world as well as within our souls is so jumbled that there will never be *only one way to happiness*. So, *what I am advocating here has nothing to do with a call on humanity.* We have to realize that different cultures exist next to each other and that the dream that all should be the same cannot be sustained – in fact, it is not even a beautiful dream. (Landauer, [1901] 2010: 90)

De Cleyre (2005) also wrote against such stagnation and fragmentation of anarchism. For her, none of the 'types' of anarchism (e.g. individualism, anarcho-communism, etc.) were satisfactory, as it was not a problem of defining a(n) (anarchist) method nor a worldview. It was about changing and daring, heterogeneity and contradiction. Rather than seeking the truth for emancipation, we found here movement, fluidity, change and diversity interwoven to oppose an ontological and epistemological defence of anarchism. For de Cleyre (2005: 70), 'it no longer seems necessary to me, therefore, that one should base [our] Anarchism upon any particular world conception'. 'Events are the true schoolmaster' asserted the Canadian anarchist; it is not a question of how to apply abstract principles. But it is, in my view, a call to engage the significance of experiences and embodiment. Through 'thoughts and feelings', anarchist landscapes are performed and are more than projections of the 'Idea', neither accumulation of innovative discourses and radical practices. These perspectives provide elements of complexity (Ferretti, 2017), portraying becoming anarchism*s*. In such a way, she opposed defining any 'anarchist' method and asked: 'do you ask Spring her method? Which is more necessary, the sunshine or the rain? They are contradictory – yes; they destroy each other – yes, but from this destruction the flowers result. Each choose that method which expresses your selfhood best, and condemn no other man because he expresses his self otherwise'.

Following these engagements with the complexity and contingency, 'truth' appears for Landauer as an inherently problematic word. He considered that 'truth is an absolutely negative word, the negation in itself, and therefore in fact subject and goal of every science, whose enduring results are always of a negative nature' (Landauer, [1903]2015: 89). Against the stagnation of knowledge and worldviews, it bears noting his critique as a renewed consternation of the dominance exerted through science. In this sense, truth as negation is a point of departure towards decentralization and non-hierarchization. Thus, the world itself is not 'truth'. The world and landscape conceptions unfold continually, as modes to make sense of them and comprehend them, but they do not entail more than that. Concepts are just moments of realities, which are at the same time necessary to their formation. We could question with de Cleyre (2005: 87) 'why, *since no one can know a perfect method,* nor even act always according to the best method he himself conceives, why fly to the defence of progress and protect destiny?'

Landscape has not been defined only by its spatiality but as having a temporal or historical trajectory as well. Evolution or histories of landscapes tended to characterize landscapes by the superposition of elements that form a palimpsest – An accumulative process that can easily come to configure a linear perception and representation. The latter has proved to be just a way to conceive landscape transformation, but mostly, a sense of linear progress has become a dominant understanding that narrows the possibility of experiencing different temporalities, imposing only one trajectory for a harmonious, equitable, just, etc. society. Far from a linear idea of progress and history, from a univocal trajectory, this 'murky' landscape gets involved with intricate understandings of space–time unfolding. Change and differentiation burst that linearity. For Landauer ([1901] 2010: 90), this would lead to 'break with the habit of seeing each improvement, each innovation, only in relation to our highest and ultimate goal, categorically allowing no other perspective'. The future, instead of representing the 'natural' way of things, the true path for non-hierarchical landscapes, is lost in the darkened horizons. And as its 'realization is in the future, and since the future holds unknown factors, it is nearly certain that the free society of the unborn *will realize itself according to no man's* [sic] *present forecast*, whether individualist, communist, mutualist, collectivist, or what-not' (de Cleyre, 2005: 87). Not to hold on a teleological account push us to consider different alternatives, as 'vorticial' or 'serpentine' temporalities with limitless curves and ascending turns. Such a view was upheld by Elisee Reclus, as Ferretti (2017) pointed out. A serpentine understanding that contested dominant and oppressive temporalities, criticizing world's representation, signalling the impossibility of a geometric modelling of it (Ferretti, 2017: 899).

A contemporary reading of Landauer and de Cleyre's work recognizes aspects currently discussed around the term pluriverse and non-teleological approach, for example in the ontological shift in anthropology or political ontology in geography. But as I would like to emphasize, the sense of 'pluriverse' has been revolving within the anarchist perspectives in different forms contending essentialist notions. Additionally, and considering current discussions, I suggest here that the 'pluriverse' idea could be enhanced and enriched by anti-hierarchical frameworks and theories (and vice versa, as I have to tried to explore here); acknowledging again the inherent tensions aroused by fixed accounts. The possibilities of bringing together anarchists frameworks and the pluriversal enhance the convergence of spatial–temporal experiences from different perspectives to expand their own limits.

Drawing on these authors, I highlight the idea that there are multiple ways of understanding the world and representing it, a pluriverse where the set of 'geographical knowledge' complement each other and enrich each other. The image that comes together side by side as the German anarchist puts it. Thus, in the pluriverse 'the real' is exposed as moment and 'the true' as negation. But it is not intended to reach relativism, but to *remove coercive* propositions or dominating totalities. Likewise, to form from the diversity of world experiences, a unitary image of the same which symbolic significance is credible, is only to conform a symbol of the world (Landauer, [1903]2015). Facing universal exclusionary perspectives, as visualizations of the world through single images, the fundamental thing is to break with the domination, the domination of a reality, of what is the 'true' nature, the true landscape. Ontologies of landscapes, and I am thinking here of my own work based on their representation through language (concepts, place names, narratives), are just moments, assemblages that coalesce, ever-emerging, fluid and tentative that do not represent a transcendental and fixed entity.

All the above said, this takes me back to the central point of this intervention, to break with domination and coercive understandings of landscapes. To move in a direction, also, towards avoiding the capture and extraction of knowledges. This is a double movement away from essentialist perspectives, not only to 'burst' landscape idea but also to acknowledge the family of non-hierarchical project in which anarchism is just one way of comprehending it. A pure or true anarchism, and for that a true anarchist landscape as the realization of its principles, represents in this vein an essentialization. It results in anarchism's crystallization as a stable entity, stopping its processual character and is used to justified exclusiveness: its trueness only represents its negation.

I therefore consider landscapes not as predefined visual entities characterized by certain elements or the expression of elite detachment and alienation, but as platforms that enable an epistemic and ontological reflection to find common ground and, fundamentally, be aware of our own limitations. From there synergies, coincidence, limits, contradiction and ambiguities can be identified and generate alternative forms of thinking and dwelling to construct solidarities for knowledge co-production. Landscapes of multiple views that accept the multiplicity and intervene in the way we think and see them in a critical and reflexive manner. And, ultimately, landscapes that provoke us to unlearn the 'archist' ways of producing and making sense of landscape.

BECOMING A DARKENED DREAM

In this chapter, landscapes have been a case or an example of how keeping open-ended and eclectic approaches maintain the possibility of dialogue and conservation. It is not the intention here to portray a definition of what ought to be an anarchist landscape or not. But to signal the potential of rethinking landscapes for non-hierarchical approaches to human–non-human interrelations. My intention is to problematize and evidence the multiple trajectories that could generate an approach that argues for a stable foundation or a defence of a system. Why and how an anarchist political ecology remains part of such problematization? I hope the murky landscapes that I try to evoke serve as cases of how within such broad field of inquiry concepts and discourse require our constant attention against stagnation and coercion in knowledge production. As example of numerous alternatives, non-hierarchical landscapes are boundless as expressions of particular conjunctions and as continually unfolding processes. Here, Landauer and de Cleyre were part of a conversation, more than ideal thinkers or holders of original radical thinking. A conversation that signals the potential inscrutability of anarchist thought becoming another narrative for the best world, creating boundaries instead of breaking them (Aragorn!, 2009). Approaches that provide resources for thinking, rethinking, make connections, problematize, contradict ourselves and be mindful of limits. Finally, we can start our journey through these murky landscapes following Landauer's suggestion: 'Only when anarchy becomes, for us, a dark, deep dream, not a vision attainable through concepts, can our ethics and our actions become one' (Landauer, [1901] 2010: 91).

NOTES

1. 'Towards an anarchist ecology' [https://www.indybay.org/uploads/2014/01/28/towards-anarchist-ecology.pdf, accessed January 2ⁿᵈ, 2018].

2. Landscapes among anarchist are not an extensively used concept. It is problematic, and may have found in the Impressionist painters one of its main expression relating anarchist principles and representation. For Reclus landscapes were vehicles of social organization, political strategy and education. As a form of contestation, he considered landscapes useful to resist romantic and bourgeoisie representations (Ferretti, 2012).

REFERENCES

Aragorn! (2009). *Two Essays. A non-European Anarchism & Locating an Indigenous Anarchism.* The Anarchist Library.

Barrera-Bassols, Narciso (2003). *Symbolism, knowledge and management of soil and land resources in indigenous communities: ethnopedology at global, regional and local scale. Vol I.* PhD Thesis (unpublished), Enschede: International Institute for Geo-Information Science and Earth Observation (ITC).

Barrera de la Torre, Gerónimo (2017). *Ontología del paisaje Chatino: hacia "otras" geografías. La(s) geografía(s) chatina(s) de la región de San Juan Lachao, Oaxaca.* México: Instituto de Investigaciones "Dr. José María Luis Mora".

Berque, Agustine (2009) *El pensamiento paisajero.* Madrid: Biblioteca Nueva.

Bessire, Lucas and Bond, David (2014). "Ontological anthropology and the deferral of critique." *American Ethnologist,* 41(3): 440–456.

Blaut, James M. (1979) "Some principles of ethnogeography", in S. Gale y G. Olsson (eds.), *Philosophy in geography.* Germany: D. Reidel, Dordrecht, pp: 1–17.

Breitbart, Myrna M. (1989). "Descentralismo anarquista en la España rural, 1936-39: la integración de comunidad y medio ambiente", in Myrna M. Breitbart (ed.), *Anarquismo y Geografía.* Barcelona: Oikos-tau, pp. 253–290.

Cruz Lorenzo, Tomas (1989). "Evitemos que nuestro futuro se nos escape de las manos". *Medio Milenio,* (5): 23–34.

Davidson, Stewart (2009). "Ecoanarchism: A critical defence." *Journal of Political Ideologies,* 14(1): 47–67.

De Cleyre, Voltairine (2005). *Exquisite Rebel: The Essays of Voltairine de Cleyre - Anarchist, Feminist, Genius* (S. Presley & C. Sartwell, Eds.). Albany: State University of New York Press.

Escobar, Aarturo (1999). "After nature: Steps to an antiessentialist political ecology." *Current Anthropology,* 40(1): 1–30.

Escobar, Arturo (2004) "Constructing nature. Elements for a post-structural political ecology", in Richard Peet and Michael Watts (eds.), *Liberation Ecologies. Environment, development and social movements.* New York: Routledge, pp. 46–68.

Ferretti, Federico (2017). "Evolution and revolution: Anarchist geographies, modernity and poststructuralism". *Environment and Planning D: Society and Space,* 35(5): 893–912.

García-Ramon, María Dolores (1989). "La concepción de un paisaje anarquista rural: aportaciones de la teoría anarquista española", in Myrna M. Breitbart (ed.), *Anarquismo y Geografía.* Barcelona: Oikos-tau, pp. 223–252.

Girón Sierra, Alvaro (1996). *Evolucionismo y anarquismo en España, 1882-1914.* Madrid: Consejo Superior de Investigaciones Científicas. Centro de Estudios Históricos.

Ince, Anthony (2012). In the Shell of the Old: Anarchist Geographies of Territorialisation. *Antipode,* 44(5): 1645–1666.

Jun, Nathan (2011). "Reconsidering post-structuralism and anarchism", in Duane Rousselle and Süreyyya Evren (eds.), *Post-anarchism. A reader*. USA: Pluto Press and Fernwood Publishing, pp. 231–249.

Knapp, Michael; Flach Anja and Ayboga, Ercan (2016). *Revolution in Rojava. Democratic autonomy and women's liberation in Syria Kurdistan*. London: Pluto Press.

Koch, Andrew M. (2011). "Post-structuralism and the epistemological bases of anarchism", in Duane Rousselle and Süreyyya Evren (eds.), *Post-anarchism. A reader*. USA: Pluto Press and Fernwood Publishing, pp. 23–40.

Landauer, Gustave ([1903]2015). *Escepticismo y mística. Aproximaciones a la Crítica del lenguaje de Mauthner*. Herder : México.

Landauer, Gustave ([1901] 2010). *Revolution and other writings: a political reader* (G. Kuhn & R. J. F. Day, Eds.). Oakland: PM Press.

Mark, D. M., Turk, A. G., Burenhult, N., y Stea, D. (eds.) 2011. *Landscape in language. Transdisciplinary perspectives*. Netherlands: John Benjamins.

Meza González, Javier (2015). *Breve introducción a la vida y obra de Rudolf Rocker*, Universidad Autónoma Metropolitana, México.

Morris, Brian (2015). *Anthropology, Ecology, and Anarchism: A Brian Morris Reader*. USA: PM Press.

Neumann, Roderick P. (2011). "Political ecology III: Theorizing landscape." *Progress in Human Geography*, 35(6): 843–850.

Pelltier, Philippe (2013). *Geographie & Anarchie. Reclus, Kropotkine and Metchnikoff.* France: Éditions du Monde libertaire and Éditions libertaires.

Ramnath, Maia (2011) *Decolonizing Anarchism. An antiauthoritarian history of Indi's liberation struggle*. USA: AK Press and Institute for Anarchist Studies.

Springer, Simon (2016) *The Anarchist Roots of Geography: Towards Spatial Emancipation*. USA: University of Minnesota Press.

Watts, Michael J. (2015) "Now and the: the origins of political ecology and the rebirth of adaptation as a form of thought", in Tom Perreault, Gavin Bridge, and James McCarthy (eds.), *The Routledge Handbook of Political Ecology*. New York: Roudtledge, pp. 19–49.

Wilcock, D., Brierley G., y Howitt R. 2013. "Ethnogeomorphology". *Progress in Physical Geography*, 37(5): 573–600.

7

Kenneth Rexroth and Paul Goodman

Poets, Writers, Anarchists and Political Ecologists

Gregory Knapp

My interest in alternative, decentralist solutions to social and environmental problems is based on my intellectual upbringing as a student at Berkeley in the 1960s, but also has been maintained by more recent generations of writers concerned with these issues. I have been intrigued by what appears to be a kind of amnesia about some American radical, public intellectual writers who flourished before the 1970s, when Michel Foucault's translations began to appear in English, and he began to visit California. My focus here is especially on two poets and writers, Paul Goodman and Kenneth Rexroth, associated with east coast and west coast anarchist intellectual life, respectively. I believe both were influential in defining issues that are still with us; both represented a kind of specifically American non-academic radicalism; and both embodied a kind of 'revolutionary hope' which all but vanished from the scene after the Vietnam War. These writers identified themes which resonate with cultural ecology, political ecology and the new cultural geography. The early identification of these themes is not just of antiquarian interest; the connections imply that the possibility exists of rooting political and cultural ecological work in some additional aspects of American literary and intellectual history.

PAUL GOODMAN

Paul Goodman was born in New York City on 9 September 1911, of German-Jewish and middle-class origins. He was educated in public schools and CCNY and pursued a bohemian life style in the New York City area, publishing stories in the Partisan Review and New Directions. His first major book, *Communitas*, was written with his older brother and architect Percival and published in 1947 (Goodman and Goodman 1960 [1947]). About this time, he taught at Black Mountain College. He completed his PhD at the University of Chicago in 1954, and then travelled in Europe. His eleven major books appeared between 1959 and 1970, and during this period, he taught at Sarah Lawrence, University of Wisconsin-Milwaukee (Urban Affairs), San Francisco State and the University of Hawaii. He purchased a farm in New Hampshire where he lived intermittently from 1961. He died of a heart attack in 1972 at the age of 61 (Widmer 1980).

Goodman was a lifelong communitarian anarchist in the tradition of Kropotkin, describing himself at times as a peasant anarchist or a practical utopian. He participated in the Worldwide General Strike for Peace, was a founder of the New York branch of Resist and was an editor of the pacifist/libertarian magazine *Liberation* (Stoehr 1994, 100–101). Goodman deliberately wrote to reach the largest possible educated audience and avoided elitist jargon. In his book *The Society I Live in is Mine*, he published a wide range of letters of protest addressed to media, government officials and leaders of institutions on topics of money, war, repression, lapse of community and failure of intellect:

> The society in which I live is mine, open to my voice or action, or I do not live there at all. The government, the school board, the church, the university, the world of publishing and communications, are my agencies as a citizen. To the extent that they are not my agencies, at least open to my voice and action, I am entirely in revolutionary opposition to them and I think they should be wiped off the slate. (Goodman 1962, viii)

Goodman was also concerned with ecology (Stoehr 1990). Part of his ecological attitude was a form of geo-piety, grounded in the romantic counter-enlightenment (Gade 2011, 65–96). Goodman cited Wordsworth's 'good insight of the beauty and morality of rural life'. 'The ecology of a country scene is so exquisitely complicated . . . [it] has been so worked over . . . that it is bound to have unity and style, heroic in scale, minute in detail' (Goodman 1994, 70). As was the case with Alexander von Humboldt (Wulf 2015, 25–38), Goodman was inspired by Goethe:

> In a passage that I often repeat, Goethe speaks of that patient finite thing, the Earth. 'The poor Earth! – I evermore repeat it – a little sun, a little rain, and it grows green again'. So the Earth repeats it Goethe repeats it, and I repeat it. (Goodman 1994, 82)

By 1970, Goodman was speaking of the environment in terms of 'delicate sequences and balances'. A simplified and modest technology would permit 'the environment to persist in its complexity, evolved for a billion years' (Goodman 1970, 12–13). This and the use of systems terminology might seem to make Goodman an eco-systemicist with an oversimplified dedication to sustainability. Elsewhere, however, Goodman makes clear that he has a strong adaptationist, evolutionary perspective. Creation is not perfect. 'The execution is often exquisitely minute. Yet there are clumsy or unfinished sentences, missing transitions, characters left hanging' (Goodman 1994, 96). The complexity makes nature unpredictable, even to systems science;

therefore, decision-making involving the environment must be decentralized, modest and subject to continual adjustment – best supported by anarchist arrangements. In this context, both positivist experimental methods and natural history methods have validity in appropriate situations (Goodman 1970, 12–15). The corresponding traditions in human ecology research would be the adaptive dynamics approach, as espoused by Bennett (1976), progressive contextualization as outlined by Vayda (1983) and a feminist political ecology focusing on chains of relation (Rocheleau 2007) as against apolitical ecosystemicism. All of these approaches prioritize agency and local actors as against *a priori* hegemonic processes and discourses.

Goodman thus saw the human organism and its environments in dynamic relationship. 'If we envisage an animal moving, continually seeing new scenes and meeting new problems to cope with, it will continually have to make a creative adjustment . . . . And the environment, for its part, must be amenable to appropriation and selection; it must be plastic to be changed and meaningful to be known' (Goodman 1994, 51).

In practical terms, Goodman favoured biological over chemical pest control, following Rachel Carson. Goodman (1970) referred admiringly to a culture that weeded out less useful plants from the forest, leaving behind only useful vegetation, probably a reference to cultural geographer Burton Gordon's discovery (1969) of orchard-garden thickets (forest fallow management); Goodman may have met Carl Sauer's student Gordon at San Francisco State (where Goodman also taught) where Gordon would have provided influences from geographical cultural ecology. Carl Sauer and his students have had a long and fruitful history of support for thought contesting the verities of capitalist modernization and supporting alternative approaches to improvement of human–environment relationships (Mathewson 2009).

GOODMAN, CULTURE AND PLACE

For Goodman, culture is the set of survivals of past thought, insight and enthusiasm to be glimpsed in religious and civic occasions, music, art, architecture, the practice of farming, cooking, child-rearing and many other learned professions and skilled crafts. Like Scott (2012), he argued in favour of respecting local creativity and knowledge. He believed that it is better to freely take on a minor tradition which can be appropriated as experience than be forced to take on a major tradition which cannot be experienced as authentic. In this sense, he would have supported contemporary indigenous politics and resistance to colonialism. Yet at the same time, he believed that many of the great historic figures of Western culture 'were real people and meant what they did', and thus could be enlisted as supportive predecessors of current struggles (Goodman 1994, 61–63).

'Vocation is taking on the business of the community so it is not a drag . . . . If I find what I am good at and good for, that my community can use and will support, securely doing this, I can find myself further'. Thus, it is lifeless to be infinitely adaptable to play various roles. The only common role that everyone plays is citizen, 'loyal pride in the place where he is thrown' (Goodman, 1994, 65).

Place was extraordinarily important in Goodman's vision of culture and education. 'For the first five school years there is no merit in the standard curriculum. To repeat Dewey's maxim, for a small child everything in the environment is educative if he attends to it with guidance' (Goodman 1970, 100). Goodman proposed a model of schooling in which field trips and opportunities in the community played a major role.

This perspective on culture and place stimulated in Goodman a continual reflection on architecture and urban landscapes as products of the battle between authenticity and arid structure, means and ends. This reflection is most visible in his 1947 book, *Communitas: Ways of Livelihood and Means of Life*, co-authored with his brother, the urban theorist and architect Percival Goodman (Goodman and Goodman 1960 [1947]). This book first reviews a variety of urban and regional plans from around the world, including socialist plans. It then presents three blueprints for future planning in America. One is called 'A New Community: the Elimination of the Difference between Production and Consumption'. This involved integrating, industrial, farming and residential activities to maximize a variety of human interactions. A second blueprint was called 'Planned Security with Minimum Regulation'; that plan provided for basic needs for those who wished to devote their lives to pursuing non- materialistic goals. Both of these blueprints could be seen as providing for a post-development trajectory towards an ideal consistent with what has recently been termed Buen Vivir (Gudynas 2011). The authors also put forward a third model, 'A City of Efficient Consumption', which maximized the production, consumption and destruction of material commodities. This model was prescient in predicting the ubiquitous spread of the shopping mall and other characteristics of capitalist life; meant as a mischievous cautionary warning it turned out to be prophetic.

GOODMAN AND SOCIETY

Goodman, like Kenneth Rexroth, was an anti-structuralist. The starting point for his social analysis was the assumption that for the most part 'society' is a fictitious and superstitious abstraction, albeit one which can have real and dangerous consequences. For Goodman, 'most people mostly live their lives' in a 'loose matrix of face to face communities, private fantasies and shifting subsocieties'. Goodman thus rejected Marxist and other frameworks based on reifying Society (Goodman 1994, 49–50).

This bears on property relations. 'The issue of property has been wrongly put ... between "private property" and "social property" . . . to be a private individual is largely pathological. For a society to be a collective is largely pathological'. 'Giving access to the young, conserving the environment, helping the needy . . . are necessary for society to be tolerable at all [and thus] . . . cannot be an object of economic activity'. As for an excessive focus on planning for the future, Goodman was worried that this could be another tool of centralization and domination: 'both socialists and capitalists make a disastrous ethical mistake, mortgaging the present to the future' (Goodman 1994, 66–67).

Goodman admired the concern of dissidents for a simpler standard of living, non-violence and direct action, and the thinkers most connected to these concerns – Kropotkin, Malatesta, Bakunin, Ferrer, William Morris and Thoreau (Goodman 1970, 145). He suggested as a viable temporary option a 'mixed economy' of big and small capitalism, producers' cooperatives, consumers' cooperatives, independent farming, municipal socialism and pure communism for decent poverty (Goodman 1970, 149). As for small-hold farmers, as extolled by Robert Netting (1993), Brookfield (Brookfield and Parsons 2007) and Altieri (Altieri and Toledo 2011), he supported them: 'freehold farming . . . kept open the possibility of anarchy . . . a farmer . . . can . . . withdraw from the market, eat his own crops, and prudently stay out of debt' (Goodman 1994, 66–67).

Goodman referred to the 1969 People's Park takeover in Berkeley (in which I participated) as an example of a clash between the inexperience of the young and reactionaries' lack of imagination. For Goodman, this episode was especially poignant because in this case his 'guess is that in the School of Architecture of the university, the do-it-yourself method of the hippies . . . is being taught as a model of correct urban landscape architecture, to encourage citizenship and eliminate vandalism, according to the ideas of Karl Linn . . . . The chancellor could just as well have given out academic credit and an A grade' (Goodman 1970, 56; see also Mitchell 1995).

Goodman was also opposed to narrow-minded nationalisms and obsessions about boundaries;

> The thing is to have a National Liberation Front that does not end up in a Nation State, but abolishes the boundaries. This was what Gandhi and Buber wanted, but they were shelved . . . . Some boundaries, of course, are just the limits of our interests . . . . But as soon as we begin to notice a boundary between us and others, we project our own unacceptable traits on those across the boundary, and they are foreigners, heretics, untouchables, persons exploited as things. By their very existence, they threaten or tempt us, and we must squelch them, or with missionary zeal make them shape up. (Goodman 1970, 194)

This quotation makes it clear that Goodman's vision, like Rexroth's, was profoundly critical of cultural particularism. It has something to say for our current moment of populist nationalism.

GOODMAN'S PLACE

Paul Goodman has been linked to the experimental Black Mountain College (1933–1957) and the Black Mountain School of Poetry, on the grounds that he taught there (in 1950), published in their journal, and was friendly with a number of the school's members. However, the college refused to endorse his request for continued employment. Soon after, the college came under the leadership of Charles Olson, who resented Goodman as a threat to his authority (Horowitz 1989, 9). In general, Goodman stands apart from the main group of the Black Mountain School of poets. Instead, Goodman became one of the major intellectual forces in the 'countercul-ture' of the 1960s (Sale 1995). Towards the end of his life, Goodman bemoaned the accelerating ahistoricity of the young. 'They no longer remember their own history ... Each incoming class is more entangled in the specious present' (Goodman 1970, 55). After his death in 1972, Paul Goodman's work was primarily kept alive by Tay-lor Stoehr (1931–2013), his friend and literary executor, and professor of English at the University of Massachusetts, Boston.

KENNETH REXROTH

Kenneth Rexroth was born in 1905 in Indiana, moving to California in the 1920s. Self-taught, he was involved in a variety of radical and bohemian activities through the 1920s and 1930s. He moved to San Francisco in 1927, living there until 1968, when he moved to Santa Barbara. He published about twenty-five books of poetry and plays and thirteen books of translations during his life. He also wrote many notable essays, beginning with his foreword to a book of D.H. Lawrence's poems in 1947. The essays have been published in eight collections between 1959 and 1974. Most of the essays were on literature, arts, or religion, but also included analyses of Northern California life and culture, global economic development, African-Amer-ican liberation, the student movement (beginning in 1960), environmentalism and urbanism. The essays of literary and art criticism frequently touch on environmental and geographical issues, particularly his essays on Lucretius, Marco Polo, Izaak Wal-ton, Gilbert White, Gary Snyder, Philip Whalen and Chinese nature poetry and landscape painting.

He taught at San Francisco State University (1964) and the University of Cali-fornia at Santa Barbara (from 1968). He wrote a series of columns for *San Francisco Magazine* and had a weekly book review programme on KPFA radio in San Fran-cisco. After 1974, he spent an increasing amount of time in Japan, and, after 1979, he suffered from increasingly poor health until his death on 6 June 1982.

Rexroth participated in a bohemian cultural milieu which anticipated many cur-rent norms. He was fond of pointing out that San Francisco's interwar culture, with its north Italian influence (largest contingent from Lucca) had a strongly Mediter-ranean flavour. The attitude of *dolce far niente*, the habit of drinking wine at parties, and an 'atmosphere of wholesome orgy' enveloped Telegraph Hill (Rexroth 1973c). Rexroth's anarchism and environmentalism were displayed in the lectures and semi-nars in the Libertarian Circle (which met in the building of the mainly Jewish and Italian Workman's Circle in the Fillmore District) about 1944; later he asserted (probably with exaggeration) that the Circle's 'whole emphasis was on ecology as a scientific foundation for a philosophy of social reorganization' (Rexroth 1969). Weekly educational meetings discussed anarchist theory and practice, there were frequent jazz and folk dances in the Mission District, picnics in Marin County and poetry readings (some marked by the use of marijuana); the Circle participated in the founding of the first listener-sponsored radio station (KPFA) and the San Francisco Poetry Center. Rexroth frequently asserted that the Libertarian Circle and its off-shoots were directly responsible for most post-war counterculture, including the San Francisco Renaissance, the Beats and the Hippies. He traced the origins of The East Village to members of the Libertarian Circle who migrated to the Lower East Side in New York City. 'The ideas and lifestyle for which we stood have spread across the world' (Rexroth 1991, 517–521). There is general agreement that Rexroth's presence was essential for the emergence to the San Francisco Renaissance (Tritica 1989). Gary Snyder was one of those affected (Snyder 1980, 39, 162); his poetry, focus on culture and ecology and relationship with geography, would merit an essay in its own right.

My notes of Rexroth's KPFA broadcasts around 1970 contain a wide range of book reviews, on Asian art, communitarian and utopian communities, anthropology, religion, urbanism and ecology. He reviewed Harner's book on the Jivaro of Ecuador, in the same broadcast with books on the Tupamaro guerillas of Uruguay, Ann Swinger's book on land above the trees and Saint Simon's anarchism. His influence in the Bay Area continued to be a force for environmentalism, decentralism and an expanded literary and cultural frame of reference up until the final years of his life.

REXROTH AND ENVIRONMENTALISM

Rexroth constantly refers to ecology in his writings, which he identified with the geography of Elisee Reclus and Peter Kropotkin – 'in those days they called them [ecologists] geographers' (Rexroth 1969). Rexroth's view of nature is conditioned by Whitehead (Rexroth 1961, 86), Buddhism, Tu Fu, Boehme and Christian sacramental theology; the universe is a 'continuing shifting and flowing organism of relationships', 'a concourse of persons, all reflecting and self-reflecting and the reflections and the reflective medium reflecting' (Rexroth 1952, 12-13). 'Space-time . . . is no more real in an absolute sense than the ruler is part of the cloth which the tailor measures' (Rexroth 1952, 31). Nature is also inherently unstable: he liked to quote Buddha, 'the combinations of the world are unstable by nature' (Rexroth 1991, 516).

Rexroth's nature poetry is based on Tu Fu and the other East Asian writers who invented the wilderness ideal and wilderness poetry. Many of Rexroth's poems are based on his long backpacking and skiing trips into the Sierra and coast ranges of California. But he also embraced the 'geo-piety' of the seventeenth-century British naturalist Izaak Walton (Rexroth 1968, 200) and the eighteenth-century naturalist Gilbert White:

a philosophy of living things, a philosophy we now call ecology . . . . The very lack of specialization gave White his enduring significance. Since he saw . . . all things together, all the time . . . his book is permeated with an unobtrusive emphasis on the interrelatedness of life . . . he is never polemical, the conclusions of Piotr Kropotkin's *Mutual Aid* . . . are immanent rather than explicit . . . . On [his book] is formed the whole very English tradition of amateur natural history . . . [he] communicates the beauty and quiet drama of the English countryside through the seasons, one of the two most beautiful, with Japan, of the thickly populated parts of the world. (Rexroth 1973b, 70–71)

Rexroth saw Western dust bowl Kansas similarly to Donald Worster (1979), 'a ruined country and a ruining people', an emblem of 'the decline and fall of the Capitalist system' (Rexroth 1952, 147). Rexroth worked on the WPA guide to California in the 1930s, writing sections on National Parks, forests, lakes and deserts; he also worked on an unpublished *Field Handbook of the Sierra Nevada* with information on plants and animals (Hamalian 1991, 83). Rexroth supported David Brower in the Sierra Club, Ed Ricketts, 'the brain trust of John Steinbeck and the "Doc" of his novels', and what he called the 'ecological revolution in the Bay Area' in the late 1960s (Rexroth 1969). In 1969, he continued to extol ecology as 'the science that automatically produces evaluation without ceasing to confine itself to purely scientific methods'. He urged his audience to read Frederick Clements as well as Kropotkin. He contrasted the ecologists with the 'value-neutral' approaches of vulgar Darwinism, Leninism and most forms of Marxism (Rexroth 1969). However, by 1972, he had come to claim that 'ecology' had become the most misused term in the American language, subject to manipulation by public relations and advertising, particularly by the oil and lumber industries. He was distinguishing between the genuine environmentalism of David Brower and what he called 'establishment conservationism' of the Sierra Club and the like (Rexroth 1972a).

REXROTH AND CULTURE

Rexroth was a passionate reader of anthropology and ethnography both popular (the eleventh edition of the Encyclopaedia Britannica) and professional (the Bureau of American Ethnology). He approached 'indigenous' poetry and art from the perspective of a practicing artist who appreciated its power and beauty, but also from the perspective of a seasoned anarchist who tried to root practices in the social context.

Rexroth refused to believe that cultures or periods constituted insuperable barriers to understanding. Rather, it is possible to find 'events and relationships that are invariant in the life of all men':

The unity of human experience is determined by the narrowness of the range of action and interaction of organisms and environments, for all men everywhere. Eskimos, Polynesians, Romans, Chicagoans – all men have the same bodies and the same kind of brains and cope with an environment in ways that would seem more uniform than not to an observer from another planet . . . the contemporary novel that embodies paradigms of the great tragic commonplaces of human life seems precisely 'novel,' fresh, and convincing, while literature that deals with contemporaneity on its own terms is hackneyed before it appears in print. (Rexroth 1968, ix–xi)

What is most impressive about Marco Polo is not that he finds men in distant lands strange and their ways outlandish but that he does not . . . He had what we have lost, an ecumenical mind, an international sensibility. As [a medieval merchant], he . . . had the tolerance that comes of thinking of one world linked together . . . the tremendous civilizing force of business as business in the face of the most anomalous customs . . . the opposite of the ruthless destructiveness of trade, flag and Bible in Victorian days. (Rexroth 1968, 151)

The fundamental unity of humankind meant that, for Rexroth, it is possible to discern a canon of classics of literature, art, music and other arts. Value judgements are possible and desirable in the arts to distinguish between the universal, dealing with 'the tragic commonplaces of human life', and the ephemeral contemporary. For him, no society or group is immune from producing bad art or bad culture, but none has a monopoly on great achievement.

Much art has a social function or is forced to serve one. Traditions and texts to serve the needs of a people (or a nation-state) are often manufactured, but invented traditions often come to play an authentic role. 'The Aeneid . . . The Kalevala, the Shah-nama . . . are all synthetic myths, made by intellectuals, which succeeded. They did provide foundations for the structural relationships through which their peoples saw themselves' (Rexroth 1961, 36).

Rexroth in 1955 described the development of a world culture, anticipating Escobar's (1995) discussion of hybridity:

Colonial & subcolonial countries have got to develop a really critical assimilation – a digestion [with] organic acceptance & rejection . . . [In] any acculturation process assimilation & revolt go hand in hand & begin [with] the deracinated . . . (Bartlett 1991, 198–199)

Rexroth constantly was attentive to the cultural landscape. One of his earliest projects was his participation in the Works Progress Administration (WPA) Guide to California, where he authored sections farm hamlets and fishing villages as well as on natural landscapes (Hamalian 1991, 83). Although he doubted that architecture was 'a direct expression of a kind of social sensibility [or] . . . Folk Soul' (Rexroth 1972c), he analysed buildings, churches, places in his poetry and criticism. Usually his analyses combine an awareness of brutal political and economic realities with a sensitivity to the role of the architect, the taste of the sponsors and the potential of place to evoke religious and community loyalty. Rexroth's analysis of the church of Sainte Cécile in Albi France is – with all its brevity, poetic licence and polemics – comparable to David Harvey's analysis of the Basilica of the Sacred Heart (Sacré-Coeur) in Montmartre, Paris (Harvey1985, 221ff):

> The finest integral work
> Of art ever produced north
> Of the Alps, a palisade
> Of sequoias, the Karnak
> Of Europe, the behemoth
> Of orthodoxy that devoured
> Langue d'Oc... (Rexroth 1952, 44)

The reference is to the Albigensian crusade, which Rexroth links to the struggle between regional economic and cultural systems. Indeed, Rexroth often tried to understand history in terms of the tension between regional and sectional cultures – North, South and West in the United States; North and South in France, Europe as a whole and China; England vs. Wales.

Rexroth was a consistent opponent of modernism in architecture and design, although he appreciated the revolutionary impulses of many of its practitioners (and some of their achievements). He called the high-rise 'the outward material sign of the inward reality of an inhumane social order'. He was a post-modernist before the term was invented. He pointed to Gaudi as the exemplar of an architecture for 'radical young people, hippies and freaks' (Rexroth 1972).

Rexroth was a lifelong reader of travel and exploration literature, 'one of the most absorbing of all forms of reading matter'; Favourite authors included Marco Polo and the geographer Owen Lattimore (Rexroth 1968, 153). In this context, it is interesting to note his 1964 proposal to write a travel book on the wine regions of Europe, which was to combine commentaries on cuisine, pre-Gothic architecture, current affairs and literary and historical connections. This 'travel book' apparently failed to attract funding and was never produced (Bartlett 1991, 235–237).

REXROTH, ANARCHISM AND URBAN POLITICAL ECOLOGY

Rexroth saw significant social processes as largely taking place outside the purview of the state:

> History assumes the State
> As the extrapersonal
> Vehicle of memory,
> What is important is what is
> Held in the sieve of polity.
> The State is the great forgetter. (Rexroth 1952, 49)

For Rexroth, the state tends to act to reduce persons to 'population units', just as the market economy tends to reduce persons to commodities (Rexroth 1952, 104). Much of Rexroth's earlier social writing is based on the Gemeinschaft–Gesellschaft distinction of the nineteenth-century sociologist Ferdinand Tönnies as developed by the twentieth-century Jewish utopian socialist and philosopher Martin Buber. In view of the radical schism between community and collectivity, the appropriate action is to attach the institutions of collectivity and nourish small scale, local community:

> It is
> Wise to keep the pattern of
> Life clear and simple and filled
> With beautiful and real things.
> The round may be narrow enough.
> The rounds of the world are narrower. (Rexroth 1952, 167)

Later in life, Rexroth called for a 'revolutionary ecology of the modern city' based on the city planning literature. Like Goodman, he stressed the continuity of reformist ideas since 1800. He emphasized environmental protection, banning automobiles from certain areas, community centres in tune with local needs, an end to high-rise commercial and residential buildings and an attack on crime in the streets (which Rexroth identified as related to organized crime) (Rexroth 1971c). This urbanism would have to be politically grounded on marginalizing the influence of organized crime, narcotics traffickers, banks and especially the small and ignorant suburban taxpayers who were the power base of Reagan republicanism in southern California at the end of the 1960s (Rexroth 1971a). Rexroth's analysis of the political and economic forces attacking the environment was as relentless as any political ecologist, but more likely to include organized crime and criminal big labour as part of the corrupt mix influencing events and policy.

Rexroth noted in early 1973 the emergence of a new national political configuration alien to the goals he had striven for all his life. This included a rightward move by students and the press. He rejected the explanations that activism accomplished nothing; that students followed their parents into the camp of Nixon; that the CIA and Mafia destroyed the movement with terror, co-optation and drugs; that activism had gone off into radical rural communes; that the abolition of the draft had removed the main reason for opposition to the war; that universities have corrected all their problems; and that television had finally conquered the mass mind of the new generation. He pointed out that he saw similar quietude emerging in France and eastern Europe. He ultimately saw this change as mysterious, a generational change (Rexroth 1973a). Late in life, he became increasingly involved in visits to Japan and became more disgusted with American life. Rexroth's work continued to sell after his death (Gardner 1980), but his reputation became more complex with the publication of a magisterial biography by Linda Hamalian (Hamalian 1991). This biography revealed the complexities of the man behind the image he presented in his writings; it at once emphasized the magnitude of his achievements and the flaws which caused some of his closest friends and associates to turn away.

REXROTH AND GOODMAN

Kenneth Rexroth and Paul Goodman were discontents to modernist centralism and its ecological and cultural consequences during and after World War II. They moved in different contexts, but their paths occasionally overlapped. Rexroth was aware of Goodman and spoke of him relatively favourably as early as 1945 (Bartlett 1991, 60, 106–115). However, when he met Goodman for the first time in 1948, he concluded that Goodman was 'really a square' (Hamalian 1991, 174). Goodman was also less than completely impressed with Rexroth, calling some of his letters 'mythomaniacal' in the 1940s (Hamalian 1991, 159). The two have deep affinities, however, reflected by *American Poetry's* decision to devote an issue (Volume 7, Number 1, Fall 1989) to essays on both of them. And on occasion, Goodman helped Rexroth out (Hamalian 1991, 322).

Both were anarcho-pacifists, marked by their opposition to American participation in World War II. After the War, both somewhat reluctantly became interpreters of the disaffiliated – Rexroth for the beats, Goodman for the juvenile delinquents, both for college protesters. Neither of them were enthusiastic partisans of the alienated young, however, since both felt that the young were in some respects the victims of their own lack of education in the traditions of local and global communities (Goodman 1994, 63).

Both were only distantly related to existentialism (Rexroth opposed it). Both were deeply involved with religious ideas; Rexroth with Buddhism and sacramental 'high church' Anglicanism and Catholicism, Goodman with Protestantism (the 'Reformers' including Luther, plus Schweitzer, Otto and Barth, although he saw himself as an agnostic). Both were fascinated with Eastern religious ideas, although with Goodman this came late in life and was coupled with his edgy agnosticism. Both practiced a kind of geo-piety. Both identified with the most noble goals of Western civilization, including its modern variants and both argued (Goodman most eloquently) for the need to finish the missed and unfinished goals of this tradition. Both contested the view that nature, including human nature, was infinitely malleable and argued that the past created truly noble, cross-culturally negotiable ideals, albeit ones subject to further refinement (Stoehr 1990).

They both were post-Leninist anarchist radicals; but, more importantly, both were alike in being widely read but sitting lightly to theory. At the end of his life, Goodman said 'I stick pretty close to the concrete and finite, that comes in sizeable chunks with a rough structure and an on-going tendency and is immersed in ignorance, a void that is sometimes fertile' (Goodman 1994, 39). Rexroth noted that 'It is wise to keep the pattern of life clear and simple and filled with beautiful and real things' (Rexroth 1952, 167).

Although not averse to the magisterial statement, both also delighted in the mischievously controversial barb. They felt free to admire authors with whom they clearly disagreed politically or religiously, and both were capable of transcending their time, place and culture. Yet both were clearly grounded and centred in Western civilization, with which both identified as intellectuals; Tritica (1989), for example, groups Rexroth with Edmund Wilson and Malcolm Cowley as premier persons of letters for their generation.

Both were also strongly concerned with environment, ecology, city and place. Thus, Rexroth taught geography to workers in San Francisco. Both admired aspects of academia; Rexroth considered pursuing a PhD (Gibson 1989) and taught at UC Santa Barbara, while Goodman had a PhD in aesthetics from the University of Chicago and taught in a variety of academic settings. But they were isolated from the academic community during most of their lives (Tritica 1989). Goodman felt that he 'was excluded from the profitable literary circles dominated by the Marxists in the thirties and ex-Marxists in the forties because [he] was anarchist' (Goodman 1994, 108). Rexroth had similar concerns (Gutierrez 1996, 10). They both came at the end of the period in which most respectable 'men of letters' were expected to make a living outside of the confines of the university system, in fields, such as high journalism and book authorship, and were expected to be part of intellectual life in major world cities, such as Paris, London, New York, Chicago, San Francisco, or Buenos Aires rather than in sleepy provincial college towns.

Another commonality was generational. Rexroth was born in 1905 at 'the end of the great experiment in Modernism' and arguably was amongst the last to share in the academic ostracism which modernism inspired. Adult life was spent in the atmosphere of the Great Depression and the War (Tritica 1989). Paul Goodman was born in 1911 and graduated from public high school in 1927; after graduation from the City College of New York in 1931, he too descended into underemployment in the atmosphere of the Great Depression. During their old age, both came to apocalyptic conclusions about the future. Rexroth publicly doubted that much of humanity would survive to the year 2000 due to the threat of nuclear war. Goodman thought the 'probability is high (95 per cent) that atom bombs will destroy my friends and children' (Goodman 1994, 101). They were both much younger than Michel Foucault (b. 1926) who visiting United States bohemian locales in the 1970s arguably contributed to appropriating American anarcho-pacifist culture for global academic audiences.

The commonalities of interests are remarkable considering the very different backgrounds of these two writers. They were amongst the last to see themselves as part of the *avant garde* of a modern Western civilization. However, their vision of culture and environment, politics and religion, the past and the future contain extraordinary parallels with the concerns of academic cultural and political ecology and cultural geography. I am uncertain as to how many academic geographers were directly influenced by their writings (I was one). Apart from the issue of direct influence, these writers responded to a perceived situation of environmental and cultural crisis which has become far more commonly shared. I suspect the indirect influences have been profound. We could profitably re-read these writers and recognize their early membership in our interpretive communities. Since their time, of course, there have been numerous public intellectuals, poets and writers whose work has bridged issues of anarchism and cultural and political ecology. Concerns about the interactions between geography and the humanities have inspired a growing body of research, including articles in the journal *GeoHumanities: Space, Place and the Humanities*.

ACKNOWLEDGEMENTS

An earlier version of this material was presented in a paper at the Annual Meeting of the Association of American Geographers at Fort Worth, Texas (Knapp 1997), which has since circulated in anarchist circles. Responses to that presentation were positive and I thank those who have helped me further develop and improve this topic.

REFERENCES

Altieri, Miguel A. and Victor Manuel Toledo. 2011. The agroecological revolution in Latin America: rescuing nature, ensuring food sovereignty and empowering peasants. *The Journal of Peasant Studies* 38(3), 587–612.

Bartlett, Lee. 1991. *Kenneth Rexroth and James Laughlin: Selected Letters*. New York: W.W. Norton and Company.

Bennett, John W. 1976. *The Ecological Transition: Cultural Anthropology and Human Adaptation*. Oxford: Pergamon.

Brookfield, Harold, and Helen Parsons. 2007. *Family Farms: Survival and Prospect*. London: Routledge.

Diamond, Jared. (2005). *Collapse*. New York: Penguin.

Escobar, Arturo. 1995. *Encountering Development: The Making and Unmaking of the Third World*. Princeton: Princeton University Press.

Gade, Daniel W. 2011. *Curiosity, Inquiry, and the Geographical Imagination*. New York: Peter Lang.

Gardner, Geoffrey, ed. 1980. For Rexroth. *The Ark* 14.

Gibson, Morgan. 1989. Reviewing Rexroth. *American Poetry* 7(1): 88–95.

Goodman, Percival, and Paul Goodman. 1960 [1947]. *Communitas*. New York: Vintage.

Goodman, Paul. 1962. *The Society I Live in is Mine*. New York: Horizon Press.

Goodman, Paul. 1969. *Five Years: Thoughts During a Useless Time*. New York: Vintage.

Goodman, Paul. 1970. *New Reformation: Notes of a Neolithic Conservative*. New York: Random House.

Goodman, Paul. 1994. *Crazy Hope and Finite Experience: Final Essays of Paul Goodman*. San Francisco: Jossey-Bass.

Gordon, Burton L. 1969. *Anthropogeography and Rainforest Ecology in Bocas del Toro Province, Panama*. Berkeley: Office of Naval Research Report, Department of Geography, University of California.

Gudynas, Eduardo. 2011. Buen Vivir: Today's tomorrow. *Development* 54: 441–447.

Gutierrez, Donald. 1996. *The Holiness of the Real: The Short Verse of Kenneth Rexroth*. Madison: Farleigh Dickinson University Press.

Hamalian, Linda. 1991. *A Life of Kenneth Rexroth*. New York: W.W. Norton and Company.

Horowitz, Steven P. 1989. An investigation of Paul Goodman and Black Mountain. *American Poetry* 7(1): 2–30.

Knapp, Gregory. 1991. *Andean Ecology: Adaptive Dynamics in Ecuador*. Boulder: Westview Press.

Knapp, Gregory. 1997. The State is the Great Forgetter: Rexroth and Goodman as Antecedents of Cultural Ecology, Political Ecology, and the New Cultural Geography, paper presented at the Association of American Geographers 93d Annual Meeting, Fort Worth.

Knapp, Gregory. 2017. Mountain agriculture for global markets: The case of greenhouse floriculture in Ecuador. *Annals of the American Association of Geographers* 107(2): 511–519.

Matheson, Kent. 2009. Carl Sauer and his critics. In W.M. Denevan and K. Mathewson (eds.), *Carl Sauer on Culture and Landscape: Readings and Commentaries*. Baton Rouge: Louisiana State University Press, pp. 9–28.

Mitchell, Don. 1995. The end of public space? People's park, definitions of the public, and democracy. *Annals of the Association of American Geographers* 85: 108–133.

Netting, Robert McC. 1993. *Smallholders, Householders: Farm Families and the Ecology of Intensive, Sustainable Agriculture*. Stanford: Stanford University Press.

Parsons, James J. 1996. 'Mr. Sauer' and the Writers. *Geographical Review* 86(1): 22–41.

Rexroth, Kenneth. 1952. *The Dragon and the Unicorn*. Norfolk, CT: New Directions Press.

Rexroth, Kenneth. 1961. *Assays*. New York City: New Directions Press.

Rexroth, Kenneth. 1968. *Classics Revisited*. Chicago: Quadrangle Books.

Rexroth, Kenneth. 1969. Revolution Now! *San Francisco Magazine* (December).

Rexroth, Kenneth. 1971a. American System's Way of Death. *San Francisco Magazine* (July).

Rexroth, Kenneth. 1971b. What's Going on in Britain. *San Francisco Magazine* (October).

Rexroth, Kenneth. 1971c. Your Move, Mayor. *San Francisco Magazine* (November).

Rexroth, Kenneth. 1972a. At Large. *San Francisco Magazine* (June).

Rexroth, Kenneth. 1972b. Radio Broadcast. KPFA broadcast transcribed by author (November 12).

Rexroth, Kenneth. 1972c. St. Mary's, A Strange Cathedral. *San Francisco Magazine* (February).

Rexroth, Kenneth. 1973a. Behind the Silence. *San Francisco Magazine* (March).

Rexroth, Kenneth. 1973b. *The Elastic Retort: Essays in Literature and Ideas*. New York: Seabury Press.

Rexroth, Kenneth. 1973c. The Last Bohemia (Continued). *San Francisco Magazine* (December).

Rexroth, Kenneth. 1973d. Radio Broadcast. KPFA broadcast transcribed by author. (February).

Rexroth, Kenneth. 1991. *An Autobiographical Novel: Revised and Expanded*. New York: New Directions.

Rocheleau, Dianne. 2007. Political ecology in the key of policy: From chains of explanation to webs of relation. *Geoforum* 39: 716–727.

Sale, Kirkpatrick. 1995. Review of Three Books on Paul Goodman by Taylor Stoehr. *The Nation*, 260.

Scott, James C. 2012. *Two Cheers for Anarchism*. Princeton: Princeton University Press.

Snyder, Gary. 1980. *The Real Work: Interviews and Talks 1964-1979*. New York: New Directions.

Stoehr, Taylor. 1990. Growing Up Absurd - Again: Rereading Paul Goodman in the Nineties. *Dissent* (Fall): 486–494.

Tritica, John. 1989. Regarding Rexroth: Interviews with Thomas Parkinson and William Everson. *American Poetry* 7(1) :71–87.

Vayda, Andrew 1983. Progressive Contextualization: Methods and Research in Human Ecology. *Human Ecology* 11(3): 265–281.

Widmer, Kingsley. 1980. *Paul Goodman*. Boston: Twayne Publishers.

Wulf, Andrea. 2015. *The Invention of Nature: Alexander von Humboldt's New World*. New York: Knopf.

Worster, Donald. 1979. *Dust Bowl: The Southern Plains in the 1930s*. Oxford: Oxford University Press.

8

The Prefigurative Politics of Going Off-Grid

Anarchist Political Ecology and Socio-material Infrastructures

Ryan Alan Sporer and Kevin Suemnicht

Travelling to Taos New Mexico, one will spot glimmers of sunlight being reflected throughout the mesa. Approaching one of these glimmers, a structure becomes clear. Barely a story tall, one side of the structure is covered in glass; the other three are covered in earth. The glimmer gives way and bright green fills the windows, contrasted by the surrounding reddish dirt. The structure is oddly shaped, like Luke Skywalker's home on Tatooine in *Star Wars* (Figure 8.1). This building is constructed with used car tyres, bottles and cans, amongst the other conventional materials of concrete, lumber and glass. It is an off-grid building and hundreds like it populate the southwest of the United States and thousands can be found around the world. They are called Earthships

The Earthship off-grid design comes from architect turned 'biotect' Michael Reynolds. Since the 1970s, Reynolds and others have developed sustainable and off-grid housing by utilizing the negative externalities of post-industrial society. Recognizing the disastrous commodity chains that provide liveable shelter, Earthship builders and dwellers have refined ways for their homes to *interface* with their surroundings in a more convivial manner. Notably, the off-grid home provides year-round sustainable food production, comfortable shelter, clean energy, on-site sewage treatment and potable water with less dependence on the socio-material infrastructures of the state and markets.

Through an investigation of the off-grid Earthship movement, this chapter draws lessons that have positive implications for the nascent literature of anarchist political ecology. We begin with a reading of the mainstream academic literature on political

Figure 8.1   Earthship exterior.

ecology and argue that these works have successfully criticized the liberal bourgeois foundations of many contemporary practices of human–nature relations, particularly in resource management and environmentalism. An essential component of this criticism has been the role of state agencies in environmental management schemes, which have consistently been shown to be ineffective at achieving environmental goals (for examples, see Mathews 2011, Peluso 1992, West 2006). Meanwhile, state-based environmentalist practices have been a vehicle for dispossession, physical and epistemic violence against autochthonous peoples, and the entrenchment of neo-liberal capitalist conservation ideologies.

While we applaud these efforts, we point out that political ecology has not been able to move beyond the critique of the state to the question of whether the state itself is a viable vehicle for sustainable environmental practices – let along environmental justice. The critique of the state and capitalism has been most thoroughly articulated in the philosophical discourse and political movement of social anarchism. Therefore, we believe that an anarchist intervention can serve as a means of superseding the state-centric thinking within political ecology. Once liberated from the statist epistemic trap, we believe that an anarchist framework can provide a radical way of rethinking ecological practice.

Towards this end, we deploy an anarchist political ecology framework to explore how Earthship building and dwelling allows people to partially escape the violence of the capitalist state and create a more egalitarian form of life. We analyse the fundamental relationship between material infrastructures and statecraft, which leads simultaneously to statist political logics and ecological disaster, and we show that through off-grid housing, people are able to create convivial human–nature assemblages based upon anarchistic practices of mutual aid and autonomy. In doing so, we demonstrate the possibilities of anarchist political ecology for articulating political practices appropriate to respond to the violence of the Anthropocene – both for humans and things.

THE ENDURING PESSIMISM OF ACADEMIC POLITICAL ECOLOGY

Since its inception in the 1970s and 1980s, the discipline of political ecology has proliferated at a remarkable rate and can refer to a wide variety of critical orientations towards the environment and human–nature relations. Briefly, we summarize the discipline of political ecology in order to provide foundations that make it clear how anarchism can serve as a means to improve the discipline. We argue that while political ecology recognizes the limitations and even contradictions of statist approaches to environmental problems, it does not go far enough in challenging the very ability of statist political forms to resolve ecological problems.

What is political ecology? According to early theorists (i.e. Blaikie 1985, Watts 1983), political ecology considers ecological problems from the general Marxian framework wherein struggles over resources are considered to fundamentally revolve around class relations. For early political ecologists, there is no ecological relationship which is not simultaneously a political relationship. For example, Peluso (1992) argues that forestry management in Java has been a vehicle of class domination, where poor indigenous Javanese are exploited by a professional class of forestry agents who have a vested interest in perpetuating the management regime which employs them. In critiquing such environmental management regimes, political ecologists posed a major challenge to traditional conservation concepts and norms, such as 'sustainability' (Isenhour et al. 2015), the moral righteousness of large park projects (Vivanco 2006, Büscher 2013), and the ideology that the poor are the primary cause of environmental degradation (Forsyth 2003).

Even more radically, political ecology challenged the very concept of nature itself. Drawing on Marxist geographer Neil Smith (2008), the environmental historian William Cronon (1996) and feminist philosopher Donna Haraway (1999), political ecologists proposed that the concept of nature developed alongside the capitalist mode of production, which led to nature being theorized within the ascent of bourgeois modernism.

For Smith (2008), the bourgeois conception of nature has two features. First, it poses an absolute separation between the human/culture sphere and the sphere of nature. Second, nature is conceived as a universal phenomenon. Within the bourgeois conception of nature, then, lies a contradiction. On the one hand, nature is universal which positions humans as a part of it, yet nature is distinct, and humans are outside it. Similarly, Cronon (1996) notes that nature is at once a moralizing force (used when describing a thing as true, natural, essential), a commodity (nature exists for humanity to pillage and commodify) and a horrifying and demonic 'other' (when nature signifies the powerlessness of humanity in the face of natural disaster).

For feminist critiques of the bourgeois conception of nature, capitalist modernity rests upon specifically patriarchal ways of considering nature which legitimize gendered ideologies of exploitation and domination. Merchant (1980) provides the seminal feminist critique of bourgeois nature. She argues that feminized conceptions of the natural (i.e. 'Mother Earth') represent nature as a fertile body which can nurture and provide for us, while equating masculinity with culture. With the rise of bourgeois modernity, which is often traced in this literature to the philosophies of Bacon and Descartes (Foster 2000), nature-as-woman shifts from a source of symbolic fertility to a concept of nature as something that can be conquered, mastered and brought under the control of Man and technology. With the rise of bourgeois modernity, sexual assault becomes a prevalent metaphor to describe the domination of nature.

Armed with its criticism of bourgeois nature, political ecology is a powerful tool to delegitimize environmental politics based on a wide variety of authoritarian and liberal premises. For example, one popular area of research within political ecology deals with the construction of large nature reserves (e.g. West 2006, Vivanco 2006, Büscher 2013). Time and again, these studies show that creating conservation parks dispossesses local people who rely on the land of their livelihood. In turn, these groups often resist the conservation regime, thereby undermining the conservation attempts. Contrary to ideologies which would then demonize these often poor people, political ecologists instead argue that the very existence of people living within 'intact nature' suggests that those people already use the land sustainably (Doane 2012).

While political ecology has effectively pointed out the ideological nature of contemporary environmental struggles, it has not posed a way to transcend these limitations. Indeed, a survey of recent ethnographic work in political ecology shows a pernicious pessimism – it is well equipped to debunk and delegitimize statist environmentalisms (both of the liberal and authoritarian varieties) while being simultaneously unable to propose a positive and affirmative environmental politics in their place. This, we suggest, creates within mainstream political ecology (even within its nominally radical Marxist wing) a pernicious and underlying pessimism. For us, this is where an explicitly anarchist political ecology comes in, which may serve as a corrective on political ecology's inability to pose lasting political solutions to environmental problems.

ANARCHIST POLITICAL ECOLOGY

Anarchism, a political theory concerned with the interrogation of all forms of hierarchy, has always been concerned with ecological questions. From Reclus to Bookchin and beyond, anarchism has consistently recognized that the capitalist mode of production and the forms of social domination which presuppose it have in short-time destroyed unfathomable swathes of the natural world. What distinguishes anarchist from other forms of socialist thought, however, is that anarchists have consistently pointed towards statist and hierarchical organizational forms as the primary obstacle in obtaining a social organization which is simultaneously egalitarian and libertarian in human and non-human worlds. Indeed, the anarchist thesis can be stated: 'without hierarchy, freedom and equality'. Or, as Bakunin famously wrote, 'We are convinced that liberty without socialism is privilege, injustice; and that socialism without liberty is slavery and brutality'.

This thesis dramatically departs from common-sense notions of social order, which states that hierarchy is necessary to prevent the violent passions of the masses.[1] Indeed, to draw on the work of Deleuze and Guattari (1986), the history of political philosophy in the Western world has created an *idea* of thought based upon the foundational concept of the state. This they simply call 'state-thought'. While Deleuze and Guattari's concept has many nuances which space precludes discussion of here, the idea of the *inevitability* of centralized hierarchical social formations can be understood, from Deleuze and Guattari's perspective, as a form of mental censorship which makes the thinking of non-state solutions to contemporary problems difficult to imagine from within a statist context.

Yet, despite these difficulties, contemporary anarchist scholarship in the social sciences has served to empirically show the inherent *limitations of state-thought*. Scott (1999), for example, discusses the practical operations used by states in solving social problems. The state must create legible objects for manipulation. This means finding ways of measuring people and land, which often involves a *reduction* of forms of social and natural complexity. Importantly, for Scott, this amounts to the state's impotency to resolve social problems because the optics available to it preclude the creation of complex solutions to complex problems. Similarly, Scott (2009) and Grubacic and O'Hearn (2016) (crucially drawing on the work of Pierre Clastres [1987, 2010]) describe the state in terms of a dialectic relation between the state's attempt to capture and secure subjects and the seemingly universal impulse to escape the state's grasp.[2]

We argue that political ecology has had the misfortune of falling prey to state-thought by failing to overcome the problem of the state *despite persistently criticizing it*. In other words, while political ecology has consistently pointed out the failures of statist ecological projects, it has not made the radical leap to anarchism which we hold as the political possibility of resolving ecological problems. In the next section, we adopt an anarchist political ecological framework, which we propose simultaneously *denaturalizes* the state as privileged political actor and which *denaturalizes* nature as that which is outside the human. Indeed, we believe that the Earthship movement, while insufficiently revolutionary, proposes a political form of life based upon convivial relations between humans and things premised upon a 'Do-It-With' (DIW) ethic and autonomous political practice. Taken together, these sensibilities – conviviality, DIW and autonomy – gesture towards a form of life alternative to the logics of the state and capital. Indeed, as Donna Haraway (2016) has recently suggested, there is a need to create wholly different worlds together. Earthships may represent such an attempt. We turn now to the Earthships themselves, as we take a tour through the material construction of these living structures.

EARTHSHIPS: BUILDING AND DWELLING IN THE REFUSE OF CAPITALISM

The first time one enters an Earthship, they are often surprised at the comfortable temperature independent of the temperature outside. This comfort is attained through 'low-technology' that makes use of geothermal energy and passive solar heating and cooling. Primarily, hundreds of discarded car tyres are packed with dirt and arranged into an upside-down U-shape.[3] Subsequent layers are added, creating a three-sided room. The southern side is then framed in glass and a slighted roof or dome is installed. This assemblage captures the heat from radioactive materials decaying within the earth and solar energy filtering through the wall of windows facing south.

During the summer, one may feel a rush of cool air inside these structures. With no air conditioner, a simple opened slot on the north wall and vents in the ceiling cools the house through convection. At night, the New Mexico mesa temperatures drop quite low, even in the summer. However, after a day of absorbing geothermal and solar energy, the dense tyre walls act as batteries and transfer energy from the dense walls to the living spaces. After a few days of living in an Earthship, one takes notice of the silence that this non-mechanical technology produces. No sounds of forced air, compressors, fans, or burners kicking on. No continual throughput of materials and no monthly bill to pay to simply maintain a liveable habitat (Figure 8.2).

The Earthship is designed to utilize rainwater to supply the dweller with their water needs.[4] Choosing to gather, store and clean water on-site instead of depending on the municipal water infrastructure resonated with many who have lost confidence in the state. Simply, the rooftop doubles as a rain catchment system. Cisterns, buried behind the building, store the rainwater. This is pressurized and filtered for human use. While wide variation exists between household water usage (see Borg et al. 2012), it is estimated that an average of 80–100 gallons a day per person of water is used by the average American household (Perlman 2016). As such, this system would only work in high rainfall locations. However, by reusing water, along with conservation, the Earthship is designed to reduce water usage for two people to 38.6 gallons a day (Reynolds 1993) – a number that is attainable even with only 12 inches of average annual rainfall in northern New Mexico.

Looking at this system closer, used water from the sinks and showers is directed to filters and an indoor botanical cell that lines the inside of the southern window wall. Here, through the process of evaporation, transpiration, oxygenation and bacterial encounter, the 'grey' water is used and cleaned by food-producing plants. Excessive water from the botanical cells is then used as toilet water. Lastly, sewage is directed

Figure 8.2   Inside an Earthship under construction.

to a solar-powered septic tank to accelerate the anaerobic processes. Outdoor botanical cells use effluent for non-edible landscape plants. This assemblage, combined with a conservational material culture, has facilitated the continual inhabitation of Earthships for decades. Furthermore, rain water has virtually zero possibility of being contaminated with rusty lead pipe infrastructure and with no water bill there is no threat of a shut off due to delinquent payments. This system is attractive in an era of water crisis.

These necessity producing-systems, however, do not reduce one to a Luddite lifestyle. While not essential, electricity has become a necessity few would choose to live without. Indeed, from big screen televisions and refrigerators to coffee makers, laptops and lamps, one finds plenty of modern appliances and devices in an Earthship. To power them, Earthships generate electricity through photovoltaic and wind technology, store it in battery banks and distribute it in the form of alternating current and direct current. Additionally, many Earthship dwellers choose to minimize their electricity use and often prefer hand-powered tools and devices with minimal energy usage.

The off-grid home is almost complete, yet there is one last dependency-producing commodity chain to be broken – food. As we have seen, the glass-framed southern wall is lined with botanical cells. Due to the retention of heat generated by the design of the building, year-round food production is possible. In general, a great variety of foods are produced in Earthships. Figs, leafy greens, bananas, papayas, peppers, broccoli, cucumbers, eggplant, carrots, peas, pineapples, strawberries, as well as a seemingly endless variety of herbs and edible flowers form an essential component of the Earthship. While pests can be a problem, dwellers have responded through the enrolment of 'good bugs', lizards and other animals which prevent pests from becoming intolerable. With growing concern over genetically modified organisms, or as one off-gridder put it, 'frankenfoods', the Earthship supplements the dwellers diet (Figure 8.3).

Having completed our tour, we can begin to see the ways in which the Earthship forms a network between human and non-human agencies, thereby creating an ecology of its own and an Interface through which the dependencies and estrangement of peoples and things from capitalist and state socio-material assemblages can begin to be repaired. To understand the ways in which these structures can be considered a form of resistance, we turn to a discussion of the state's infrastructural-basis.

Figure 8.3 Earthship garden.

THE INFRASTRUCTURAL STATE
AND ITS DISCONTENTS

What are infrastructures? At their most banal, 'infrastructures are matter that enable the movement of other matter' (Larkin 2013). Often, because of their ubiquity, they have been dismissed as boring and mundane things (Star 1999; Anand 2015). Yet, such trivializing words conceal the greater political and ontological significance of infrastructures. What if, instead, as recent theorists have been apt to do, we think carefully about the political importance of infrastructure? Anand (2012), for example, shows how Muslim settlers in Mumbai are systematically excluded from accessing and utilizing the city's water works, which positions this squatter community outside the 'biopolitical care of the state'. Strang (2016) similarly argues that water infrastructures globally continue to shift towards the despotism of evoking exceptions in the provisioning of basic services.

Other theorists have shown the relation between material infrastructures and resistance, which suggests that social movements cannot be considered outside broader human–material assemblages. Mitchell (2011), for example, shows that the early worker's movement in England was able to successfully press for democratic and socialist reforms through their ability to shut down the railways and coal production, which in turn shut down the early carbon economy.

Indeed, taken from this angle, infrastructure not only is an essential component of contemporary forms of government and the repertoires of contention but is also essential to the state itself. Following Agamben (2009) and Mitchell (1991, 2011), the state can be understood in terms of a territorially bounded assemblage of apparatuses of control. The electrical grid, the roads, the pipelines and so on – all of these material things are so intrinsically bound up within the calculations of government that they must be seen as themselves *agencies* in the act of governing itself (Bennett 2010). Taken one step further, infrastructure and the 'grid' can be understood not only as a part of the state, but quite literally (though not exhaustively) to *be* the state. Indeed, the particular infrastructural assemblages produce quite different forms of governmentality. Collier (2011), in an influential study within this 'infrastructural turn' in social theory, shows how the development of heating infrastructure in the Soviet Union has affected the Russian state's imposition of neo-liberal reforms. Whereas in the United States, infrastructure was built within the individualizing logics of commodity markets through the metering of heating systems[5] (which allows for precise calculations of energy expenditures), the Soviet system was built instead along collectivist lines with large-scale central boilers providing heat throughout the city. Now, with liberalization, as Collier puts it, the 'intransigence of things' *resists* the atomization and marketization of energy resources. While we do not in any way wish to condone the particularities of Soviet modernism, the case study instructively shows how infrastructure continuously affects political, governmental and economic logics regardless of the particular configuration of governing logistics or social forms.

More directly related to our case study, the centralization and monopolization of infrastructures in the United States has led to a concomitant centralization and monopolization of political authority (Boyer 2017). In turn, this dramatically limits the ability of those affected to conceive of politics outside the infrastructural imperatives of the capitalist state. As such, it is imperative for anarchist social movements to directly address the infrastructural nature of governmentality. With this in mind, we return to those who have *already* taken the powers of infrastructure seriously – the Earthship builders and dwellers. We show how, through the creation of *alternative* non-state infrastructures, the off-grid population creates a form of life which deviates from the analytical imperatives of the capitalist state, both at the level of material practices and at the level of thought. Our ethnography focuses on four key features of life in the Earthship: conviviality, do-it-with, mutual aid and autonomy.

CONVIVIALITY: MAKING PEACE BETWEEN HUMANS, NON-HUMANS AND THINGS

Conviviality[6] is a conception of living premised on the equality of human beings, non-human life and things. For Earthship builders and dwellers, conviviality means being attentive to the non-human world and responsive to its limits. While living amongst Earthship dwellers, we found an enduring attentiveness to the creation of convivial relations – and an opposition to destructive, or 'agonvivial', environmental relations. Ovidiu, for example, a 40-year-old Romanian immigrant who left his work in the finance industry to lead a Spartan life building Earthships finds similarity amongst others who lead this lifestyle. According to him, 'A lot of people I talk with are interested in living in harmony with nature, as oppose[d] to against it'. Similarly, Michael, an early-20s, ex-film student who works with Reynolds discussed his view of humanity's relationship to the planet:

> We need the environment, we need these things, we thrive on this, we can't keep destroying and combating nature . . . . We have to be symbiotic with it if we're ever going to survive. And that's the honest truth . . . . We need to be tenders of the Earth, not competitors with it.

For Michael and many other off-gridders, there is a belief that humans have 'dissociated ourselves from nature' and we have not 'lived by nature's rules'.

For the Earthship population, living by 'nature's rule' is creating a material culture of 'voluntary simplicity', which is an ethical-material practice, coined by philosopher Richard Gregg (1936) and popularized by Elgin (1993), which seeks to reduce dependency on various technologies. Instead of viewing domestic technology as something which saves us time, it is viewed as a trap which makes us all the more hurried in our daily lives. Lachlan, an Earthship dweller, provides an example of reducing one's dependence on material culture. He desired to leave his native Australia to work on Earthships, but he needed to make many changes before he embarked on this journey. He tells us 'I had a mortgage and a house, a full-time job. I was sort of *stuck* in society. I just ended up selling [my house], sold my car, sold pretty much everything . . . . It just came slowly. I was sick of this routine Monday to Friday working the same job'. With a black Sea Shepherd T-Shirt and a peaceful demeanour, Lachlan's abandonment of his material belongings to live in a simpler way, in conviviality with nature, is impressive.

Living in an Earthship requires that one does not 'stress the system', as off-gridders often joke. Omeika, for example, who literally dreamed of living in the rainforest, was attracted to the practice of indoor food production. Knowledge that daily life, such as washing your hands or brushing your teeth, was materially connected to the growth of food was a great pride amongst Earthship dwellers, giving them a connection and sense of wholeness. Commenting on the experience of conviviality in Earthships, Omeika says, 'we need to be more in touch with where nature is going. And I think Earthships help us do that. Make us pay attention to daily rainfall, temperature, material, [and] maintenance'. Mia, a self-described 'blue–green Marxist architect' who has lived for years in an Earthship, describes this bodily practice of attentiveness to ecological processes:

> When I enter the building, it's like I'm in a relationship. I'm in this cooperative, collaborative relationship and I adapt my activities into nature, whether it's hot or cold outside and I'm adjusting windows and skylights or not to keep the temperature just how I like it. Like, I mean, it's almost this being that cares about me. And I'm sorry conventional buildings are not like that.

Mia goes on to discuss how her 'body rhythms just set to sunrise and sunset'. She concludes, 'there's a qualitative life that's so different, so nurturing. Like even though you're in a building you're still in nature and you're interacting with nature'. Finally, Jackie, a retired nurse, discusses how the weather may dictate what she does or does not do, suggesting a marked difference from modernist sensibilities of 'overcoming' and 'dominating' nature. She tells us that she is 'A lot more careful' in how she consumes. 'If it is cloudy like this in the morning', she explains, 'I know it is taking a while to creep up to 100% on the batteries. I know I am going to not iron. So, you know you watch those kinds of things. *I try to use electricity as it comes to me'* (our emphasis).

The off-grid movement is about finding and building the capacity to live-with and to live-with-less. Yet, despite intentionally fostering relations of conviviality with nature, the off-grid home does not display a fervour of asceticism. Each off-grid life is different, and while some choose to live similar to outdoor camping, many others fill their homes with modern devices of all sorts. In this way, Earthships do not evoke a return to 'primitive' forms of life. Rather, off-gridders create a simpler material culture and an awareness, acceptance and embracing of limitations.

'DO-IT-WITH': OFF-GRIDDERS OVERCOMING SPECIALIZATION

For those interested in Earthships, the first step is to find others who already have left the grid. In this way, those who wish to disconnect find themselves needing to make new connections. Earthship Biotecture, Reynolds' small renegade architecture firm, functioned as a central hub for aspiring Earthship dwellers. Through their internship programmes and advocacy of off-the-grid living, Earthship Biotecture is a central node to distribute the knowledge and skills necessary for successful Earthship construction and the broader off-grid movement. Indeed, each year, thousands of people travel to Taos, New Mexico, to attend internships and academy sessions that teach people building skills, and to see the visitor centre. Through these practices, Earthship Biotecture acts as a waystation that transforms an impossible 'Do-It-Yourself' project of fabricating a convivial Earthship into a 'Do-It-With' reality.

While the DIY ethics has been considered in divergent ways – some consider DIY revolutionary, while for others it is a consumerist practice – when it comes to off-grid living, the DIY title obscures more than it reveals, because it relies upon fundamentally individualistic notions of self-sufficiency. For this reason, Vannini and Taggart (2015) suggest replacing the DIY label with the collectively oriented Do-It-With moniker. For Earthshippers, the goal of DIW projects is to overcome specialization. While labour specialization has been a hallmark in archaeological interpretations of development of complex social organizations, to live off-grid requires becoming a generalist and an amateur (Merrifield 2017). Through the experience of fabricating their (or another's) Earthship, the would-be off-gridder learns to overcome specialization through the necessarily collective act of building.

Shane, a student of Earthship Biotecture's academy and a self-described 'working poor anarchist', believes that society has 'infantilized' people. He explains, 'I think most people are kind of infantilized by how we do things . . . people lack the skill sets to directly interact with the Earth and perhaps leverage their knowledge in order to survive'. Shane, who is planning to build several off-grid shelters with his wife and friends, finds 'direct engagement with your surroundings for survival fascinating . . . and pragmatic'. Shane came to Taos to learn how to 'provide for oneself a little bit more'. Every year, hundreds of others descend on the high-altitude mesa to learn together, and, despite frequent mistakes and a common lack of knowledge, they learn everything from carpentry and mixing concrete to plumbing and electrical wiring. Through the collective building practice, everyone learns the necessary building skills, and many who complete the Earthship Biotecture trainings move on to create their own off-grid Earthship (Figure 8.4).

Within the Earthship community, it is common for Earthshippers to come together and throw 'tyre pounding parties' which brings together local off-grid enthusiasts organized online to volunteer their labour in the building of an Earthship. Rarely do individuals feel capable of building their own Earthship completely by themselves, and indeed for many the communal aspect of building is integral to the whole process. This is illustrated, for example with Able – a 30-year-old software engineer from Eastern Europe – who, after a successful academy session, explained that

> I now feel like I can build something. Not an Earthship, but I feel like I could build this passive solar greenhouse . . . and I think I understood the systems of the house and I also seen several phases of the building and it brought, this experience, brought me more closer. I mean, I think it's doable, *at least with other people*. It's not impossible.

Figure 8.4   Earthshippers come together.

Danny, an 'independent to conservative' Texan echoes this sentiment. 'So I guess I understand the systems more in-depth and . . . the whole process of how it works. Obviously learned how to work on these houses. How to build them to some extent'. But he confesses,

> I'm not comfortable building one entirely by myself, but I feel like at least if I had a crew I would be able to direct it enough and work off those plans I'd be able to knock out a big chunk of it.

Danny, who describes himself as 'pretty community-driven' was concerned that off-grid may mean living in the 'boonies'. Now, having completed building an Earthship as an academy student and living in another Earthship during the construction, he believes 'Earthships enhance the human life and the human experience and it builds that community'.

As we see, rather than being a form of hermetic isolation and autarchy, Earthship builders and dwellers show themselves to exist in a living community. But what about the structure after it is built? Again, we find that living off-grid is less about separating connections than about constructing new ones. Consider Evan, a Midwesterner with a sociology degree who works part-time in landscape and construction. He notes that 'Yeah you're off the grid, but you are still part of a community. The grid doesn't tie you into community at all, it just ties you to corporations'. Also consider Hannah, who is interested in 'cooperative business' and 'flat non-hierarchical organizations' and who echoes the collective aspects of off-grid life:

Off the grid is, on the one hand, more independent and, on the other hand, more con-
ducive to a real source of community. Rather than floating signifiers, it encourages that
face-to-face. And I love that barn-raising feel. And I am very interested and I am looking
at how do you create the culture that at once honors the needs and creativities of the
community but also honors and creates the space for unique individuals.

Perhaps with some irony, to do things by yourself and go off-grid requires doing
things with others. To create infrastructure which allows one to live off of (or adja-
cent to) dominant social and material relations is a process that requires overcoming
specialization with others. This creation of face-to-face and virtual communities
expands the conviviality of social relations, as well as human and non-human
relations.

AUTONOMY: A PRACTICE OF RESPONSIBILITY
AND A TERRITORY OF FREEDOM

At the end of the road for the off-gridder is a home and a life that is more autonomous, a life where one can take responsibility for oneself and for others without
allowing these relations to be mediated by outside forces. Indeed, we find that the
off-gridder is fundamentally concerned with the ethical practices of autonomy –
with a care and conduct which respects human and non-human beings and things.
Italian theorist Virno (1996) articulates a similar form of politics which he terms
'exodus'. For him, the exodus from the hierarchies and violence of capitalism and
the state is the condition for the flourishing of alternative forms of life. In his words,
'Disobedience and flight are not in any case a negative gesture that exempts one
from actions and responsibility. On the contrary, to desert means to modify the
conditions within which the conflicts is played instead of submitting to them' (Virno
1996: 20). In this section, we focus on how life off-grid is intimately entangled in the
concern for the others and an ethical reflection on the impacts of ones' action on the
world.

Daryl, 41, was living in rural Canada in a self-converted trailer while he saved
the money and learned the skills necessary to build his Earthship. While in Taos,
he noticed that there was 'this sort of unifying idea of living better and . . . just sort
of gaining a certain amount of independence so you can be responsible for yourself.
That sort of unifies everyone'. Daryl and his partner have been learning how to be
responsible for themselves. They grow some of their own food and are incrementally
retrofitting their trailer by adding a wood stove, a framed greenhouse space and other
modifications. He reflects on his experiences:

It's like I take as much responsibility for myself as I can, which leads to another interesting thing. There are areas in your life, once you decide to try to live in an Earthship,
where you realize just how little freedom you actually had in certain ways. You are not
allowed to take responsibility for yourself.

For Daryl and many others, the goal is to take back some power for sustaining one-self. This we hold is an ethical practice of living by circumventing the socio-material infrastructures of modernity, the state and capitalism.

Furthermore, this ethical practice is turned outwards to those human and non-human others the Earthship builder and dweller lives with. Bobby, for example, who is a civil engineering PhD student (and who 'generally abstains from voting') understands the current role of his discipline in constructing a world built upon a sensibility of ethical absence to others.

> In the past, we all relied on each other. We knew that if we pissed in the well that we're not only going to screw ourselves over, but we're going to screw over everybody else. And we civil engineers and other folks have eliminated . . . the requirement for people to contemplate those potential risks, and I think it's dangerous because now it's filtering over into other areas that, that will have pretty negative consequences.

To spread the practice of off-grid living, Bobby has tried to show the philosophical and technical specifics of Earthships to his colleagues and superiors to little avail. This, however, has not stopped Bobby from making repeated trips to Earthship construction sites. He continues to find that the grid 'causes you to be disconnected from other things than just your electricity or your water. It disconnects you from society'.

People living off-grid often find that only by becoming more autonomous and responsible for yourself, can you become responsible to others. Essie, a young 20-something living in an on-grid communal housing arrangement, says it is dif-ficult, but she 'tries to be constantly aware of the ways that I participate in the evils, even in a passive way'. She continues,

> It's not by people who are aware and conscious of all the destruction that are choosing to continue doing it. You feel like you are not responsible and that you are separated from it because the destruction is not right in your face all the time.

Essie, like many others, finds that life on-grid becomes unbearable in part due to their knowledge of the harms their participation causes others. As another Earthship Biotecture academy graduate put it, 'I'm not fucking with anybody else's shit by drinking this water or listening to this music. It feels good. Every song isn't one more step towards the apocalypse because of me burning coal'. As a native of West Virginia coal country he knows first-hand the destruction he references.

Indeed, for many off-gridders, the evaluation of personal responsibilities and autonomy is often linked to a critique of on-grid lifestyles. Saul, for example, a 46-year-old part-time screen writer and handyman, recently acquired a parcel of land and is preparing to build his Earthship. When discussing on-gridders, he says 'they're still just tied to the same grid – that same corporate beast'. He criticizes their responsibility to others. 'They just want to be comfortable. They don't want to think about it, they don't want to worry about their kids. They don't want to worry about the next generation. They don't want to be responsible'. In counterintuitive way, we find that off-gridders have a deep responsibility, which is why they seek to reduce their social and material relations to those who they deem to be ethically complicit in perpetuating the injustices of grid society.

While the narratives of responsibility are ever-present, the theme of autonomy also emerges in the search for freedom and through relations with other humans and nature. For most, depending on faceless assemblages, understood as centralized and hierarchical, is a condition they find unbearable. Shannon, a 36-year-old East Coast native now living in an older Earthship in Taos, tells us directly,

> I like having power over all my own shit. I like being in control of it. I like knowing how much is going in and out. I like knowing where it is going. I am really engaged in the whole process and I think it is really empowering.

Shannon, who 'has always been on the lower end of the income spectrum', is searching for autonomy from 'busy work' and 'bullshit'. She now lives a much simpler life, and her Earthship has neither a refrigerator nor many other modern 'conveniences'. She continues, 'I think when basic survival needs are in somebody else's hands there is something inherently wrong about that'. She has gained greater autonomy, but she has also made some significant choices about her comfort.

The discussion of the grid as a controlling instrument is common. Jacob confidently states, 'Being dependent on the grid if the grid fails us, we're fucked!' He understands that being off-grid is not 'necessarily easier', but that he 'would have more control over the situation. I'd be growing my own food, collecting my own water. I'd live by myself, instead of some bear trap'. The bear trap for him is the grid – that social and material relationship that he is compelled to maintain in order to survive. He waxes a bit more. 'The grid is an interconnected system that makes people dependent on the powers that be . . . . It's all a system of enslavement'.

Through off-grid living, some degree of autonomy is obtained. Yet, none believe that they have disconnected entirely, and indeed few even desire to do so. Rather, they want to have 'this feeling of not being tied down – of just being free' as off-grid enthusiast Scott remarked. 'If the different systems we live in today kind of keep us isolated, keep us dependent' as another Earthship Biotecture intern remarked, the political struggle is to 'decentralize and relocalize those systems upon which humans depend. To make it so that human beings are more in control of their own livelihood'. By creating different social relations to overcome specialization and pernicious material relations with nature, life off-grid is one filled with greater responsibility to oneself and others and to different material relations with nature.

CONCLUSION

Despite the promises of off-grid living for imagining alternatives to the state and neo-liberal capitalist modes of production, the anchoring of alternative practices has some limitations worth considering. First, generally off-gridders are uninterested at broader social mobilization against the logics of capitalism. Indeed, while the analytic of the grid is useful in pointing to the actual materiality of power in capitalist society, the off-gridders to whom we spoke did not necessarily connect their practices to the possibility of generalized resistance. Jokingly, we describe their politics in terms of 'If you build it, they will come. Or they won't. Whatever'. Furthermore, we worry that the off-grid movement could move from a DIY phenomenon to a commodity itself. Reynolds and his firm have built Earthships for actors and millionaires, often using this to fund their various 'humanitarian builds' around the world. Alternatively, if the movement where to pose a problem for the authorities by undermining administrative legitimacy or reducing the overall 'market' for infrastructural services, the practice could be outlawed through a mobilization of building code violations. Reynolds himself has had to deal with this in the early 2000s (Hodge 2007). This has also been seen in cases of condemning off-grid homes in Florida (Abrams 2014) and the historical legislation against rain catchment systems and grey water reuse systems.

Finally, even though the Earthship dwellers are explicitly not out to fix the world's wrongs, they nevertheless do not fix them.[7] It is a politics of exodus and as such it does not directly confront the political and material constraints the majority of humanity faces. We are adamant that realistic urban alternatives and direct action should be part of a larger politics that includes creating spaces of refuge, but which is not limited to them.

Nevertheless, as we hope to have shown in this chapter, the Earthship movement does provide the anarchist political ecologists with some important insights. First, the creation of convivial relations between humans, objects and nature begins to undo the problematic constructions of 'Human/Nature' which has been a critical ideological formation in the development of capitalism, contemporary forms of patriarchy and colonialism. While the problematic construction remains, we believe that grassroots experiments in convivial practices will become an increasingly important political dynamic for social movements in the Anthropocene and which, furthermore, gestures towards a politics unencumbered by modernist fantasies of the domination of the natural world.

In creating such convivial relations, too, we have shown that off-grid living is not productive of isolation and the Earthship and its dweller do not relinquish their ethical commitments to others but rather reformulates them. Off-grid people build and dwell together thereby creating worlds not fully subsumed within the operative logics of domination which code social and material life in grid society. Finally, in doing so, the off-gridders have created a form of 'minor' autonomy – an autonomous form of life which does not seek generalization. In this way, their movement, perhaps, escapes from the violent proscriptive politics that historically have characterized hierarchical communist political formations.

We hope to have contributed, alongside the other chapters of this volume, to an anarchist political ecology. Whereas political ecology has largely been unable to move beyond criticism of the state, we show amongst off-gridders a form of life that is not reducible to the state. Whereas the state fundamentally relies upon the grid to

164 Ryan Alan Sporer and Kevin Suemnicht

animate the violent apparatuses of government and capitalist interests, off-gridders animate their livelihood in a more convivial nature.

NOTES

1. For an anarchist intellectual history of the role of *arche* in political philosophy see Barnett (2016).

2. See Scott (2009); Ste. Croix (1981); Kahan (1985) for historical cases of flight in Southeast Asia, ancient Greece and feudal Russia, respectfully.

3. For Earthships built in the southern hemisphere the north side of the building is framed in glass.

4. Sporer's fieldwork to Taos coincided with two crises concerning water. The water shuts in Detroit in 2014 and the Flint, Michigan, water crisis. Speaking with visitors to the Earthship Biotecture, these public concerns often were invoked in relation to the off-grid water system that Earthships use.

5. Several Earthship dwellers spoke to the concern that the 'smart grid' would be used as another mechanism for government surveillance. See Halpern et al. (2017) for a Foucauldian critique of 'smart' infrastructures.

6. Here, we draw off the philosopher Ivan Illich's (1973) definition of convivial relations as that which 'enlarges the range of each person's competence, control and initiative'. (12). This he contrasts with manipulative relations, which 'isolates people from each other and locks them into a man-made shell' (11).

7. In this way, they are similar to the back-to-the-land homestead movement of the nineteenth century, which sought a way out but was not concerned with the struggle for liberation (Brown 2011).

REFERENCES

Abrams, Lindsay. 2014. "Florida woman living off the grid forced to connect to city utilities." *Salon Media Group*. Retrieved 11.16.2017. <https://www.salon.com/2014/02/26/florid a_woman_living_off_the_grid_forced_to_connect_to_city_utilities/>.

Agamben, Giorgio. 2009. *What Is an Apparatus? And Other Essays*. Stanford, CA: Stanford University Press.

Anand, Nikhil. 2012. "Municipal Disconnect: On Abject Water and Its Urban Infrastructures." *Ethnography* 13 (4), 487–509.

Anand, Nikhil. 2015 "Leaky States: Water Audits, Ignorance, and the Politics of Infrastructure." *Public Culture* 27 (2), 306–330.

Barnett, Derek. 2016. "The Primacy of Resistance: Anarchism, Foucault, and the Art of Not Being Governed." Dissertation, University of Western Ontario.

Bennett, Jane. 2010. *Vibrant Matter: A Political Ecology of Things*. Duke University Press.

Blaikie, Piers M. 1985. *The Political Economy of Soil Erosion in Developing Countries*. London: Longman. Reprinted by Pearson Education in 2000.

Borg, Maisie, Orion Edwards and Sarah Kimpel. 2012. A Study of Individual Household Water Consumption. *Water Science and Management*. Retrieved 11.16.2017. <http://watermanagement.ucdavis.edu/files/2113/8255/4515/01_Group_Borg_Edwards_Kimpel.pdf>.

Boyer, Dominic. 2017. "Revolutionary Infrastructure." In *Infrastructures and Social Complexity: A Companion*, Harvey, Penelope, Casper Bruun Jensen, and Atsuro Morita, eds. New York: Routledge.

Brown, Dona. 2011. *Back to the Land: The Enduring Dream of Self-Sufficiency in Modern America*. The University of Wisconsin Press.

Büscher, Bram. 2013. *Transforming the Frontier: Peace Parks and the Politics of Neoliberal Conservation in Southern Africa*. Durham, NC: Duke University Press.

Clastres, Pierre. 1987. *Society against the State: Essays in Political Anthropology*. Translated by Robert Hurley and Abe Stein. Cambridge, MA: MIT Press.

Clastres, Pierre. 2010. *Archeology of Violence*. New York: Zone Books.

Collier, Stephen J. 2011. *Post-Soviet Social: Neoliberalism, Social Modernity, Biopolitics*. Princeton, NJ: Princeton University Press.

Cronon, William. 1996 *Uncommon Ground: Rethinking the Human Place in Nature*. New York: W.W. Norton.

Deleuze, Gilles, and Felix Guattari. 1986. *A Thousand Plateaus: Capitalism and Schizophrenia*. Minneapolis: University of Minnesota Press.

Doane, Molly. 2017. *Stealing Shining Rivers: Agrarian Logic, Market Conflict, and Conservation in a Mexican Forest*. University of Arizona Press.

Elgin, Duane. 1993. *Voluntary Simplicity: Towards a Way of Life that is Outwardly Simple, Inwardly Rich*. Harper Collins Publishers.

Forsyth, Tim. 2003. *Critical Political Ecology: The Politics of Environmental Science*. New York: Routledge.

Foster, John Bellamy. 2000. *Marx's Ecology: Materialism and Nature*. New York: Monthly Review Press.

Gregg, Richard. 1936. "The Value of Voluntary Simplicity." *Visva-Bharti Quarterly*.

Grubacic, Andrej, and Denis O'Hearn. 2016. *Living at the Edge of Capitalism: Adventures in Exile and Mutual Aid*. Berkeley: University of California Press.

Halpren, Orit, Robert Mitchell, and Bernard Dionysius Geoghegan. 2017. "The Smartness Mandate: Notes toward a Critique". *Grey Room* 68: 106–129.

Haraway, Donna J. 1999. *Simians, Cyborgs, and Women: The Reinvention of Nature*. New York: Routledge.

Haraway, Donna J. 2016. *Staying with the Trouble: Making Kin in the Chtulucene*. Durham, NC: Duke University Press.

Hodge, Oliver. 2007. *Garbage Warrior*. Open Eye Media UK.

Illich, Ivan. 1973. *Tools for Conviviality*. Harper and Row.

Isenhour, Cindy, Melissa Checker, and Gary McDonogh. 2015 *Sustainability in the Global City: Myth and Practice*. New York: Cambridge University Press.

Kahan, Arcadius. 1985. *The Plow, The Hammer, and The Knout: An Economic History of Eighteenth-Century Russia*. The University of Chicago Press.

Larkin, Brian. 2013. "The Politics and Poetics of Infrastructure." *Annual Review of Anthropology* 42, 327–343.

Mathews, Andrew. 2012. *Instituting Nature: Authority, Expertise, and Power in Mexican Forests*. MIT Press.

Merchant, Carolyn. 1980. *The Death of Nature: Women, Ecology and the Scientific Revolution*. New York: HarperCollins Publishers.

Merrifield, Andy. 2017. *The Amateur: The Pleasures of Doing What You Love*. Verso.

Mitchell, Timothy. 1991 "The Limits of the State: Beyond Statist Approaches and Their Critics." *American Political Science Review* 85 (1): 77–96.

Mitchell, Timothy. 2011. *Carbon Democracy: Political Power in the Age of Oil.* New York: Verso.

Peluso, Nancy Lee. 1992. *Rich Forests, Poor People: Resources Control and Resistance in Java.* Berkeley, CA: University of California Press.

Perlman, Howard. 2016. "Water Questions & Answers: How much water does the average person use at home per day?" USGS. Retrieved 11.16.2016. <http://water.usgs.gov/edu/qa-home-percapita.html>.

Reynolds, Michael. 1993. *Earthship Volume 3.* Solar Survival Press.

Scott, Scott. 1999. *Seeing Like a State: How Certain Schemes to Improve the Human Condition Have Failed.* New Haven, CT: Yale University Press.

Scott, James. 2009. *The Art of Not Being Governed: An Anarchist History of Upland Southeast Asia.* New Haven: Yale University Press.

Smith, Neil. 2008. *Uneven Development: Nature, Capital, and the Production of Space* (3rd Edition). University of Georgia Press.

Starr, Susan Leigh. "The Ethnography of Infrastructure." *American Behavioral Scientist* 43, 377–391.

Ste. Croix, G.E.M de. 1981. *Class Struggle in the Ancient Greek World: From the Archaic Age to the Arab Conquests.* Cornell University Press.

Strang, Veronica. 2016. "Infrastructural relations: Water, political power and the rise of a new 'despotic regime'". *Water Alternatives* 9(2): 292–318,

Vannini, Philip and Jonathan Taggart. 2015. *Off the Grid: Re-Assembling Domestic Life.* Routledge. New York.

Virno, Paolo. 1996 "Virtuosity and Revolution: The Political Theory of Exodus." *Radical Thought in Italy: A Potential Politics*, Michael Hardt and Paolo Virno, eds. Minneapolis: University of Minnesota.

Vivanco, Luis. 2006. *Green Encounters: Shaping and Contesting Environmentalism in Rural Costa Rica.* New York: Berghahn Books.

Watts, Michael. 1983. *Silent Violence: Food, Famine and Peasantry in Northern Nigeria.* Berkeley: University of California Press.

West, Paige. 2006. *Conservation Is Our Government Now: The Politics of Ecology in Papua New Guinea.* Durham, NC: Duke University Press.

9

Escape from Ecology

Necrophilia and the Left's Internalized Green Scare

Dan Fischer

In 1963, the psychologist and libertarian Marxist theorist Erich Fromm pondered why there was not more widespread and effective resistance to war. He hypothesized that 'people are not afraid of total destruction because they do not love life; or even, because many are attracted to death'. Fromm described this death-desiring orientation as 'necrophilia' and explained that it develops when people lack fulfilling social connections, chances to be creative and freedom of thought and action. It predominates, he argued, in capitalist societies, where corporate and state bureaucracies treat people as 'numbers', and captivating screens endlessly project slaughter and sterility. It is likely that Fromm would have offered the same explanation today as to why there are not more widespread and effective responses to ecological breakdown. Fromm (1976) understood these 'ecological dangers and the dangers of nuclear war, either or both of which may put an end to all civilization and possibly to all life'.

This chapter, written from an Anarchist perspective, posits that a social necrophilia has prevented dominant sections of the global Left (in the United States and Latin America) from developing effective responses to ecological breakdown. Although Anarchists share leftist goals of social emancipation, they tend to act autonomously from the hierarchical, bureaucratic institutions – top-down unions, political parties and large non-profits – comprising the "official Left" or "the official institutions of the Left" (Hardt and Negri 2000; Van Meter 2017). These Anarchists argue that the official Left ultimately protects capitalism, the state and other structures of domination. As Peter Gelderloos (2010) suggested, 'The Left, to a large extent subconsciously, has as its primary role to make resistance harmless'.

While the official Left has sometimes helped achieve important reforms, its internalization of at least two necrophilous capitalist strategies has hindered more subversive and constructive forms of ecological resistance and reconstruction. These internalizations reflect Fromm's (1947) description of how people in unfree societies tend to develop an 'authoritarian conscience', which is 'the voice of an internalized external authority, the parents, the state, or whoever the authorities of a culture happen to be'. First, dominant Leftist institutions internalize capitalism's *Green Scare* targeting radical ecological movements with state repression. It is common for the official Left to denounce, inform on and arrest people who take direct action against ecological devastation. Second, the official Left internalizes capitalism's technique of *greenwashing*, falsely defending destructive corporate and state policies as green and sustainable. This greenwashing reflects Fromm's (1968) description of necrophilous policymaking: 'Those who are attracted to the non-alive are the people who prefer "law and order" to living structure, bureaucratic to spontaneous methods, gadgets to living beings, repetition to originality'.

I focus on two sections of the official Left that portray themselves as responsible defenders of life on Earth: first, Left institutions in the United States including large environmental non-profits, and second, Left parties that took state power as part of Latin America's Pink Tide since the late 1990s. With these case studies, I attempt to demonstrate that the official Left performs a role of preventing people from building a society in harmony with non-human nature. In large part, this role results from many Left institutions' elite funding sources and pro-capitalist or reformist ideologies. However, a social psychological basis is a necessary condition. As Fromm (1963) argued, 'If all [humans] loved life, had reverence for life, were independent and critical, the human basis for war would be lacking'. Similarly, if the official Left cultivated a genuine love of life, there is hardly any way it could continue marching willingly with capitalism towards omnicide (the murder of everything). Over the course of the chapter, I mention examples where some avowed anti-capitalist and even Anarchist groups, who do not accept any corporate funding or subscribe to capitalist ideology, have internalized aspects of the Green Scare and greenwashing strategies. Therefore, a satisfying explanation must involve more than *just* economic and ideological factors. In the conclusion, then, I return to Erich Fromm's theory and suggest that effective ecological movements will need to undo necrophilous internalizations and create a culture of biophilia, meaning a love of life. These movements will find that outside of the official Left, countless humans, animals and ecosystems already engage in everyday direct action and mutual aid, prefiguring a world resonating with Fromm's (1941) Anarchist-leaning commitment to 'victory over all kinds of authoritarian systems'.

GREEN SCARE IN THE UNITED STATES

'All over the globe, environmental activists are currently facing a growing backlash, which is designed to intimidate them into inactivity and silence', Andrew Rowell wrote in 1996. The prior year, a Nigerian military junta murdered the Ogoni environmental campaigner Ken Saro-Wiwa, who had organized communities against Shell Oil's devastation. Hundreds of Ogoni had been killed and 30,000 had been made homeless. Since then, the targeting of grassroots environmental campaigners has continued to expand worldwide. Global Witness (2017) reported that at least 200 land and environmental defenders in twenty-four countries had been killed in 2016. Forty per cent of the victims were indigenous, and 60 per cent lived in Latin America. The deadliest countries were Brazil, Colombia, the Philippines, India and Honduras. Almost 1,000 land and environmental defenders had been murdered between 2010 and 2016, and 197 were killed in 2017 (Watts 2018).

In the United States, the Right's 'Wise Use' movement and the federal government have claimed since the 1980s that radical environmental defenders are 'eco-terrorists' and 'extremists'. The Federal Bureau of Investigations (FBI) targeted prominent members of Earth First!, waking up a sleeping Dave Foreman with guns pointed at him in 1989, and, evidence suggests, non-fatally car-bombing Judi Bari in 1990 (St. Clair and Frank 2015; Ongerth 2014). The Heritage Foundation, a Right think-tank, advocated in 1990, 'Strangle the environmental movement. It's the greatest single threat to the American economy. It doesn't just include a few extremists. It is extremist' (Rowell 1996). Following Al Qaeda's September 2001 terror attacks, the Right and the federal government increased their use of 'eco-terrorist' accusations. One of the major targets was the Earth Liberation Front (ELF), an anti-authoritarian network whose carefully orchestrated acts of vandalism have cost Earth-destroying corporations many millions of dollars. Only targeting property, the ELF has never harmed a human being. ELF's communiqués espoused life-loving and anarchistic ideas of 'social and deep ecology', that 'Property is theft' and a commitment to 'non-hierarchical' structure (1997). By 2004, 'extreme animal rights and environmental activists' had caused more than $100 million in estimated damage to corporate property (Anti-Defamation League 2004). That year, the FBI began its 'Operation Backfire', culminating in arrests and prosecutions of ELF members for terrorism. Pointing centrally to the ELF, the FBI warned in 2005, 'The No. 1 domestic terrorism threat is the eco-terrorism, animal-rights movement' (Schuster 2005). Activists identified an on-going 'Green Scare' reminiscent 'of tactics used against Americans during the communist Red Scare of the 1940s and 1950s' (Potter 2008). The Green Scare must be understood as just one component of the U.S. government's long-standing pattern of attacking dissidents and minorities (Churchill and Vander Wall 1990).

The official Left, including major environmental non-profits, quickly adopted Green Scare rhetoric and behaviours, signalling its internalization of capitalist values. In 1989, the National Wildlife Federation's president Jay Hair condemned Earth First! as 'outlaws and terrorists' (Green 1989). The Sierra Club offered financial rewards for information that could lead to eco-saboteurs' arrest (Tolme 2001; Potter 2011). The group's executive Carl Pope elaborated to the *Wall Street Journal*, 'In fact, when a Forest Service facility in the Wilamette National Forest was torched in 1996, perhaps by ecoterrorists, the Sierra Club offered a reward to anyone who could help identify the perpetrators' (Pope 2001). According to former North American ELF Press Office spokesperson Craig Rosebraugh (2014), 'The Sierra Club had even gone so far as to work with the FBI in the Colorado Vail arson investigation' after the ELF burned down a ski resort that threatened lynx habitat in 1998.

On 30 October 2001, U.S. Congressional Representative Scott McInnis addressed a letter to the Left's major environmental non-profits. Expressing concern over green radicals' vandalism of corporate property, the letter announced, '[W]e are calling on you and your organization to publicly disavow the actions of eco-terrorist organizations like the Earth Liberation Front (ELF) and Animal Liberation Front (ALF)' (Rosebraugh 2014). With few exceptions, the non-profits capitulated. Greenpeace's director John Passacanto responded, 'If we define eco-terrorism as violence, violence to people or to property, we disavow it' (Oko 2002). The Sierra Club's Carl Pope insisted, 'We have been denouncing eco-terrorism since before Scott [McInnis] knew it even existed' (Tolme 2001).

The Southern Poverty Law Center (SPLC), a Left watchdog of far-right groups, has also devoted resources to monitoring the Earth Liberation Front and so-called 'eco-violence'. Despite acknowledging that the ELF has never harmed a human being and that it advocates 'equality, social justice and . . . compassion for all life', the SPLC (2001) voiced concern about the ELF's green radicalism: 'But like most groups on the radical right today, the ELF sees global capitalism as an enemy'.

The official Left has also attacked life-loving anarchistic currents using the 'black bloc' tactic during Seattle's 1999 mobilization against the World Trade Organization. Wearing black clothing and masks to protect their identities, these predominantly Anarchist affinity groups damaged the property of ecologically and socially destructive large corporations (ACME Collective 1999). As documented by communications scholars, their acts of vandalism 'catapulted the protests into national headlines', drawing media 'attention to the issues' (DeLuca and Peeples 2002). Left non-profits and unionists infamously assaulted the black bloc participants. Lori Wallach of Public Citizen proudly recounted: 'Our people actually picked up the anarchists. Because we had with us steelworkers and longshoremen who, by sheer bulk, were three or four times larger. So we had them literally, just sort of, a teamster on either side, just pick up an anarchist. We'd walk him over to the cops and say this boy just broke a window [. . .] Please arrest him'. The next day, Medea Benjamin of the non-profit Global Exchange asked the *New York Times*, 'Where are the police? These anarchists should have been arrested' (Dupuis-Déri 2014). Effectively agreeing with Frommian theory, Van Deusen (2010) described such Left opponents of the black bloc as 'weighed down in indecision and tacit acceptance of the status quo [. . .] Despite their professed goals, they become the harbingers of defeat and alienation'.

Moreover, animal liberation groups have found themselves abandoned and denounced by the Left's official institutions. The American Civil Liberties Union decided in 2006 not to oppose the Animal Enterprise Terrorism Act signed into law by President George W. Bush. Designed to target opponents of the fur, factory farming and animal research industries, the law expanded the legal definition of 'terrorism' to include First Amendment-protected activities – including whistleblowing and nonviolent civil disobedience – deemed 'damaging' to business operations. Will Potter (2011) argued that the ACLU effectively allowed the bill to pass: 'When the civil liberties watchdog says, "The ACLU does not oppose this bill", as it did in an

October 30, 2006, letter to Sensenbrenner, it's like a bank security guard turning his back with the vault's doors swung wide'. Other mainstream non-profits have publicly denounced radical animal liberationists. The Humane Society has condemned the 'illegal conduct' of the Animal Liberation Front, and Greenpeace has denounced the Sea Shepherd Conservation Society's sinking of unmanned whaling ships (Yates 2013; Pellow 2014).

The internalized Green Scare has furthermore pervaded the mainstream climate change movement, as demonstrated in November 2015 when the United States-based 350.org helped coordinate protests at the United Nations' climate conference in Paris, France. When Parisian officials enacted a citywide protest ban, 350.org complied and cancelled a march it had planned along with other non-profits (Rodriguez and Case 2015). However, hundreds of unarmed Anarchists and other anti-capitalists violated the ban, forming black blocs and defending themselves from police in order to maintain a presence on the streets. Rather than cheering on these protesters (or even denouncing the riot police tear gassing and arresting them), 350.org denounced the demonstrators as 'unaffiliated with the climate movement' (Phipps, Vaughan and Milman 2015).

During the 2016 struggle at North Dakota's Standing Rock Sioux reservation against the construction of the oil-transporting Dakota Access Pipeline, indigenous land defenders faced extreme state repression, including about 800 arrests and forcible eviction by '[l]aw enforcement officials, heavily armed with military equipment and riot gear'. The pipeline's construction company, Energy Transfer Partners (ETP), hired a security firm that labelled the pipeline's opponents as 'jihadists' (Global Witness 2017). In September 2016, reporters filmed a security force's dogs biting indigenous land defenders, drawing blood (Goodman 2016). ETP's CEO Kelcy Warren has since called for pipeline opponents to be 'removed from the gene pool' (Hand 2018). While repressive activity originated with corporate forces, some Leftists internalized it and tried to replace militant tactics with harmless ones. As one anonymous participant complained, 'Much of the camp's rhetoric is of the "Non-violent Direct Action" type. Lock your arm to this piece of deconstruction equipment and take a picture with a banner for Facebook'. Such activities led an indigenous man to lament, 'I don't know who these "leaders" are. They're not my elders' (Anonymous 2017). One Standing Rock participant warned that 'nonviolent direct action' trainers brought to the camp taught 'protestors how to "de-escalate" even to the point of pulling young men (warriors) aside and chastising them (gently of course) for their anger. They were also told not to wear bandanas over their faces but to proudly be identified. A chill went up and down me' (Wrong Kind of Green 2016). When Jessica Reznicek and Ruby Montoya publicly claimed responsibility in July 2017 for arsons that cost the pipeline's builders a reported $3 million, Sierra Club lawyer Wally Taylor condemned the direct actions: 'Certainly, we had absolutely no knowledge about what these women were doing or were going to do, and we condemn any kind of damage or anything like that' (Petroski 2017).

Even radical, autonomous leftists have sometimes internalized Green Scare rhetoric, demonstrating the authoritarian conscience's far-reaching effects. The Industrial

Workers of the World (IWW), a radical union (of which I'm a member) with deeply rooted Anarchist tendencies, does not accept corporate funding. To its credit, the IWW has done highly important organizing towards an 'ecological general strike' and its constitution aspires to 'live in harmony with the Earth' (Hughes and Ongerth 2014). The union supports deep reductions of the workweek, which would make the economy less polluting and wasteful (Schneider 2014). Overall, the IWW has adopted an infinitely greener stance than did, for example, the business-friendly union the AFL-CIO which supported construction of the Keystone XL and Dakota Access oil pipelines (Solomon 2017). However, when the IWW member Marius Mason was arrested for alleged vandalisms committed under the Earth Liberation Front name, the IWW's General Executive Board (2008) issued a statement *condemning* Mason's alleged tactics: '[T]he charges (simply put, arson and property destruction done to halt bio-engineering experiments and logging) are unrelated to union activity. Additionally, our union opposes these tactics, which stem from isolation and powerlessness'. The statement did not denounce the state repression that Mason faced.

Anarchistic eco-resistance groups have sometimes self-imposed a rigid pacifism, effectively adopting the state's rejection of vandalizing corporate property. Earth First! has 'self-consciously started to adopt the restrictive rhetoric of non-violence', according to one critic who supplies plenty of examples since 2011 that sometimes involved a hyper-focus on collaborations with non-profits on performative actions posing little direct challenge to capitalists (Oxalis 2014). The anarchistic Rising Tide network has also collaborated with non-profits on largely performative actions, leading a critic to argue that Rising Tide 'operates in lockstep with Greenpeace and 350.org' (Raymond 2015). The network insists in bold letters on its website, 'People and groups do not engage in property destruction under the name Rising Tide'. In all fairness, there can be strong contextual reasons for certain groups to adopt non-violent tactics, and moreover, it must be noted that the networks mentioned here have often courageously defended human and non-human communities (*Earth First! Journal* 2014). Still, their adoption of pacifist discourse may indicate a certain closeness with the official Left's limitations on resistance. As the North American ELF Press Office (2007) explained, 'No one in his right mind can honestly state that the popular environmental movement using state-sanctioned tactics has been successful. It is very obvious something more is needed'. When members of these eco-resistance groups have sometimes supported a broader diversity of methods necessary for defending life, they have broken from what Ward Churchill (2012) called the 'death wish' embedded in the 'pathology of pacifism'.

PINK TIDE AND CRIMINALIZATION
OF ANTI-EXTRACTIVISTS

Struggles in Latin America have often clashed between strategies of *buen vivir* (living well) and extractivism. The buen vivir strategy, inspired largely by Quechua, Aymara,

Guaraní and other indigenous traditions, emphasizes living harmoniously with social and ecological communities (Ford 2014). It 'puts the emphasis on doing, rather than consuming' (Esteva, Babones and Babcicky 2013). Its worldview overlaps significantly with Fromm's (1976) suggestion that people live more fulfilling lives by focusing on 'being' (which 'refers to *experience*') rather than 'having' (which 'refers to *things*'). By contrast, the official Left's strategy of taking of state power, responsible for the 'Pink Tide' of Left electoral victories since the late 1990s, has often tended towards extractivism, relying centrally on extracting and exporting oil, natural gas, timber and other natural resources for export to overdeveloped nations. According to critic Alberto Acosta (2013), extractivism has historically 'led to widespread poverty', and although Pink Tide governments have distributed revenues more fairly, they have not engaged in any radical redistribution of income and wealth'. Acosta added that extractivist governments tend to 'criminalize' forms of 'protest against the extractivist activities'. John Holloway (2010) warned that Pink Tide states relate to their populations as 'a quantity of undifferentiated, abstract atoms, with limited capacities [. . .] This is not a politics of dignity'. Following the necrophilous trajectory, the Left in power has targeted ecological resistance in Bolivia, Venezuela, Ecuador, Brazil and Mexico.

In 2010, Bolivia's Left government convened in Cochabamba the World People's Conference on Climate Change and the Rights of Mother Earth. Some 35,000 people from 142 countries attended. The conference produced a radical document denouncing capitalism and calling for a variety of local solutions respecting ecosystem and planetary health. However, outside of the conference, a national indigenous council known as Conamaq held a parallel summit that critiqued the Bolivian government's extractivist policies. Organizers called this conference the 18th Mesa or 18th table, since the official World People's Conference had 17 working groups (Building Bridges Collective 2010). In their declaration, the 18th Mesa denounced 'imperialism, transnationals and the so-called progressive Latin American governments that implement mega energy and infrastructure projects under the [Integration of Regional Infrastructure in South America (IIRSA)]'. In addition to critiquing the Pink Tide governments, the 18th Mesa declaration implicated other parts of the Left including 'those NGOs which support projects of the aforementioned corporations' (18th Mesa 2010).

The Bolivian government, in turn, has targeted indigenous and grassroots critics with violence and smears. In December 2013, the government 'helped to violently oust the Conamaq from their offices in La Paz'. A Conamaq member claimed, 'Our crime was defending Mother Earth' (Peralta M 2014). After members of the People's Guarani Assembly of Takova Mora blocked a highway in Chaco on 19 August 2015, protesting oil extraction in indigenous territories, police broke up the rally using tear gas and batons and detained twenty-seven people. Seventeen were punished with extrajudicial sanctions preventing them from publicly participating in events related to this local ecological struggle (Cregan 2015).

In Venezuela, environmental campaigners and indigenous peoples have complained about repression accompanying extractive activities enabled by the Left government and military. Survival International reported in 2015, 'Indians have denounced the Venezuelan military for failing to tackle the illegal mining and for "creating a climate of terror and fear". Some officers are known to be involved in the illegal gold trade'. In 2016, President Nicolás Maduro opened the Arco Minero, a major mining zone, without consent from local indigenous communities. The local indigenous leader Brian Clark lamented the intimidating presence of the Venezuelan military: 'The presence of the army here is not for the people. It's for their [the state's and military's] own benefit' (Ebus 2018).

Ecuador's Pink Tide government – under Rafael Correa (2007–2017) and his successor Lenín Moreno – has also taken aim at environmental defenders, smearing and arbitrarily punishing campaigners and going so far as forcibly shutting down the Pachamama Foundation, a prominent environmental non-profit, in 2016. Human rights researchers found a lack of sufficient evidence to support the charges in three of the government's cases against indigenous and environmental campaigners (Human Rights Watch 2018). First, in 2013, indigenous Shuar campaigner José Acacho, was convicted of 'terrorism' and sentenced to twelve years in prison for allegedly inciting violence at a 2009 protest against new mining laws. Not a single trial witness testified that Acacho was even present at the demonstration. A second case responded to a clash between the government and mining opponents in December 2016. Following the confrontation, Correa's government tried to dissolve the organization Ecological Action, although the group successfully appealed its closure. The Shuar campaigner Augustín Wachapá was charged with inciting violence through a Facebook post and says he was held in a maximum-security prison for four months. Researchers called the government's case 'devoid of meaningful evidentiary support'. Finally, seven indigenous leaders and environmental defenders who demonstrated against oil drilling in 2013 'remain subject to a criminal investigation that has failed to yield any evidence against them for over four years'. The Pachamama Foundation had helped organize the protest against foreign investors bidding on drilling rights on indigenous territories. On television, Correa smeared the defendants as 'violent people, bad people' and four days later, on 4 December 2013, his government ordered the Pachamama Foundation to close down. While the current administration has reinstated the Pachamama Foundation and has made overtures to environmentalists, 'the provision used to shut down Pachamama Foundation remains in place' and problems of arbitrary prosecution remain unresolved. Researchers concluded that Ecuador's government has 'abused' executive powers 'to harass, intimidate, and punish Ecuadorians who opposed oil and mining projects that the president endorsed' (Human Rights Watch 2018).

When the Brazilian Worker's Party held power from 2003 to 2016 as part of the Pink Tide, they were criticized for doing little to stop the murder of land defenders by landowners and logging companies. In 2011, rubber tapper and ecological campaigner José Claudio Ribeiro da Silva, known as Ze Claudio, was murdered by vigilantes. It was reported a few years later, 'The outcry over Ze Claudio's killing spurred the government to announce it would provide activists with protection, but few have actually received it' (Miller 2015).

Since the Left-leaning President Andrés Manuel Lopez Obrador took power in Mexico in 2018, the state has repeatedly sent soldiers, tanks and helicopters into the territories of the Zapatista National Liberation Army and their indigenous supporters. The Zapatistas, who staunchly oppose Lopez Obrador's proposed infrastructure megaprojects in their region, have complained that 'the military, police, and paramilitary presence has increased, as has that of spies, listening ears, and informants' (Pinto 2019; Telesur 2019).

While indigenous and grassroots environmental campaigners in Latin America have often advanced life-loving resistance, the Left in power is acting to repress and marginalize those approaches. While sometimes co-opting ecological rhetoric, Pink Tide governments have maintained the centrality of destructive extraction. Raúl Zibechi (2015) appropriately observed, 'The extractivist model tends to generate a society without subjects. This is because there cannot be subjects within a scorched-earth model such as extractivism. There can only be objects'. Such disrespect of people's health, homes and dignity matches Fromm's characterization of necrophilia.

GREENWASHING THE STATUS QUO

Dedicated to preserving the status quo, the official Left claims that solutions will be top-down and led by technical experts instead of by communities. For example, Environmental Defense Fund's President Fred Krupp insisted, '[W]hat the environmental movement needs is more scientists and engineers and economists' (St. Clair 2011). Even despite their professed dedication to data, however, the official Left enthusiastically supports policies and technologies expected to bring ecological breakdown well past safe levels, locking in at least 3 or 4° Celsius of global warming above pre-industrial levels. Leading climate scientists confirm that no level of warming above 1 or 1.5° is remotely safe: Already an estimated 400,000 human beings currently die each year from climate change impacts. 2° of warming could submerge the world's coastal cities with rising seas. 4° of warming could even kill off 90 per cent of human beings (Fischer 2017). Just slightly higher levels could completely 'annihilate planetary life' (Strona and Bradshaw 2018). While failing to prevent catastrophic warming, the Left's preferred policies also exacerbate comparable threats, such as water contamination, nuclear radiation, methane leaks, mountaintop destruction and indigenous people's dispossession. Simply put, there is no way that a life-loving Left would promote these false solutions.

Theoretically, society could rapidly transition towards a fully renewable and greenhouse gas-free economy, leaving some chance of minimizing catastrophe. As Energy Justice Network (2018) summarized, '[S]tudies say it can be done by 2030, but with enough political will and a shifting of subsidies from dirty energy and militarism to clean solutions, it can likely be done much sooner'. According to Hansen (2018), decarbonization at this pace, combined with greener agriculture and forestry, could return global temperatures to safe levels this century. For many decades, grassroots movements and intellectuals have proposed indigenous, Anarchist, syndicalist,

Communalist and ecosocialist visions of a sustainable world free from capitalism's grow-or-die imperative (Bookchin 1964; Sethhness Castro 2012). Demonstrating these radical visions' mass potential, the Environmental Justice movement has campaigned for community-controlled clean energy and efficiency programmes (Raval 2015) with principles affirming 'the sacredness of Mother Earth, ecological unity and the interdependence of all species' (People of Color Environmental Leadership Summit 1991). Other groups have begun constructing fragments of an ecological society by creating direct democratic assemblies and syndicates, planting community gardens, installing renewable power and collectively constructing non-consumerist lifestyles compatible with the philosophy of buen vivir. Examples include the Global Ecovillage Network, the Right to the City, and Transition Towns, which all prefigure a 'libertarian communist future' (Carson 2018). Instead of replicating these important experiments on a massive scale, the mainstream Left has focused primarily on greenwashing the present capitalist society.

In 2009 and 2010, the U.S. Democratic Party and like-minded non-profits advocated for federal cap-and-trade legislation largely crafted by BP, Shell, Duke Energy, DuPont, General Electric and Dow Chemical (Klein 2014). While mainstream scientists called for the United States to cut carbon emissions by at least 40 per cent below 1990 levels by 2020, the potential legislation only aimed for a 0.7 per cent cut below 1990 levels during that period. Moreover, the bills allowed companies to avoid even these minuscule pollution cuts as long as they paid for fraud-prone 'carbon offset' schemes that purportedly but unreliably reduced pollution abroad. The bills were estimated to allow a 92 per cent chance of an extremely dangerous 2° of warming and a 40 per cent chance of 4° of warming. The bills also subsidized and otherwise offered incentives promoting polluting energy sources such as offshore oil, so-called 'clean coal' and nuclear power (Center for Biological Diversity 2010). Climate scientist James Hansen (2009) warned that the legislation 'would only assure continued coal use, making it implausible that carbon dioxide emissions would decline sharply'.

Despite staunch criticisms from leading scientists and grassroots activists alike, the official Left celebrated these corporate-crafted cap-and-trade bills as if they were sent from the heavens. The Sierra Club called the House bill a 'step toward unleashing a true clean energy revolution'. The League of Conservation Voters deemed it 'the most important environmental vote to date in the House of Representatives', and the Environmental Defense Fund called it 'a strong bill' and 'the most important environmental and energy legislation in our nation's history' (Sierra Club 2008; Thrush 2009; Parry 2009; Krupp 2009). The denialism required to celebrate a 0.7 per cent emissions reduction (compared to a necessary reduction of at least 40 per cent) as a 'step toward . . . . revolution' was staggering. In any case, the bill failed in the Senate and never became law.

The pattern of greenwashing continued in subsequent years as the Left cheered enthusiastically for the 2015 Paris Climate Agreement despite the fact that the treaty protected capitalist growth instead of rebuilding society along ecological lines. Even in the unlikely event that the treaty's emissions reductions pledges are implemented, they are estimated to warm the planet by more than 3° and by as much as 4° (Climate Action Tracker 2018). However, the Paris agreement did not contain any mechanism to actually enforce these pledges, leading Dr. Hansen to call the treaty 'a fraud, really, a fake . . . It's just bullshit' (Milman 2015). Grassroots analyses explained how the treaty gave a green light to commercial logging, fraudulent offsets, genetically modified organism monocultures, large-scale animal agriculture, hydroelectric dams and nuclear power (Reid Ross 2015). For example, La Via Campesina (2018), a global network of small farmers, observed that the agreement 'further commodifies Mother Earth and dispossesses peasants and indigenous people'. Despite such glaring inadequacies, the Sierra Club celebrated the Paris Agreement as a 'turning point for humanity' and praised 'President Obama's leadership'. The Left-leaning Avaaz.org exclaimed, 'World leaders at the UN climate talks have just set a landmark goal that can save everything we love!' 350.org cheered, 'Today is a historic day' at the passage of 'a deal that sends a signal that it's time to keep fossil fuels in the ground' (Sierra Club 2015; Adler 2015; 350.org 2015). Among the U.S. Left, bureaucracy and delusion won over creativity and realism.

Latin America's Pink Tide governments, despite their 'green' and 'ecosocialist' rhetoric, are not much more committed to systemic transformation than the U.S. Left is. Evo Morales's regime in Bolivia has claimed green credentials based on its role in convening the Cochabamba climate summit. Nonetheless, the administration has brought natural gas extraction levels to 'unprecedented heights' (Webber 2017). It also shifted the country's agricultural sector away from small farming by subsidizing larger and more destructive industrial farms (Tilzey 2017). In 2015, Morales implausibly assured reporters that a planned $300 million nuclear reactor 'poses no risk to humans or to mother Earth' (AFP 2015). While Venezuela's president Hugo Chávez (1999–2013) claimed his regime had embraced an ecologically oriented '21st century socialism', Maria Pilar Garcia Guadilla (2010), in an Anarchist journal in Venezuela, exposed this green rhetoric as grounded in 'myth' and pointed to government plans for increased coal and oil extraction and mega-damming. Although Chávez and his successor Nicholás Maduro promised to diversify the country's oil extraction-based economy, the promises remained empty. OPEC (2018) reported, 'Venezuela's oil revenues account for about 95 per cent of export earnings. The oil and gas sector is around 25 per cent of gross domestic product'.

Ecuador's government recognized the 'rights of nature' in its 2008 constitution and in the following year promoted a National Plan for Buen Vivir, adopting the language of grassroots indigenous and environmental campaigners. Despite the rhetoric, the government followed an extractivist model and opened its Yasuní National Park to oil, gold and copper extraction megaprojects owned by transnational corporations, endangering lives and homes of the park's indigenous residents. Ecuadorian philosopher David Cortez observed that the government's rhetorical commitment to buen vivir has become simply '"a tool to legitimize policies of aggressive *extractivismo*' (Sacher and Báez 2017).

Brazil's Pink Tide government, despite committing to 'zero illegal deforestation' by 2030, allowed deforestation at rates expected to drive most Amazonian tree species extinct by mid-century. Moreover, the government encouraged the construction of hundreds of dams that adversely impacted indigenous peoples, farmers and ecosystems (Akemi and Sethness Castro 2018). Brazil's pledges in the Paris Agreement have been ranked 'insufficient' for keeping global temperatures below 2° (Climate Action Tracker 2018).

Mexico's Lopez Obrador went through a performance of asking Mother Earth for permission to build a destructive railway megaproject through the territories of indigenous people including the Zapatistas. Subcomandante Moisés, a Zapatista spokesperson, responded, 'We don't buy it. Mother Earth doesn't speak, but if she did, she'd say clearly, *No! Go fuck yourself*' (Baschet 2019).

There sometimes seem to be few limits to the official Left's engagement with destroying life. In 1995, the Wildlife Society's millionaire president Jon Rousch sold $150,000 worth of timber from sensitive lands on his own ranch to Plum Creek Timber Company (St. Clair 2010). The Nature Conservancy allowed natural gas drilling on its Texas bird sanctuary in 1999 and drilled an oil well there in 2007 that still operated as of 2014. The Sierra Club accepted millions from the fracking industry from 2007 to 2010 and has continued to take funds from fracking investor Michael Bloomberg (Klein 2014). Conservation Northwest endorsed Washington state's 2017 plan to kill wolves deemed a threat to ranchers' cattle. The group offered the meek excuse, 'While heart-rending it is our hope that this action . . . will cease further livestock depredations and prevent the need for additional lethal actions' (Mapes 2017). The Marxist *Jacobin Magazine* has run articles supporting geoengineering and nuclear power (Angus 2017). Environmental groups have even tacitly supported mass-murderous and ecologically disastrous wars. The Sierra Club forbade chapters from opposing the 2003 U.S. invasion of Iraq (Bustillo 2002). The campaign website of the Green Party's 2016 presidential candidate Jill Stein called on the United States and Russia to 'restore all of Syria to control' by Bashar al-Assad's regime massacring its population. Stein also picked an openly pro-Assad running mate (Weinberg 2016).

TOWARDS BIOPHILOUS REVOLUTION

In contrast to necrophilia, Fromm coined 'biophilia' to describe the life-loving orientation that ordinarily develops in free, healthy societies. Biophilia encompasses not only a love of humanity but also of all 'living beings'. Certain passages in his work even suggested that biophilia (one could more precisely say ecophilia) extends to entire ecosystems including their non-living structures. For example, Fromm (1960) mentioned the possibility of relating 'creatively, actively' to mountains and rivers and seeing them as intrinsically valuable. Crucially, he argued that love of life involves an *active* practice: 'If a woman told us that she loved flowers, and we saw that she forgot to water them, we would not believe in her "love" for flowers' (1956).

Biophilous responses to ecological breakdown would be guided by the 'biophilous conscience', 'motivated by its attraction to life and joy' (Fromm 1963). Biophilous resistance would involve, I contend, a diversity of tactics grounded in a situational assessment of what is effective and ethical rather than rigid criteria, such as what is legal, what is the 'most militant', or what is pacifist. Regarding the last of these dogmas, Fromm (1964) spoke highly of non-violent actions and opposed unnecessary and adventuristic violence, but he also rejected strict pacifism since 'violence in defense of life is of a different nature than violence which aims at destructiveness'. Biophilious responses would aim at social transformation, laying the groundwork of a life-loving society. Practitioners would 'try to achieve a new style of life' through projects, such as 'local councils', 'purposeful agricultural communities' and 'community living in cities' (Fromm 1968). They would seek to overcome what Fromm (1961) called 'alienation from oneself, one's fellow [hu]man and from nature'.

Necrophilia is not inescapable, and Fromm therefore held out active hope – neither optimism nor pessimism – for the working class to engage in anarchistic revolution. This hope 'is impatient and active, looking for every possibility of action within the realm of real possibilities' (Fromm 1973). Revolution for Fromm (1968) entailed neither 'tired reformism' nor 'pseudo-radical adventurism', and it can be inferred that revolution today would occur autonomously from the Left's dominant strains. His hope sprang from a view that living beings inherently engage in a project of (often-collective) self-preservation: 'And yet it would not be wrong to say the tree hopes for sunlight and expresses this hope by twisting its trunk toward the sun. Is it different with the child that is born?'

Confirming Fromm's hypothesis, non-human beings regularly find ways to preserve life and resist domination, dispossession and destruction (Hribal 2010). These resisters are often wild animals, such as the young gorillas who cooperate to dismantle hunters' traps in Rwanda (Diskin 2018), or the deer that entered an Indianapolis computer store, smashing commodities and using antlers to fling away a police officer (Tulhoy 2017). Even captive cows routinely flee slaughter and exploitation, with one recently joining a herd of wild bison and learning to survive in Poland's Bialowieza Forest (News from Elsewhere 2018). Another cow escaped with its calf from a Texas farm, and the two travelled to an animal sanctuary, according to reports: 'She swam across a pond with her baby, ran through a forest for hours, until she ended up jumping our very high fence and getting into our pasture' (Schweig 2018). Raoul Vaneigem (1998) observed that nature sometimes 'refuses to produce' for capitalist ends and instead delivers 'sudden jolts that threaten the edifice' of the social system. Given chances to heal, damaged ecosystems regenerate vibrant, diverse networks of life after suffering intensive domestication or even nuclear power meltdowns (Tree 2018; Barras 2016).

Outside the official Left, humans globally have also been refusing to engage in the daily process of reproducing death-desiring capitalist society. This chapter has supplied some examples including grassroots proponents of buen vivir and Environmental Justice, members of ecological communes and so-called eco-terrorists. People find countless ways to replace life-numbing work and consumption with life-affirming activities: they might call in sick to go bird-watching, sneak hours away at the office to read Ursula Le Guin stories, form a choir with friends, grow their own food in a garden, or squat a vacant house. Holloway (2010) speculates, 'There is nothing special about being an anti-capitalist revolutionary. This is the story of many, many people, of millions, perhaps billions'. Keven Van Meter (2017) claims such everyday resistance comprises a 'factor of revolution', challenging capital accumulation while also laying groundwork for more overt, coordinated and sustained struggle. Within Anarchist and anti-authoritarian movements, Nick Montgomery and carla bergman's (2017) call for 'joyful militancy' offers a biophilous attempt at overcoming the often rigid and joyless cultures surrounding activism. More organizing will be needed to make systemic transformation possible and to build resilient, biophilous communities capable of collectively surviving state repression and adequately combating corporate propaganda. The good news is that biophilia, when cultivated and maintained, spreads to other people with ease. Fromm (1963) noted, 'Love of life is just as contagious as love of death'.

REFERENCES

18th Mesa. 2010. "Mesa 18 Declaration (English & Spanish)." http://cochabamba2010.typ epad.com/blog/2010/05/mesa-18-declaration-english-spanish.html.

350.org. 2015. "The Paris Agreement, and What the Future Holds." December 12, 2015. https://350.org/the-paris-agreement-and-what-the-future-holds/.

ACME Collective. 1999. "Peasant Revolt! N30 Black Bloc Communique by ACME Collective (A Communique from One Section of the Black Bloc: N30 in Seattle)." In 2010. *The Black Bloc Papers*. Edited by Xavier Massot and David Van Deusen. Kansas: Breaking Glass Press. https://libcom.org/library/black-bloc-papers.

Acosta, Alberto. 2013. "Extractivism and Neoextractivism: Two Sides of the Same Curse." In Permanent Working Group on Alternatives to Development. *Beyond Development: Alternative Visions From Latin America*. Edited by M. Lang and D. Mokrani. Amsterdam: Transnational Institute.

Adler, Ben. 2015. "Green Groups Are Deeply Divided on Whether the Paris Agreement Is a Win or Loss." *Grist*. December 14, 2015. https://grist.org/climate-energy/green-groups -are-deeply-divided-on-whether-the-paris-agreement-is-a-win-or-loss/.

AFP. 2015. "Bolivia Plans to Build $300m Nuclear Complex with Research Reactor." *The Guardian*. October 29, 2015. https://www.theguardian.com/world/2015/oct/29/bolivia-n uclear-complex-reactor-russia-environment.

Akemi, Romina and Javier Sethness Castro. 2018. "Introduction: Anarchism in Latin America." In Cappelletti, Ángel. *Anarchism in Latin America*. Translated by Gabriel Palmer-Fernández. Oakland: AK Press.

Angus, Ian. 2017. "Memo to Jacobin: Ecomodernism Is Not Ecosocialism." *Climate & Capitalism*. September 25, 2017. http://climateandcapitalism.com/2017/09/25/memo-to-jaco bin-ecomodernism-is-not-ecosocialism/.

Anonymous. 2017. *Dispatches from Standing Rock: Against the Dakota Access Pipeline & its World*. 2017. https://itsgoingdown.org/wp-content/uploads/2017/02/dispatches_from_st anding_rock_print.pdf.

Anti-Defamation League. 2004. "Ecoterrorism: Extremism in the Animal Rights and Environmentalist Movements." https://web.archive.org/web/20041129153921/http://www.adl .org/learn/ext_us/Ecoterrorism_print.asp.

Barras, Colin. 2016. "The Chernobyl Exclusion Zone Is Arguably a Nature Reserve." *BBC*. April 22, 2016. http://www.bbc.com/earth/story/20160421-the-chernobyl-exclusion-zone -is-arguably-a-nature-reserve.

Baschet, Jérôme. 2019. "Zapatistas Take on President AMLO at 25th Anniversary." *ROAR*. Feburary 26, 2019.

Bookchin, Murray. 1964. "Ecology and Revolutionary Thought." *The Anarchist Library*. https://theanarchistlibrary.org/library/lewis-herber-murray-bookchin-ecology-and-revo lutionary-thought.

Building Bridges Collective. 2010. *Space for Movement? Reflections from Bolivia on Climate Justice, Social Movements and the State*. Leeds: Footprint Workers Co-op. https://spacefo rmovement.files.wordpress.com/2010/08/space_for_movement2.pdf.

Bustillo, Miguel. 2002. "Sierra Club Rift Opens Over Stance on Iraq." *Los Angeles Times*. December 3, 2002. http://articles.latimes.com/2002/dec/03/nation/na-sierra3.

Carson, Kevin. 2018. *Libertarian Municipalism: Networked Cities as Resilient Platforms for Post-Capitalist Transition*. Center for a Stateless Society. https://c4ss.org/content/ 50407.

Center for Biological Diversity. 2010. "Analysis of Key Provisions of the American Power Act of 2010 (APA)." May 13, 2010. https://www.biologicaldiversity.org/programs/climate_law _institute/legislating_for_a_new_climate/pdfs/Bill_Analysis_6-22-2010.pdf.

Climate Action Tracker. 2018. April 30, 2018. https://climateactiontracker.org/.

Churchill, Ward. 2012. *Pacifism as Pathology*. Internet Archive. https://ia600604.us.archive.or g/28/items/PathologyOfPacifism/pap_imposed.pdf.

Churchill, Ward and Vander Wall. 1990. *Agents of Repression: The FBI's Secret Wars Against the Black Panther Party and the American Indian Movement*. Boston: South End Press.

Cregan, Fionuala. 2015. "Rising Tensions in Bolivia over Oil and Gas Exploitation on Indig- enous Lands." *Intercontinental Cry*. August 31, 2015. https://intercontinentalcry.org/rising -tensions-in-bolivia-over-oil-and-gas-exploitation-on-indigenous-lands/.

DeLuca, Kevin Michael and Jennifer Peeples. 2002. "From Public Sphere to Public Screen: Democracy, Activism, and the 'Violence' of Seattle." *Critical Studies in Media Communica- tion* 19, no. 2: 125–151.

Diskin, Eben. 2018. "Young Gorillas Are Working Together to Destroy Poachers' Traps in Rwanda." *Matador*. June 5, 2018. https://matadornetwork.com/read/young-gorillas-wor king-together-destroy-poachers-traps-rwanda/.

Dupuis-Déri, Francis. 2014. *Who's Afraid of the Black Blocs?: Anarchy in Action around the World*. Translated by Lazer Lederhendler. Oakland: PM Press.

Earth First! Journal. 2014. "A Decade of Earth First! Action in the 'Climate Movement'." *Earth First! Newswire*. January 19, 2014. https://earthfirstjournal.org/newswire/2014/01 /19/a-decade-of-earth-first-action-in-the-climate-movement/.

Earth Liberation Front. 1997. "Beltane." In *Igniting a Revolution: Voices in Defense of the Earth*. Edited by Steven Best and Anthony J. Nocella, II. Oakland: AK Press, 2006.

Ebus, Bram. 2018. "Venezuela's Mining Arc Boom Sweeps up Indigenous People and Cultures." *Mongabay*. https://news.mongabay.com/2018/01/venezuelas-mining-arc-boom -sweeps-up-indigenous-people-and-cultures/.

Energy Justice Network. 2018. "Solutions." Accessed May 1, 2018, http://www.energyjustice .net/solutions.

Esteva, Gustavo, Salvatore Babones, and Philipp Babcicky. 2013. *The Future of Development: A Radical Manifesto*. Chicago: University of Chicago Press.

Fischer, Dan. 2017. "Answering Annihilation: Some Notes on Earth's Execution." *It's Going Down.* July 17, 2017. https://itsgoingdown.org/answering-annihilation-notes-earths-exec ution/.

Ford, Matt. 2014. "Re-contextualizing Anti-Extractivism: Buen Vivir and the New Left in the Andes." *Climate & Capitalism.* June 1, 2014. http://climateandcapitalism.com/wp-content /uploads/sites/2/2014/06/Ford-Recontextualizing-Anti-Extractivism.pdf.

Fromm, Erich. 1941. *Escape from Freedom.* New York: Holt, Rinehart and Winston.

———. 1947. *Man for Himself: An Inquiry into the Psychology of Ethics.* New York: Henry Holt and Company.

———. 1956. *The Art of Loving.* New York: Harper & Row.

———. 1960. "Psychoanalysis and Zen Buddhism." In Suzuki, D.T. and Erich Fromm. *Zen Buddhism and Psychoanalysis.* London: Ruskin House.

———. 1961. *Marx's Concept of Man.* New York: Frederick Ungar Publishing. https://www .marxists.org/archive/fromm/works/1961/man/ch05.htm.

———. 1963. *War Within Man: A Psychological Enquiry into the Roots of Destructiveness.* Philadelphia: American Friends Service Committee.

———. 1964. *The Heart of Man: Its Genius for Good and Evil.* New York: Harper & Row.

———. 1968. *The Revolution of Hope: Toward a Humanized Technology.* New York: Harper & Row.

———. 1973. *The Anatomy of Human Destructiveness.* New York: Henry, Holt and Company.

———. 1976. *To Have or To Be?* New York: Harper & Row.

Garcia Guadilla, Maria Pilar. 2010. "Venezuela: The Myth of 'Eco-socialism of the XXI Century'." Translated by Julio Pacheco. *El Libertario.* https://www.nodo50.org/ellibertario /english/mithecosocialism-ingles.txt.

Gelderloos, Peter. 2010. "How Nonviolence Protects the State." Interview by the Stimulator. *SubMedia.* Video, 9:44. https://sub.media/video/non-violence-protects-state/.

General Executive Board of the Industrial Workers of the World. 2008. "Direct Action Empowers Workers to Get the Goods." *Industrial Worker.* https://www.iww.org/PDF/I ndustrialWorker/IWMay08.pdf.

Global Witness. 2017. *Defenders of the Earth: Global Killings of Land and Environmental Defenders in 2016.* July 13, 2017. https://www.globalwitness.org/en/campaigns/environ mental-activists/defenders-earth/.

Goodman, Amy. 2016. "Video: Dakota Access Pipeline Company Attacks Native American Protesters with Dogs and Pepper Spray." *Democracy Now!* September 4, 2016. https://ww w.democracynow.org/2016/9/4/dakota_access_pipeline_company_attacks_native.

Green, Frank. 1989. "Their Motto: 'No Compromise in Defense of Mother Earth.'; Wilder- ness Guerrillas." *San Diego Union-Tribune.* January 14, 1989.

Hand, Mark. 2018. "Pipeline Exec Says Whoever Vandalized Dakota Access Pipeline Should Be 'Removed from the Gene Pool'." *ThinkProgress.* March 8, 2018. https://thinkprogress .org/pipeline-execs-discuss-opposition-c1d029836d9b/.

Hansen, James. 2009. "Cap and Fade." *New York Times.* December 6, 2009. https://www.nyt imes.com/2009/12/07/opinion/07hansen.html.

———. 2018. "Climate Change in a Nutshell: The Gathering Storm." December 18, 2018, http://www.columbia.edu/~jeh1/mailings/2018/20181206_Nutshell.pdf/.

Hardt, Michael and Antonio Negri. 2000. *Empire.* Cambridge: Harvard University Press.

Holloway, John. 2010. *Crack Capitalism.* London: Pluto Press.

Hribal, Jason. 2010. *Fear of the Animal Planet: The Hidden History of Animal Resistance.* Petrolia: Counterpunch.

Hughes, Morgen and Steve Ongerth. 2014. "Towards an Ecological General Strike—Days of Direct Action in Bay Area, CA." *Earth First! Newswire.* April 7, 2014. https://earthfirstjo urnal.org/newswire/2014/04/07/towards-an-ecological-general-strike-days-of-direct-action -in-bay-area-ca/.

Human Rights Watch. 2018. *Amazonians on Trial: Judicial Harassment of Indigenous Leaders and Environmentalists in Ecuador.* March 2018. https://www.hrw.org/report/2018/03/26/ amazonians-trial/judicial-harassment-indigenous-leaders-and-environmentalists.

Klein, Naomi. 2014. *This Changes Everything: Capitalism vs. the Climate.* New York: Simon & Schuster.

Krupp, Fred. 2009. "House Passes Most Important Environmental and Energy Legislation in U.S. History." *Environmental Defense Fund.* June 26, 2009. http://blogs.edf.org/climate41 1/2009/06/26/house-passes-most-important-environmental-and-energy-legislation-in-us-h lstory/.

La Via Campesina. 2018. "La Via Campesina in Action for Climate Justice." In *Radical Realism for Climate Justice.* Edited by Heinrich Böll Foundation. https://www.boell.de/sites/def ault/files/radical_realism_for_climate_justice_volume_44_6_1.pdf?dimension1=ds_radica lrealism.

Mapes, Lynda. 2017. "Washington State to Kill More Wolves to Protect Livestock." *The Seattle Times.* July 20, 2017. https://www.seattletimes.com/seattle-news/environment/w ashington-state-to-kill-more-wolves-to-protect-livestock/.

Miller, Michael. 2015. "Why are Brazil's Environmentalists Being Murdered?" *Washington Post.* August 27, 2015. https://www.washingtonpost.com/news/morning-mix/wp/2015/08 /27/why-are-brazils-environmentalists-being-murdered/?utm_term=.de764f4483fb.

Milman, Oliver. 2015. "James Hansen, Father of Climate Change Awareness, Calls Paris Talks 'a Fraud'." *The Guardian.* December 12, 2015. https://www.theguardian.com/en vironment/2015/dec/12/james-hansen-climate-change-paris-talks-fraud.

Montgomery, Nick and Carla Bergman. 2017. *Joyful Militancy: Building Thriving Resistance in Toxic Times.* Oakland: AK Press.

News from Elsewhere. 2018. "Cow Walks on Wild Side with Polish Bison." *BBC.* January 24, 2018. http://www.bbc.com/news/blogs-news-from-elsewhere-42803471.

North American Earth Liberation Front Press Office. 2007. "ELF FAQs." In Pickering, Leslie James, *Earth Liberation Front 1997-2002.* Portland: Arissa.

Oko, Dan. 2002. "Ecoterrororists Under Fire." *Mother Jones.* February 8, 2002, http://www .motherjones.com/politics/2002/02/ecoterrororists-under-fire/.

Ongerth, Steve. 2014. *Redwood Uprising: The Story of Judi Bari and Earth First!-IWW Local #1.* https://www.judibari.info/book/37.

OPEC. 2018. "Venezuela." Accessed April 29, 2018. http://www.opec.org/opec_web/en/abo ut_us/171.htm.

Oxalis. 2014. "Two Steps Back." *Anarchist Library.* May 1, 2014. https://theanarchistlibrary .org/library/oxalis-two-steps-back-black-seed-issue-one.

Parry, Sam. 2009. "Why This Is the Pivotal Climate Vote of Our Lives." *Environmental Defense Fund.* June 25, 2009. http://blogs.edf.org/climate411/2009/06/25/why-this-is-the -pivotal-climate-vote-of-our-lives/.

Pellow, David Naguib. 2014. *Total Liberation: The Power and Promise of Animal Rights and the Radical Earth Movement.* Minneapolis: University of Minnesota Press.

Peralta M., Pablo. 2014. "Bolivia's Conamaq Indigenous Movement: 'We Will Not Sell Ourselves to Any Government or Political Party.'" Translated by Benjamin Dangl. *Upside Down World*. May 26, 2014. http://upsidedownworld.org/archives/bolivia/bolivias-co namaq-indigenous-movement-we-will-not-sell-ourselves-to-any-government-or-political-p arty/.

People of Color Environmental Leadership Summit. 1991. "Principles of Environmental Justice." https://www.ejnet.org/ej/principles.pdf.

Petroski, William. 2017. "Dakota Access Protesters Claim Responsibility for Pipeline Sabotage." *The Des Moines Register*. July 24, 2017. http://www.desmoinesregister.com/story/news /2017/07/24/dakota-access-protesters-claim-responsibility-pipeline-sabotage/504136001/.

Phipps, Claire, Adam Vaughan, and Oliver Milman. 2015. "Global Climate March 2015: Hundreds of Thousands March Around the World—As It Happened." *The Guardian*. November 29, 2015, https://www.theguardian.com/environment/live/2015/nov/29/global -peoples-climate-change-march-2015-day-of-action-live.

Pinto, Ñaní. 2019. "Militarization Increases in Zapatista and Campesino Territories in Chiapas." *Avispa Midia*. May 7, 2019, https://avispa.org/militarization-increases-in-zapatista -and-campesino-territories-in-chiapas/.

Pope, Carl. 2001. "Sierra Club Denounces ELF's Ecoterrorists." *Wall Street Journal*. November 29, 2001. https://www.wsj.com/articles/SB1006990341185533000.

Potter, Will. 2011. *Green is the New Red: An Insider's Account of a Social Movement Under Fire*. San Francisco: City Lights Books

———. "The Green Scare." *Vermont Law Review* 33, no. 67 (2008). http://lawreview.ver montlaw.edu/wp-content/uploads/2012/02/15-Potter-Book-4-Vol-33.pdf.

Raval, Amee. 2018. "Weathering the Storm: Building Community Resilience in Environmental Justice Communities." *UCS Science Network*. May 30, 2018. https://blog.ucsusa. org/science-blogger/weathering-the-storm-building-community-resilience-in-environment al-justice-communities.

Raymond, Lorenzo. 2015. "What the Climate Movement Can Learn from Black Lives Matter." September 7, 2015. *Earth First! Newswire*. https://earthfirstjournal.org/newswire/2015 /09/07/what-the-climate-movement-can-learn-from-black-lives-matter/.

Reid Ross, Alexander. 2015. "Grey not Green: Technocratic Climate Agreement and Police State Terror." *Earth First! Newswire*. December 13, 2015. https://earthfirstjournal.org/ newswire/2015/12/13/grey-not-green-technocratic-climate-agreement-and-police-state-te rror/.

Rising Tide North America. "Our Principles." Accessed April 28, 2018. https://risingtideno rthamerica.org/features/principles/.

Rodriguez, Belinda and Ben Case. 2015. "Why Big NGOs Won't Lead the Fight on Climate Change." *Roar*. December 6, 2015, https://roarmag.org/essays/paris-ngo-cop21-climate -march/.

Rosebraugh, Craig. 2004. *Burning Rage of a Dying Planet: Speaking for the Earth Liberation Front*. New York: Lantern Books.

Rowell, Andrew. 1996. *Green Backlash: Global Subversion of the Environmental Movement*. London: Routledge.

Sacher, William and Michelle Báez. 2017. "Extractivism vs. Buen Vivir in Ecuador." *Global Dialogue* 7, no. 4 (December). http://globaldialogue.isa-sociology.org/extractivism-vs-buen -vivir-in-ecuador/.

Schneider, Nathan. 2014. "Who Stole the Four-Hour Workday?" *Vice*. December 30, 2014. https://www.vice.com/en_us/article/yvqqxw/who-stole-the-four-hour-workday-0000406 -v21n8.

Schuster, Henry. 2005. "Domestic Terror: Who's Most Dangerous?" *CNN*, August 24, 2005. http://www.cnn.com/2005/US/08/24/schuster.column/.

Schweig, Sarah V. 2018. "Cow and Her Baby Break Free and Run Away to Animal Sanctuary." *The Dodo*. 11 April 2018. https://www.thedodo.com/on-the-farm/wild-cow-escapes -with-baby.

Sethness Castro, Javier. 2012. *Imperiled Life: Revolution Against Climate Catastrophe*. Oakland: AK Press.

Sierra Club. 2009. "Clean Energy Jobs Plan Clears House in Historic Vote." June 26, 2008. http://action.sierraclub.org/site/MessageViewer?em_id=116923.0.

———. 2015. "Sierra Club on the Paris Climate Agreement: 'A Turning Point for Humanity.'" December 12, 2015. https://content.sierraclub.org/press-releases/2015/12/sierra-club -paris-climate-agreement-turning-point-humanity.

Solomon, Norman. 2017. "AFL-CIO To Planet Earth: Drop Dead." *Huffington Post*. September 19, 2017. https://www.huffingtonpost.com/norman-solomon/afl-cio-to-planet-e arth-d_b_12080618.html.

Southern Poverty Law Center. 2001. "Left Wing Earth Liberation Front Advocates Extremist Agenda." May 8, 2001. https://www.splcenter.org/fighting-hate/intelligence-report/2001/ left-wing-earth-liberation-front-advocates-extremist-agenda.

St. Clair, Jeffrey. 2010. "How Green Became the Color of Money." *Counterpunch*. December 31, 2010. https://www.counterpunch.org/2010/12/31/how-green-became-the-color-of- money-2/.

———. 2011. "How Green Became the Color of Money." *Counterpunch*. January 7, 2011. https://www.counterpunch.org/2011/01/07/how-green-became-the-color-of-money/.

St. Clair, Jeffrey and Joshua Frank. 2015. "Dave Foreman and the First Green Scare Case." *Counterpunch*. November 20, 2015.

Strona, Giovanni and Corey J.A. Bradshaw. 2018. "Co-extinctions Annihilate Planetary Life During Extreme Environmental Change." *Scientific Reports* 8. https://www.nature.com/ar ticles/s41598-018-35068-1.

Survival International. 2015. "Venezuelan Tribes Protest Against Violent Mining Gangs." *Earth First! Newswire*. June 18, 2015. http://earthfirstjournal.org/newswire/2015/06/18/v enezuelan-tribes-protest-against-violent-mining-gangs/.

Telesur. 2019. "Zapatistas Warn Mexico: 'We Won't Back AMLO Projects'." *Telesur*. January 1, 2019, https://www.telesurenglish.net/news/Zapatistas-Warn-Mexico-We-Wont-Bac k-AMLO-Projects-20190101-0025.html.

Thrush, Glenn. 2009. "LCV: No Endorsement for Climate Bill Foes." *Politico*. May 23, 2009. https://www.politico.com/blogs/on-congress/2009/06/lcv-no-endorsement-for-climate-bil l-foes-019306.

Tilzey, Mark. 2017. "Neo-extractivism, Populism, and the Agrarian Question in Bolivia and Ecuador." Paper presented at the 5th International Conference of the BRICS Initiative for Critical Agrarian Studies, Moscow, Russia, October 2017. https://www.tni.org/ en/publication/neo-extractivism-populism-and-the-agrarian-question-in-bolivia-and-ecu ador.

Tolme, Paul. 2001. "Terrorizing the Environmental Movement." *Slate*. November 26, 2001, https://www.salon.com/2001/11/26/ecoterror/.

Tree, Isabella. 2018. "Back to the Wild!" *Daily Mail*, April 20, 2018. http://www.dailymail.co .uk/news/article-5640191/How-letting-Mother-Nature-reclaim-prime-farmland-produced -breathtaking-results.html.

Tuhoy, John. 2017. "Indiana: Deer Smashes Up Computer Store, Flings Cop with Antlers." *Earth First! Newswire*. October 10, 2017. http://earthfirstjournal.org/newswire/2017/10/30 /indiana-deer-smashes-up-computer-store-flings-cop-with-antlers/.

Van Deusen, David. 2010. "The Emergence of the Black Bloc and the Movement Towards Anarchism." In *The Black Bloc Papers*.

Vaneigem, Raoul. 1998. *The Movement of the Free Spirit*. Translated by Randall Cherry and Ian Patterson. New York: Zone Books.

Van Meter, Kevin. 2017. *Guerrillas of Desire: Notes on Everyday Resistance and Organizing to Make a Revolution Possible*. Oakland: AK Press.

Watts, Jonathan. 2018. "Almost Four Environmental Defenders a Week Killed in 2017." *The Guardian*. February 2, 2018. https://www.theguardian.com/environment/2018/feb/02/ almost-four-environmental-defenders-a-week-killed-in-2017.

Webber, Jeffery R. 2017. *The Last Day of Oppression, and the First Day of the Same: The Politics and Economics of the New Latin American Left*. Chicago: Haymarket.

Weinberg, Bill. 2016. "Jill Stein's Assad-shilling Saved from Memory Hole... Again." *Countervortex*. October 24, 2016. https://countervortex.org/node/14955.

Wrong Kind of Green. 2016. "Non-violence Training Teaches White Paternalism at Camp Standing Rock." *Warrior Publications* September 18, 2016. https://warriorpublications.wo rdpress.com/2016/09/18/non-violence-training-teaches-white-paternalism-at-camp-standi ng-rock/.

Yates, Jon. 2003. "2 Strategies, Same Goal in Activism for Animals." *Chicago Tribune*. February 16, 2003. http://articles.chicagotribune.com/2003-02-16/news/0302160225_1_alf-vil la-park-brakes.

Zibechi, Raúl. 2015. "Extractivism Creates a Society without Subjects: Raúl Zibechi on Latin American Social Movements." *Upside Down World*. July 20, 2015. http://upsidedownwor ld.org/archives/international/extractivism-creates-a-society-without-subjects-raul-zibechi -on-latin-american-social-movements/.

10

Are the State and Public Institutions Compatible with De-growth?

An Anarchist Perspective

Francisco J. Toro

> *The light which puts out our eyes is darkness to us*
>
> – Henry David Thoreau, *Walden*

THE MATTER OF THE STATE: AN OBLIGATORY CHALLENGE FOR DE-GROWTH

Double Standards around the State and Environmental Management

Over the last forty years, the management of environmental and development issues have undoubtedly been marked by the irruption and ecumenical spread of the sustainability paradigm throughout the political commitments and environmental policies. The role that the State and public institutions have played in this scenario is determinant, but may be characterized as a worrying ambivalence. On the one hand, capitalist states have operated as a determinant executive branch of the neo-liberal system, yielding to the influencing decisions of global multinational corporations and financial institutions. Such participation and involvement into the neo-liberal game is both active and passive. In fact, governments and public organizations have usually been a mere marionette in this game, and they have not reconsidered the axiom of economic growth, designing policies of development as usual.[1] On the other hand, governments have introduced significant reforms in the management of environmental issues, responding to an assumed responsibility in a wide and multi-scalar range of commitments and agreements. In the developed countries, as a part of the so-called 'Welfare State', the care and conservation of a healthy environment is a central tenet, and public institutions are behind the protection of wild and fragile habitats, the implementation and stimulation of the production of renewable energies or the fashionable emphasis on 'sustainable' and non-motorized alternatives of transport within the cities.

Substantially, this binary and ambiguous position of the State is, in fact, quite representative of its current political status in order to respond to a 'double predicament' (Bauman & Bordoni, 2014): the electorate, and its capacity to allow and depose national governments, and the global forces, with the capacity to abort or encourage political decisions according to their pecuniary interests. It makes it quite difficult to assert whether the feedback of relationship between the State and environmental management has offered positive and effective outcomes. One of the most controversial points is if these progresses towards sustainable practices are really successful when they are driven by technocratic and governmental-centralized procedures. Albeit all international conferences and meetings since Rio 92 insist on the role and involvement of citizenship as a crucial part of the environmental agendas, this implication has broadly been marginal and testimonial.[2] As an example, many NGOs and especially left-wing movements have been organizing alternative forums and meetings in order to give voice to communities which are not represented by the political leadership. This disappointed environmentalist activism also denounces that the State, the economic institutions and big corporations are members of a partnership driven to ensure their status of power and hierarchical system of decision-making, in which the latter have the last word. Therefore, it would be an extremely risky and worrying future scenario if the steps ahead of a sustainable transition ultimately depended from those institutions and agents which do not cease to degrade the environment and enlarge the socioeconomic drift amongst regions and societies, by favouring processes of concentration of capital and power.

Certainly, the emergence of de-growth is a logic reaction to the incompetence and counter-productiveness of the State and power institutions in the environmental arena, which do not challenge the orthodoxy of the market and the hegemonic economic paradigm. The public institutions have been inoculating and inculcating a style of environmental management to the population by means of widely legitimated regulative and interventionist tools (education, legislation, tax policies, subsidies, etc.), in which the quota of participation by the citizenry is at most testimonial. In other words, public institutions are determinant agents for colonizing the social imaginary with neo-liberal and capitalist values. According to anarchists, 'the purpose of the State is not only to stabilize and facilitate capitalism . . . capital and state developed in tandem as a mutually-reinforcing system of societal organization' (Ince & Barrera de la Torre 2016).

De-growth within a Statist Society? An Undefined Position

De-growth, implicitly, is aiming to undress the mythology of growth and neo-liberal praxis fully installed in the governmental and normative framework of capitalist states. A non-traumatic future of scarcity of resources and successful adaptive patterns to climate change effects will demand skilled and participatory forms of policy-making and implementing cross-scale political strategies. Thereby, at the core of de-growth is guaranteeing a set of political requirements to be implemented by means of a voluntary transition in fields, such as consumption, work and system of values (Latouche 2009, Kallis et al. 2015, Trainer 2015). In a nutshell, de-growth partisans are convinced that a monitored and guided de-growth has to be based on bottom-up strategies rather than top-down practices which have characterized the policies for sustainability by both capitalist and socialist regimes, usually following the dictation of transnational corporations and financial lobbies.

Despite the State being a key issue in any reflection on how de-growth should be conceived and embodied, it has received little and rare attention in the academic world. The analyses have been focused in the critique against the economy and techno-science rather than politics and State (Ariès 2015). Serge Latouche, the forerunner of the recent spread of de-growth ideas in France, expresses this non-defined position, emphasizing that de-growth is first and foremost a slogan, and there are not 'ready-made political solutions' (Latouche 2009). This is, on the one hand, reasonable insofar as he intentionally wants to dissociate it from the hegemonic model of development, which have been monolithically applied, without taking into account specific context and realities. For him, de-growth is not a real alternative to economic growth, as it does not pretend universal recipes but the advocacy of diverse forms of implementation. De-growth, in this sense, reinforces the power of local against the globalizing driving forces of the neo-liberal system. On the other hand, there is not a concrete project of how this transition to de-growth would be, and the role of the State and public institutions within it.

Probably, a latent confidence by the majority of de-growth thinkers exists in the possibilities of the State to regulate softly the de-growth transition, insofar as it organizes the democratic structure of modern societies. For instance, Asara et al. (2015: 378) think that 'the role of the state is hence deemed crucial to facilitate the degrowth transformation through the implementation of "non-reformist reforms"'. In fact, the State will be necessary because of its capacity of governing from its upper position over the lay society, as Kallis (2015) asserts: 'A certain degree of hierarchy is unavoidable because the redistribution of burdens and resources among more and less privileged localities will require intermediation and decision-making at broad geographic levels. Some of the degrowth reforms . . . are, in fact, quite interventionist and would require strong state action'.

Decolonizing De-growth from the State

Such arguments around the role of State by 'degrowthers' seem ambiguous and need to be discussed through a deep examination of the ideological roots of the current economic system. The machinery of the market and some fetish concepts of modernity, such as growth, development and progress, have been crucial in the configuration and legitimation of democratic system (Deriu 2012). In fact, the own ideas of economic system and democratic system share the same source of inspiration in the

Western tradition: society as a corpuscle of individuals who seek for own political and economic interests, optimized by suffrage or market, respectively (Naredo 2006). Economic liberalism was in its irruption a call for individual rights (such as private property) and an opposition to a repressing and monolithic State. Therefore, 'the emancipatory role played by free economic initiative in the construction of political democracy cannot be denied' (Deriu 2012: 554). During the twentieth century, the birth and consolidation of welfare state in capitalist countries, synonym of a more prosperous, fair and democratic society, was articulated through the application of monetary measures, in order to relieve social problems but ensuring the national economic growth (Garland 2016). In sum, the marriage between the State and the market is what K. Polanyi interpreted and coined as the 'The Great Transformation' (1944), or 'the progressive disembedding of the economic life, individualization and the enthronement of state/market as the predominant axis of integration' (Kish & Quilley 2017: 310)

In addition, this rise of the State to a normative category, and even a right in itself, is also a result of the dominant influence of the modernity-coloniality view in Western culture. The State is seen as something innate, natural to any developed society, the point of culmination of a modern and mature society (Ince & Barrera de la Torre 2013). According to this insight, if de-growth is to be the new status of humankind in its progressive adaption to a scenario of dramatic exhaustion of material resources, it will necessarily be within complex and statist societies. No one (non-anarchist) will advocate for a non-statist society, which would be an obstacle to introduce the anarchist discourse into the de-growth proposals. Yet, considering some of the precepts of any de-growth agenda, such as designing self-sufficient communities, empowering citizenship and local stakeholders, localizing and decentralizing the production, etc., that is, *à-la-anarchist* reforms, are radically opposed to a hierarchic organization and representative methods of solving political challenges. The more complex is a society, the more influential are the State and its bureaucracy in the political life, complicating participative and assembly processes in voluntary and desirable implementation of de-growth.

This vague and non-clarified position around the question of the State leads de-growth to an undefined terrain that might feed, according to P. Ariès, an advocacy of the 'good State', somewhat in line with those who believe in a 'clean' or 'green' growth (Ariès 2015). So much so that de-growth risks falling into neo-liberal discourse clutches, being paradoxically 'colonized' as occurred with the precedents ideals of human welfare, as the popular 'sustainable development', as Gómez-Baggethun and Naredo (2015) caution: 'Sustainability principles have been over time re-shaped to fit dominant economic ideas, including the axiomatic necessity of unconstrained growth' (in Asara et al. 2015: 379). In fact, recent warnings in the framework of public services cuts and severe adjustments, casted by the national governments of some European countries, such as Greece, Italy and Spain, during the economic downturn, push towards a forced austerity and the self-culpability for the imprudence of 'living over the possibilities'. In other words, such reforms may be identified with de-growth reforms, when they are actually not. This appeal to austerity 'represents the consolidation and extension of the same neoliberal policies than produced the very problems (of recession, debt and unemployment) it is purported to solve' (Choat 2016: 96). As we know, such moralizing message intentionally confers the responsibility of the crisis on the careless behaviours and consumerist decisions of the masses, instead of questioning the own internal logic of the financial-neo-liberal system and the strategies of big corporations, as determinant actors who control the fate and drift of the economic cycles.

Such dilemma drives to rethink de-growth by facing the issue of the State and public institutions. Accordingly, an anarchist approach, insofar as its radical critique of the State and power structure is essential in the configuration of a more fair and autonomous society (as de-growth attempts to suggest), would offer valid and rich insights and elements. Therefore, the aim of this work is, first, to question the role that capitalist state and institutions would have in a scenario of voluntary and participative contraction of the economy and a new ethos of Nature–society relationship. Subsequently, this work will also offer some reflections about how important might be the anarchist utopia in order to think about a *post-statist* de-growth, in which bottom-up initiatives must be developed, such as cooperation, the commons and self-sufficiency.

OPENING UP INSIGHTS AND CRITICAL APPROACHES AROUND THE STATE FOR DE-GROWTH

Though there is not a unified and consolidated theoretical corpus around the State and public policies, de-growth partisans have attempted to approach the mechanisms by which the national governments have essentially served as a way of naturalizing politically the capitalism, through neo-liberal and economic growth policies. Yet, they need to be nourished by other radical approaches. For instance, the great and diverse amount of political ecology studies could help to situate or deem the role of the State in societal-environmental conflicts. Moreover, the State needs to be discussed on its condition of hierarchic way of government and technocratic strategies to manage environmental issues, demanding a collaborative work with Social Ecology and anarchist studies. Also, attention has to be paid to how political parties, with aspirations of power and government, incorporate or propagate in their agendas practices and targets favouring the national economic growth and stimulating consumption in their electorate. Obviously, there are multiple foci that deserve more detailed research. Nevertheless, in order to sort in a preliminary way some of these insights, three fundamental critiques to the State have been identified, following Ariès (2015), to which de-growth partisans have paid or should pay more attention:

a) As a repressive machine serving the economic status quo. In the neo-liberal era, some public institutions working in surveillance and defence are actually positioned on the side of proper performance of the market and the most powerful global economic actors. Thereby, they attempt to subdue any form of insurgency and overshadow alternative languages of valuation.

b) As an ideological machine serving the axiom of economic growth. The State articulates through its institutions the spread of neo-liberal metanarratives and central values such as growth, competitiveness and consumerism. In doing so, the State acts as a colonizing agent, with preconceived ideas of progress, development, technological power and material welfare.

c) As the main agent of productivism, Public economic sectors are contributing to high degrees of environmental degradation and overexploitation of resources beyond the real needs and demands of the citizenry. This process is affecting the internal resources, as well as foreign land and resources. The social support and the required demands (or the artificial creation of those) offer legitimacy to its performance as a productivist and degrading agent.

As a Repressive Machine Serving the Economic Status Quo

The last economic breakdown has had moralizing effects, a kind of 'disaster pedagogy' (Latouche 2015), in the way of conceiving how to go into politics and discussing the real role of our political institutions. Since 2011, numerous and diverse groups of citizens (*Indignados 15-M, Occupy Wall Street, Yo Soy 132, Nuit debout* – to which we have to add the *Arab Spring*, insofar as they emerged as a radical opposition to authoritarian and repressive governments) have shown their huge discontent with the political class and the permissiveness and facilities given by national governments to neo-liberal strategies and exigencies of big corporations, ignoring urgent and basic structural demands of the citizenship. Many of these movements flirt with the de-growth philosophy and are also quite 'guilty' of its penetration in the social sphere (D'Alisa et al. 2015, Demaria et al. 2015, Asara & Muraca 2015, Asara 2016).

The recently ill-fated sociologist Zygmunt Bauman considered at that time that these protests made up for the lack of global politics. The influence of neo-liberal capitalism is ecumenical, whereas the application of policies is made at a national or regional-local scale. The sudden and extraordinary power of social calling was possible due to the virtual social networks, but he asserted that 'if emotion is suitable for destroying it is especially incompetent for creating anything' (Bauman 2011).

Yet, what Bauman actually underlined is not the faded illusion of *Indignados*, once the popular support finally diversified (and consequently fragmented) this discontent in the polls, but the incapacity of the State for driving a rampant and out of control capitalist machine. In other words, for the State, in a context of crisis, it is much easier to defend a chance of an economic recovery (that would be temporary, as all we should know) than be another *indignado*.

Accordingly, the State plays the devil's advocate to convince the citizenry that any deregulation of the labour market or reductions in the budget for public services are sacrifices for a more and immediate prosperous future. This is a way of depoliticization, according to E. Swyngedouw (2011), using non-authorized political bureaucracy and experts (in economics, marketing, technical science, etc.) to command the arrangement of policies. Therefore, the most effective mechanism of repression is not the violent action against the uprisings (the Arab spring is a proof of the subsequent origin of undefined internal conflicts and civil wars), but the reactivation of the individualist and consumerist ego of the population, because the global prosperity of the economy depends on their voracious (and non-sensical) consumption. In doing so, the formal democracy, guaranteed by the State, is not corrupted with blood and violence.[3] Real politics,[4] once more, will be substituted by measures and results only understandable using a capitalist and monetary rationality: wages, economic growth, incomes, taxes, subsidies, pensions, etc. Whereas the State and citizens use this same language, a new way of repression, understood as the impossibility of thinking/imagining alternative conceptions of welfare, will subtly remain in the colonized minds.

Notwithstanding, classical repression is still a common formula used by the State in order to protect the interests of national or multinational corporations, and there is an abundance of cases linked to environmental conflicts, both in the North and in the South. Indeed, the role of the State has to be assessed according to its position in these struggles, in which national governments and public institutions are just some of the multiple actors involved in the environmental governance (Wolford et al. 2013). Recent cross-national mega-projects of infrastructures in Europe have given rise to social protests that have been seriously repressed by police forces (Ariès 2015). Yet, the glaring cases are in developing countries, in which the conflict between extractivist companies and indigenous people are commonly resolved in favour of the first by the police, criminalizing the protests and violating in many cases human rights (Rasch 2017). In the exercise of the force, they are just following the orders derived from the agreements signed between national governments and extractivist agencies. As a corollary, Gerber (2011) listed dozens of conflicts over industrial tree plantations which appeared since the mid of twentieth century, most of them still active, concluding that 'authorities have overall more often reacted by repression than by negotiation, sometimes with extreme violence' (Gerber 2011: 173). Along with it, mining conflicts in South America have been managed with analogous repressive methods to facilitate raw material extractions (Martínez-Alier & Walter 2016).

As an Ideological Machine Serving the Axiom of Economic Growth

It was previously mentioned that concepts such as production, development and economic growth are part of the consolidation of any welfare state, being associated with a more prosperous and democratic society. The roots of liberalism and capitalism are thus bonded with the modern idea of democracy. This marriage has its best proof in the credibility and authority acquired by the economic rationality and its legitimacy by reinforcing two central principles of human rights: equality and liberty. Both tenets have been transformed into neo-liberal codes: homogeneity, in the sense of a standardization of lifestyles and individualism, in the sense of an egocentric attitude of making profits and accumulating goods. The consolidation of Western modern states responds to the definition of national projects seeking for an ever-improving state of welfare, and thus reinforcing a shared feeling of common belonging to the cause. The State is still perceived 'as the pinnacle of development, an "Omega point" beyond which progress is not possible' (Ince & Barrera 2016).

Indeed, given that the economic imaginary is fully installed in the conceptions and practices of population, no government will support anything unpopular like de-growth: 'calling for degrowth explicitly is electoral suicide in an environment dominated by corporate media' (Kallis 2015) which denotes a vicious circle around this economic colonization. A good example is the political agenda of left-parties such as Podemos, in Spain, which embrace de-growth in some parts of its program, but finally has to succumb to the hegemonic and unique thought.[5]

Such identification is even more consistent and dramatic in developing countries. The political emancipation of old colonies had in the creation of State institutions the key element of a national development. Nevertheless, they sudden became overnight 'underdeveloped' by the grace of Truman's inaugural address. This has been one of the more effective mediums of ideological colonization by the wealthier states, without the need of a formal and direct political and military control of peoples and land. For Brand and Wissen (2012), the relationship between the State and the capital defines 'an imperial mode of living', that, according to Gramsci, 'turns the state into an "educator" that aims to "make certain habits and practices disappear, while seeking to spread others"'.

De-growth partisans, under the influence of Cornelius Castoriadis, push forward the idea of 'colonization of the imaginary'. In this regard, the State is a powerful tool for producing and disseminating symbols and metanarratives in pursuing the constitution of shared imaginaries in the citizenry. As Whitehead (2013) asserts, 'the primary political priority was to return us to the collective safety and prosperity that only growth could secure'. For Serge Latouche, the 'colonization' of the imaginary resulted from the myth of economic growth. Few dares to call any governmental-sponsored policy or project into question, which aims to create more employment, to materially increase the infrastructure and equipment, and, in short, to raise the incomes of the population, in general.

Latouche differentiates three driving forces of colonization: education, media manipulation and daily consumption (Latouche 2006); all of them driven to inoculate an economic rationality over social behaviours. Albeit he does not refer explicitly to the State as an ontological agent of colonization, those three forces are usually influenced and favoured by public institutions. Educational policies, whether at primary, secondary, or university level, explicitly or subliminally introduce a neo-liberal narrative in the curriculum, praising the economic growth as a natural law of every national economy or the innate positive value of technological advances and innovation for achieving this purpose (Ecologistas en Acción 2006, LeFay 2006, Winter & Cotton 2012, Cotton et al. 2013). Instead of looking after an emancipatory education inclined to form a more sensible, concerned and fair society, the State is adapting education to the principles and practices of the market, in order to rise the international competitiveness and profits (Díez 2010), to an extent which enables financial corporations lecturing in this regard. For instance, the Spanish bank, Banco Santander, is developing a project for schoolchildren in financial education, with lessons such as 'intelligent indebtedness' (Banco Santander 2016).

Nevertheless, this issue is extremely relevant, even more by showing how education is not only spreading the neo-liberal imaginary for making new potential 'soldiers' for productivist aims, but educational institutions are also literally assaulted by consumerist messages and attractions. The direct exposition to advertising in the school centres is ever more evident (Latouche 2006, Díez 2010). The advertising colonization of the French school space has increased during the 1990s by 539 per cent and 1,875 per cent in the school materials (Groupe Marcuse 2004).

Such critiques of education as an alienating tool of the State are not a new topic within the radical and anarchist theory. But surprisingly, this issue is hardly analysed amongst de-growth scholars. Indeed, they do not completely abandon the idea of economic growth: '(the) explicit opposition to the motto of sustained growth does not imply an exact opposition to economic growth' (Martínez-Alier et al. 2010). This assertion is similar to that of Latouche, when he still believes in a future scenario of compatibility between capitalism and environmental management: 'drastically reducing environmental damage does mean losing the monetary value in material goods. But it does not necessarily mean ceasing to create value through non-material products. In part, these could keep their market forms' (Latouche 2003), even advocating the subsistence of market, profit and representative democracy patterns (Fotopoulos 2010).

As the Main Productivist Agent

There is no doubt that economic growth has become a 'state matter' since the middle of twentieth century. All the efforts made by public policies are ultimately aimed at sustaining an annual positive rate of economic growth, using the GDP and analogous macroeconomic indexes as indicators of 'everything goes' for this aim. The social legitimation of this belief is very simple: if economy grows, employment, pensions, public investment in health, education, etc., will do as well. Yet, such target actually hides an evil illusion: state expenditures and investments are driven to improve the GDP figures without a real evaluation of how it is achieved. This issue has concerned the majority of de-growth scholars, who are particularly working in order to report the environmental and social large-scale devastation behind economic growth policies. In other words, the challenge is to get a decoupling of economic growth from its high matter and energy charge and from its social inequalities (Kallis 2011) (Bergh & Kallis 2012). Even more, de-growth makes sense by proposing a decoupling of economic growth from any non-material dimension of welfare, as happiness and good life (Muraca 2012). Though the green discourse of capitalism (eco-efficiency, green technologies, etc.) is insisting that 'dematerialization' is a reality, the truth is that this prophecy has no consistency while the rates of exhaustion of some crucial resources or the emissions of greenhouse emissions do not cease, or even have grown in cycles of positive growth (Jackson 2009, Polimeni et al. 2009, Kallis 2011, Demaria et al. 2013, Mauerhofer 2013, Sekulova et al. 2013).

However, such task would be incomplete without analysing the state economic structure, internal running and guidelines of public policies and how they are facilitating these damages. As Kish and Quilley (2017) advise:

> 'The structure of the liberal state in general and all its constituent ideational and legal forms (e.g. the idea of individual human rights, gender rights, disability rights, anti-racism, the concept of the individual, the institution of legal aid, welfare safety nets etc.) are all associated with an energetic, ecological, human cost. The political corollary of this is that sustaining or extending such state forms implies further costs that should at least be acknowledged'.

Thereby, the innate maintenance of the State (including the most reasonable and beneficial practices for the community) implies a significant ecological footprint that makes it difficult to think of a scenario of material de-growth in which State and bureaucracy practice what one preaches. This gets us back to the 1970s, when H. T. Odum (1971) exposed the intimate and direct relationship between the level of complexity of societal-political systems and their production of emergy, that is, the consumed energy in direct and indirect transformations needed to make a product or service.

Also, de-growth entails to analyse the role of the State as an environmentally destructive force, seeking desperately to increase national incomes and macroeconomic rates. Ultimately, it is the State or an association of states (e.g., the European Union) which define the authorized thresholds, limitations and perspectives of growth, all of which will affect to a bigger or lesser extent the quality and carrying capacity of the environment. This self-capacity to regulate (fully acknowledged amongst the electorship and citizenship) has usually been a right to be more permissive regarding overexploitation or wasteful policies with natural resources when the situations and particular interests have so required. It is well known that the chances given to dramatic interventions for environment have been laxer in developing countries, favouring practices such as monocultures, land grabbing, extractivism or the conservation of natural spaces to enable an intense touristic activity. But, precisely, some of the governments of the most powerful economies of the world (or corporations controlled direct or non-directly by them) are officially involved in this new modality of plundering and land colonization, with the approval of the affected countries governments (Borras Jr. et al. 2012, Grajales 2013, Wolford et al. 2013, Constantino 2016).

Nevertheless, it is paradigmatic how states of wealthier countries also deteriorate their internal natural resources and ecosystems to justify a high-income model of development or, even, the promotion of growth after a harsh cycle of recession. An example of that may be found in Spain. The prelude of the economic crisis in this country may be described as a 'wastefulness party'. No other country has built more apartments and houses in the transition from twentieth to twenty-first century in Europe (Fernández & Collado 2017). The deregulation (or regulation according to neo-liberal precepts) promoted by the Land Act approved in 1998 has been determinant. Spain is also leader in Europe in kilometres of highway and high-speed railway (the second in the world after China) (Page 2015). A great number of civil infrastructures were made (airports, highways, *starchitectures*, etc.), but they did not respond to real demands of the population. Rather, they contain a symbolic and ideological purpose: reinforce the centralization of the state territory and define a political tactic to ensure a considerable number of voters, in the name of welfare state. All of these infrastructures were directly or non-directly fostered by national and regional administrations, whether left or right ideology.

Capitalist and neo-liberal states and sustainable de-growth are profoundly incompatible, but a scenario of forced de-growth will lead to higher levels of competitiveness in the economy, struggling for a greater concentration and appropriation of resources and productive means. In this context, the direction of national policies in a resource-scarce scenario will be likely managed by more technocratic governments with less political involvement of citizens. De-growth is aiming to dismantle capitalism and economic growth, but capitalist strategies may transform the discourse of de-growth into a new state of concentration, monopolistic activities and oppression.

BRIDGING THE GAP BETWEEN ANARCHISM AND DE-GROWTH: AN INEVITABLE DIALOGUE IN THEORY AND IN PRACTICE

Anarchism and de-growth are two utopias with many meeting points, so they are 'condemned' to understand each other. It cannot be denied that the social ecology approach of anarchism has many bonds with de-growth. Some acknowledged libertarian authors are potential and real sources of inspiration for the intellectual framework of this movement. The main exponent of the contemporary environmentalist strand in anarchism is Murray Bookchin, as Marshall (1992) asserts: 'just as Kropotkin renewed anarchism at the end of the nineteenth century by giving it an evolutionary dimension, so Bookchin has gone further to give it a much needed ecological perspective'. He advanced that an anarchist project of society is an indispensable condition for constructing a more sustainable future and balanced relationship with Nature (Ward 2004: 96). Any de-growth partisan would sign the following assertion of M. Bookchin, which would be on the basis of every radical environmentalist movement: 'decentralize, restore bioregional forms of production and food cultivation, diversify our technologies, scale them to human dimensions and establish face-to-face forms of democracy' (Bookchin 1980). As an anarchist, Bookchin did not evade the question of the State, and he was really sceptical if a sustainable economy could be managed by a centralized state and its bureaucratic apparatus. In fact, in an essay written along with J. Biehl, they advocated for the abolition of the State and capitalism in order to face environmental crisis: 'addressing the ecological crisis requires engaging in social and political activity to confront and ultimately eliminate its objective social causes: capitalism, social hierarchy, and the nation-state' (Biehl & Bookchin 1995).

Yet, it is worth reminding that the early anarchist geographers, Reclus[6] and Kropotkin, laid the foundations of the social ecology and political ecology, by concluding that environmental degradation is intimately connected to social injustice and political conflicts (Toro 2016, 2017). An environmentalist anarchist approach spins, as it could not be otherwise, around the idea of freedom. The aspiration of liberty in societies and the preservation and caring of Nature are two intimately intertwined aims.

This idea of liberty, as a pre-condition to autonomy, is also a central issue in de-growth proposals. Regarding social justice, it is receiving a growing attention amongst experts of de-growth, but critiques focus especially on deconstructing the economic science, to decolonize us from the myth of an unlimited but unsustainable growth. Therefore, this less attention paid on the social dimension, and in general terms, on politics, needs to trace a line of collaborative work between anarchism and de-growth. Yet, first and foremost, this necessary positive feedback has to overcome some disagreements and gaps, likely attributed to a classical clash between socialism and anarchism. Referring exclusively to the academic arena, many of the de-growth scholars have a socialist-Marxist background rather than anarchist-libertarian one (di Donato 2009, Martínez-Alier et al. 2010, Kallis et al. 2015, Kallis 2017). As an example of this ideological rift, the French intellectual anarchist Philippe Pelletier (2014) launched a tough critique towards de-growth scholars, precisely accusing them of making wrong diagnostics and proposals, as they keep siding with the capital (private property, wages and money) and the State (as a neutral and regulative institution).[7] Thereby, the points of friction between de-growth and anarchism are in the conception and the scope given to the State, and consequently, how the State manages and adapts to capitalist conditions.

Nevertheless, Pelletier extended his hand to de-growth as he opens his pamphlet by inviting its partisans to adopt 'the anarchist proposals' (Pelletier 2014). In addition, and regarding the practical facet of de-growth, it is necessary to remind oneself of the great importance that anarchist trends have had in the irruption and consolidation of many initiatives and associations that share the basic tenets of a de-growth ethos. This reminds us that the perception of problems and the elaboration of arguments may be quite different depending on whether de-growth is at the academic level or the empiric level. Therefore, much of the literature written around de-growth has to go beyond the economic-analytic level, to absorb the wide range of subjectivities and sensibilities around empirical strategies of self-sufficiency, cooperative organizations, social empowerment of spaces and resources, and environmentalist movements and uprisings, amongst others.

REFORMS AND PROPOSALS FOR A NON-STATIST DE-GROWTH: KEEPING A QUOTA OF THE PUBLIC

The downscaling of the economic production and the redefinition of consumption patterns will necessary demand a powerful and considerable awkward decision-making process. First, it is obvious that these decisions cannot be taken overnight.

An effective redefinition of lifestyles will require sudden changes in daily aspects, such as shopping, mobility, food and even housing. These changes depend on developing radical processes of education and self-learning of de-growth, which are really difficult to predicate in the context of affluent and onerous societies. Even so, these changes may become revolutionary and traumatic in some cases, according to social classes, generations, occupations, ethnic groups, etc. Second, this transition toward de-growth has to be voluntary; it would be a kind of self-imposition by estimating the positive outcomes resulting of practices, such as frugality, reduction of consumerism, rejection of motorized transport, etc. But it also has to be organized and ecumenical; all the stakeholders should be guided by the same aim. In this scenario, new democratic and participative alternatives have to proliferate, in the form of associations, commons, or federalisms. And, in this regard, not all the countries and communities, despite their democratic setting, have the same tradition in bottom-up and real participatory politics. Third, the system of production is not itself prepared for responding to the demands of de-growth; the State (or any alternative political corpus) will have a giant work to do in order to promote reforms in the national economic policies, having to resort to different and radical tools (taxes, subsidies, dismantle of unsustainable practices, fostering local businesses and initiatives, etc.). Some of them may threat its hierarchic and centralized power (local currencies, cooperative production, barter and non-money market exchanges, etc.) (Kallis 2015), and some of the tax-financed tools have been counterproductive, being a factor of overexploiting nature and destroying the natural conditions of life (Brand & Wissen 2012).

In theory, de-growth entails a new social and political utopia, according to Kallis (2015): 'those of us who write about degrowth envision a future wherein societies live within their ecological means, with localized economies, which distribute resources more equally through new forms of democratic institutions'. All these reforms contradict the direct control by governments for pursuing a de-growth transition (Cosme et al. 2017). Therefore, de-growth will necessarily imply a deep reconversion of political systems and institutions, which have been traditionally built upon a representative democracy and a hierarchical delegation of responsibilities. In a nutshell, de-growth partisans are convinced that a monitored and guided de-growth requires a voluntary and democratic downshift, conceding more relevance to the civil society in this change (Deriu 2012, Ott 2012, Muraca 2013, Kallis et al. 2015). Is this a call for an abolition of the State and bureaucracy?

On this point, there can be conflicting positions about preserving to a greater or lesser extent the political institutions subjugated to the capitalist state. Thus, on the one hand, some de-growth partisans defend the current democratic institutions 'considering the risks of losing what we have achieved' (Demaria et al. 2013). Some bottom-up proposals would be, for instance, to promote frugal, downshifted lifestyles; decentralise and deepen democratic institutions; promote alternative political systems and credit institutions, etc. (Schneider et al. 2010, Kallis 2011, Mauerhofer 2013). On the other hand, a radical strand 'demand(s) completely new institutions based on direct and participatory democracy (more alternative, or post-capitalist vision)' (Demaria et al. 2013). It is surprising that 'although degrowth is often described as a bottom-up local process, the proposals are largely top-down with a national focus' (Cosme et al. 2017), in which public institutions have a determinant involvement: create funds to finance low economic cost, high welfare public investments; reduce working hours; create salary caps; promote work-sharing and job-sharing, etc. Such a position denotes a certain resistance in de-growth intellectuals to completely reject the State as the main organizational force.

In this regard, T. Trainer (2015) advocates similar proposals to de-growth, but he prefers, from his anarchist approach, to call it 'The Simpler Way' (TSW). For Trainer: 'desirable socialism cannot denote a centralized form or involve state power, but must be thoroughly participatory, and would be best described as a form of anarchism' (Trainer 2015). But his treatment of the question of the State seems ambiguous: 'Certainly, TSW envisages the need for (a small amount of) centralised bureaucracy, but it would be entirely under the control of the local assemblies'. Kallis (2015) reaches to a similar conclusion, but in this case with a socialist connotation: 'A certain degree of hierarchy is unavoidable because the redistribution of burdens and resources among more and less privileged localities will require intermediation and decision-making at broad geographic levels. Some of the degrowth reforms . . . are, in fact, quite interventionist and would require strong state action'. Trainer (2015) justifies it because of the capacity of the State to initiate a considerable restructuring of the productive settings, but provided that the State would work in the decolonization of the economic imaginary, that is, 'if everyone shared the vision and was willing to shift to an extremely different way of life'.

Another crucial topic considering the implementation of de-growth out of state management are communal spaces and initiatives. An anarchist view will advocate systems of local management based on the interactions and mutual dependences of the community (Trainer 2012), which may reach more efficient and socially sincere outcomes. Governments (whether local or national) may provide spaces for social demands but an excess of interventionism could denaturalize the essence and self-managed initiatives. The experiences of peri-urban agricultures are an ideal laboratory to analyse the involvement of local governments, national regulations and a wide range of stakeholders (farmers, unions, cooperatives, neighbourhood associations, etc.). The question is whether a non-statist de-growth society will dispense with all the so-called 'public institutions'. Demaria et al. (2013) suggest that 'some institutions need to be defended' as reasonable achievements of welfare state. Yet, the maintenance of these institutions is usually seen (and especially in times of economic recession) according to a financial mentality, as an 'expenditure' of the State rather than a social investment with any expectations of monetary benefits. We may wonder if there would be social institutions like these without the sponsorship of the State.

CONCLUSION

We should think of future steps towards de-growth in a non-statist society and there is a lack of literature advocating encounters and feedbacks between anarchism and de-growth. That necessarily demands a collaborative work between them, and not only in the issue of the State and public institutions. Without this feedback, de-growth will be completely embedded in the State praxis and, so, will enable a way of (once again) reinventing the neo-liberal discourse. For its part, anarchism will distance itself from the radical ecology that de-growth requires. The main challenge is not in reducing the amount of goods a society needs and/or enhancing the environmental quality of our cities and towns. Such progresses could be done in dictatorships, elitist and specific local contexts. The question is how to achieve this aim without the intermediation of power system, hierarchical and unfair policies, and above all, forced and isolated from the will and involvement of citizenship. For that, stimulating the decolonization of societies and abandoning the fetish elements of the capitalist and neo-liberal imaginary are priorities. In order to facilitate the encounter between anarchist social ecology and de-growth, we must abandon the classical dualism 'State (or bureaucracy)/citizenship', opting for a more integral idea of citizenry, in which the State has no any other distinctive quality than offering a reasonable organization to a transitional society towards de-growth.

NOTES

1. Negotiations between labour unions and governments have achieved great advances in the rights of workers and determining a minimum wage, but they have not been able to impede the abroad delocalization of companies and the closure of factories and centers of production, leading to the redundancy of local workers.

2. In this regard, G. Kallis (2015: 11) criticizes the ineffectiveness of all these conferences, as following: 'After years of intergovernmental deliberations following the Stockholm and Rio environmental conferences, and tons of ink spilled in the name of "sustainable development", the only concrete declines in CO_2 emissions came since 2008 as a result of the recent economic crisis'.

3. However, there were quite a few protests stifled with harshness by the public security corps.

4. It may be differentiated from the politics as a public management, according to Swyngedouw (2015).

5. However, this political sensibility of Left-parties has been contested by Drews and van der Bergh (2016), concluding in a survey that about one-third of respondant prefers either ignoring growth as a policy aim (*agrowth*), or stopping it altogether (*degrowth*) to achieve the environmental sustainability; but 'a majority views growth and environmental sustainability as compatible' (Drews & Bergh 2016).

6. I explored that E. Reclus encompasses essential issues which are in the core of degrowth theory and his point of view usually moves in the same direction: a critical view of progress and the instrumental aims; the concern about our environmental implications and the degradation of nature; the idealization of local, self-managed, emancipated and balanced communities with environmental qualities; the denounciation of injustice between the rich and the poor at diverse scales; and the estimation of primitive and traditional cultures as references for a good living (Toro 2017).

7. In my opinion, his interpretation is seriously inappropriate, simplified and biased. Pelletier is quite pertinent in pointing out the sensationalism that affects environmentalism and how technological solutions are staining capitalism with green. Yet he confusingly

encompasses environmental thinkers and trends in the same group though they correspond to diverse and heterogeneous discourses: from the most conservative to the most radical. He is not rigorous and fair referring to S. Latouche and P. Ehrlich as partisans of a supposed unique environmentalism, addressing both in the same way. Pelletier compares degrowth and environmentalism with a powerful religion: the elaboration of a catastrophic litany based on the spreading of fear and announcing an ecological collapse. He does not probably know –or avoid– that austerity may be desirable if is first and foremost voluntary and not imposed as he attempts to make believe in comparison with Catholicism. Voluntary is a basic condition of reaffirmation of freedom and autonomy, which are, in fact, basic values of the anarchist utopia.

REFERENCES

Ariès, P. (2015) "État". In G. D'Alisa, F. Demaria & G. Kallis, *Décroissance. Vocabulaire pour une nouvelle ère*, Neuvy-en-Champagne, *Éditions le passager clandestine*, pp. 231–238.

Asara, V. (2016). "The Indignados as a socio-environmental movement: Framing the crisis and democracy". *Environmental Policy and Governance*, 26(6), 527–542.

Banco Santander (2016). ""Aprende Finanzas" una iniciativa para acercar la Educación Financiera a los jóvenes".

Bauman, Z. & Bordoni, C. (2014) *State of Crisis*, Cambridge: Policy.

van den Bergh, J. C. J. M., & Kallis, G. (2012). "Growth, A-growth or degrowth to stay within planetary boundaries?" *Journal of Economic Issues*, 46(4), 909–920.

Biehl, J. & Bookchin, M. (1995). "Theses on Social Ecology and Deep Ecology". (http ://social-ecology.org/1995/08/theses-on-social-ecology-and-deep-ecology). (Last visited: 11/18/2017).

Bookchin, M. (1980). *Toward and Ecological Society*. Montreal: Black Rose.

Borras, S. M., Franco, J. C., Gómez, S., Kay, C., & Spoor, M. (2012). "Land grabbing in Latin America and the Caribbean". *Journal of Peasant Studies*, 39(3–4), 845–872.

Brand U., & Wissen M. (2012) "Global environmental politics and the imperial mode of living: articulations of state–capital relations in the multiple crisis". *Globalizations*, 9(4): 547–560.

Castoriadis, C. (1987/1975). *The Imaginary Institution of Society* (trans. Kathleen Blamey). Cambridge, MA: MIT Press.

Choat, S. (2016). "Marxism and anarchism in an age of neoliberal crisis". *Capital & Class*, 1–15.

Constantino, A. (2016). "El capital extranjero y el acaparamiento de tierras conflictos sociales y acumulación por desposesión en Argentina". *Revista de estudios sociales*, 55, 137–149.

Cosme, I., Santos, R., & O'Neill, D. W. (2017). "Assessing the degrowth discourse: A review and analysis of academic degrowth policy proposals". *Journal of Cleaner Production*, 149, 321–334.

Cotton, D., Winter, J. & Bailey, I. (2013). "Researching the hidden curriculum: Intentional and unintended messages." *Journal of Geography in Higher Education* 37, 192–203.

D'Alisa, G., Forno, F. & Maurano, S. (2015). "Grassroots (economic) activism in times of crisis. Mapping the redundancy of collective actions". *Partecipazione e Conflicto. The Open Journal of Sociopolitical Studies*, 8(2), 328–342.

Demaria, F., Schneider, F., Sekulova, F. & Martínez-Alier, J. (2013). "What is Degrowth? From an Activist Slogan to a Social Movement". *Environmental Values*, 22, 191–215.

Deriu, M. (2012). "Democracies with a future: Degrowth and the democratic transition". *Futures* 44, 553–561.

Díez, E. (2010). "Decrecimiento y Educación". In Taibo, C. (coord.). Decrecimientos. Sobre lo que hay que cambiar en la vida cotidiana. Madrid: Los Libros de la Catarata.

di Donato, M. (2009). "Decrecimiento o barbarie. Entrevista a Serge Latouche". *Papeles de relaciones ecosociales y cambio global*, 107, 159–170.

Drews, S., & van den Bergh, J. C. J. M. (2016). "Public views on economic growth, the environment and prosperity: Results of a questionnaire survey". *Global Environmental Change*, 39, 1–14.

Ecologistas en Acción. (2006). *Estudio del Currículum Oculto Antiecológico de los Libros de Texto*. Madrid: Ecologistas en Acción.

Fernández, S. & Collado, I. (2017). "What has happened in Spain? The real estate bubble, corruption and housing development: A view from the local level". *Geoforum*, 85, 206–213.

Fotopoulos, T. (2010). "The de-growth Utopia: The incompatibility of de-growth within an internationalised market economy". In Q. Huan (ed.), *Eco-socialism as Politics. Rebuilding the Basis of Our Modern Civilisation*. Springer-Dordrecht-Heidelberg-London-New York: Springer, 103–122.

Garland, D. (2016). *The Welfare State. A Very Short Introduction*. New York: Oxford University Press.

Gerber, J. F. (2011). "Conflicts over industrial tree plantations in the South: Who, how and why?" *Global Environmental Change*, 21(1), 165–176.

Grajales, J. (2013). "State involvement, land grabbing and counter-insurgency in Colombia". *Development and Change*, 44(2), 211–232.

Groupe Marcuse (2004). *De la misère humaine en milieu publicitaire. Comment le monde se meurt de notre mode de vie*. Paris: Éditions La Découverte.

Ince, A. And Barrera de la Torre, Gerónimo (2016). "For post-statist geographies", *Political Geography*, 55, 10–19.

Kallis, G. (2011). "In defence of degrowth". *Ecological Economics*, 70(5), 873–880.

Kallis, G. (2015). In defense of degrowth. Edited by Aaron Vansintjan, https://indefenseofdegrowth.com/.

Kallis, G. (2017). "Socialism without Growth". *Capitalism, Nature and Socialism*, 30(2), 189–206.

Kallis, G. & Colectivo Recerca i Decreixement (2015). "Diez propuestas de políticas públicas". en G. D'Alisa, F. Demaria, and G. Kallis (eds.), *Decreixement. Vocabulario para una nueva era*. New York: Routledge, pp. 323–329.

Kallis, G., Demaria, F., & D'Alisa, G. (2015). "Introduction: degrowth". In G. D'Alisa, F. Demaria, and G. Kallis (eds.), *Degrowth: A Vocabulary for a New Era*. Barcelona: Icaria Editorial, pp. 1–17.

Kish, K., & Quilley, S. (2017). "Wicked dilemmas of scale and complexity in the politics of degrowth". *Ecological Economics*, 142, 306–317.

Latouche, S. (2003). Will the West actually be happier with less? The world downscaled. Le Monde diplomatique, December.

Latouche, S. (2006). *Le pari de la décroissance*. Paris: Librairie Arthème Fayard.

Latouche, S. (2009). *Farewell to Growth*. Cambridge-Malden: Polity Press.

LeFay, R. (2006). "An ecological critique of education". *International Journal of Children's Spirituality* 11, 35–45.

Martínez-Alier, Joan, Pascual, Unai, Vivien, Franck-Dominique, & Zaccai, Edwin. (2010). "Sustainable de-growth: Mapping the context, criticisms and future prospects of an emergent paradigm". *Ecological Economics* 69, 1741–1747.

Martínez-Alier, J. & Walter, M. (2016). "Social metabolism and conflicts over extractivism". In F. Castro, B. Hogenboom & M. Baud (eds.), *Environmental Governance in Latin America*. New York: Palgrave MacMillan, 58–85.

Mauerhofer, V. (2013). "Lose less instead of win more: The failure of decoupling and perspectives for competition in a degrowth economy". *Environmental Values* 22, 43–57.

Muraca, B. (2012). "Towards a fair degrowth-society: Justice and the right to a "good life" beyond growth." *Futures*, 44(6), 535–545.

Naredo, J. M. (2006). *Raíces económicas del deterioro ecológico y social. Más allá de los dogmas.* Madrid: Siglo XXI.

Odum. H. T. (1971). *Environment, Power and Society.* John Wiley & Sons.

Page, D. (2015). "España, el país donde hay más AVE y donde menos se utiliza", Expansión, March, 9th 2015. (http://www.expansion.com/2015/03/09/empresas/transporte/14258968 48.html) (last visited: 11/18/2017).

Pelletier, P. (2014). "La misma cantinela". Tierra y Libertad 308, pp.

Polanyi, K., 1944. *The Great Transformation.* Farrar & Rinehart.

Polimeni, J.M., Mayumi, K., Giampietro, M., & Alcott, B. (2009). *The Myth of Resource Efficiency: The Jevons Paradox.* Earthscan.

Purchase, Graham. 1993. "Social Ecology, Anarchism and Trades Unionism". In Murray Bookchin, Graham Purchase, Brian Morris, Rodney Aitchtey,, Robert Hart, Chris Wilbert, *Deep Ecology & Anarchism. A Polemic.* London: Freedom Press, pp. 23–36.

Rash, E. D. 2017. "Citizens, criminalization and violence in natural resource conflicts in Latin America". *European Review of Latin American and Caribbean Studies*, 103, 131–142.

Sekulova, F., Kallis, G., Rodríguez-Labajos, B., & Schneider, F. (2013). "Degrowth: from theory to practice". *Journal of Cleaner Production*, 38, 1–6.

Swyngedouw, E. (2011). "Interrogating post-democracy: Reclaiming egalitarian political spaces". *Political Geography*, 30, 370–380.

Swyngedouw, E. (2015). "Despolitización («lo político»)". In G. D'Alisa, F. Demaria, and G. Kallis (eds.), *Degrowth: A Vocabulary for a New Era.* New York: Routledge, pp. 149–154.

Toro, F. (2016). "Educating for earth consciousness: Ecopedagogy within early anarchist geography". in S. Springer, M. Lopes de Souza, R. White, *The Radicalization of Pedagogy Anarchism, Geography, and the Spirit of Revolt.* Rowman & Littlefield.

Toro, F. (2017). "The thought of Élisée Reclus as a source of inspiration for degrowth ethos". in F. Ferretti, G. Barrera de la Torre, A. Ince and F. Toro (eds.), *Historical Geographies of Anarchism.* London: Routledge, pp. 89–112.

Trainer, T. (2012). "De-growth: Do you realise what it means?" *Futures* 44, 590–599.

Trainer, T. (2015). "The degrowth movement from the perspective of the simpler way". *Capitalism, Nature, Socialism*, 26, 58–75.

Ward, Colin. (2004). *Anarchism: A Very Short Introduction.* Oxford: Oxford University Press.

Whitehead, M. (2013). "Degrowth or Regrowth?" *Environmental Values* 22, 141–145.

Winter, J. & Cotton, D. (2012). "Making the hidden curriculum visible: sustainability literacy in higher education". *Environmental Education Research*, 18, 783–796.

Wolford, W., Borras, S. M., Hall, R., Scoones, I., & White, B. (2013). "Governing global land deals: The role of the state in the rush for land". *Development and Change*, 44(2), 1–279.

Index

205

About the Contributors

John P. Clark is an eco-communitarian anarchist writer, activist, and educator. He lives and works in New Orleans, where his family has lived for twelve generations, and at Bayou La Terre, in the forest of the Mississippi Gulf Coast. His most recent book is *Between Earth and Empire: From the Necrocene to the Beloved Community.*

Simon Springer is professor of human geography, head of discipline for geography and environmental studies and director of the Centre for Urban and Regional studies at the University of Newcastle, Australia.

Martin Locret-Collet is a Paris-based geographer, urban designer and political ecologist who holds a PhD from the University of Birmingham (UK). His interests lay in community planning, governance, open democracy and the commons. Martin is either a hands-on, very practical researcher or a rather thoughtful and daydreaming practitioner, depending on who you ask!

Jennifer Mateer is assistant teaching professor in the Department of Geography at the University of Victoria, Canada. She is also a SSHRC-funded post-doctoral research fellow at the University of British Columbia, Canada. Her research focuses on the intersections of environmental justice, political ecology, animal geographies and participatory action research. These projects have allowed Jennifer to live and work across Turtle Island (Canada, the USA and Mexico) as well as India and Rwanda.

Maleea Acker teaches geography and Canadian studies at the University of Victoria, Canada. Her work takes multiple forms, from scholarly to journalistic, literary to artistic. She serves on the editorial board of *The Malahat Review*. Her book of essays,

Gardens Aflame: Garry Oak Meadows of BC's South Coast, charts the Indigenous history and restoration of an endangered Vancouver Island ecosystem; her third poetry collection is forthcoming in 2022 from Nightwood Editions.

Andrej Fideršek is the cofounder and an active member of the Zero Waste Žalec collective as well as an independent researcher who seeks paths towards a utopian society through the theory and praxis of social ecology. After graduating from Glasgow Caledonian University, he returned to his home town of Žalec, Slovenia. There he works on various community-orientated projects with a cosmolocal outlook. His main fields of interest are social ecology, de-growth, circular economy, aquaponics, urban gardening, regenerative design and solarpunk fiction.

Elizabeth Auclair has a PhD in geography; she is a senior lecturer in planning in the geography department at CY Cergy Paris University, France. In charge of the master's degree in cultural development and heritage valorisation for twenty years, she is since 2019 the head of the geography research centre MRTE. The general theme underlying her work concerns the articulation between artistic, cultural and heritage projects and alternative approaches for sustainable cities and territories. Her main research questions concern social inequalities, governance process and participation methods. She is presently working on cultural sustainability and "degrowth" theories applied to culture, art and heritage.

Jérôme Pélenc is lecturer at University of Toulouse 2, France, and researcher at the UMR LISST.

Anahita Grisoni is associate researcher at the l'UMR Environnement, Ville, Société, Université de Lyon.

Julien Milanesi is lecturer at University of Toulouse 1, France, and researcher at the UMR CERTOP.

Léa Sébastien is lecturer at University of Toulouse 2, France, and researcher at the UMR GEODE.

Manuel Cervera-Marzal is chargé de recherche at the FNRS in Liège University in Belgium.

Cassidy Thomas is originally from Boise, Idaho. He holds a BA in political science and an MA in community leadership from Westminster College of Salt Lake City, Utah. He is currently a PhD student in social science at Syracuse University. His work frequently incorporates scholarship from the fields of political science, sociology, and geography—often engaging (eco)feminist, (eco)marxist and anarchist thought. Much of his research explores the twenty-first century manifestations of (eco)fascism, as well as leadership and organizational structures within decentralized social movements.

Leonardo E. Figueroa-Helland (he/him/his) is an anti-colonial scholar-activist of mestizo heritage with mixed Indigenous Mesoamerican (detribalized Zoque and Maya) and Euro-American (Nordic) ancestry. He chairs the environmental policy and sustainability management programme at The New School. His work focuses on how Indigenous and decolonizing approaches intersect with diverse counterhegemonic paradigms to constitute lifeways beyond the systems that drive systemic injustice and socio-environmental crises. He centres the revitalization of Indigenous cosmovision-based communal land governance practices as keys to resurgence, re-Indigenization and the reconstitution of communal sacred territories through land rematriation. His work triangulates Indigenous and decolonizing agendas with critical political ecology, critical global studies, biocultural diversity, political agroecology and food sovereignty, complex intersectional ecologism, world-systems ecology, ecofeminism, feminisms of colour, regenerative ecologies, BIPOC and Global South liberation, and post-extractivisms to articulate systemic alternatives. He leads the Indigeneity, Decolonization and Just Sustainabilities Initiative of the Tishman Environment and Design Center.

Gerónimo Barrera de la Torre is a PhD student in the Institute of Latin American Studies at the University of Texas at Austin. His research focuses on the political ecology of forest conservation, historical geography, post-statist geographies and critical cartographies. He has worked with Indigenous Chatino people and campesino communities in Oaxaca, México, regarding local knowledges about their environment and Chatino understanding of their landscape through their language. He is working with the same communities to research the conservation and management programmes of their communal forests and codirecting a collaborative documentary on carbon offsetting projects in the region.

Gregory Knapp is associate professor and director of sustainability studies in the Department of Geography and Environment at the University of Texas at Austin. Knapp's research has focused on four themes in cultural and regional geography: adaptive dynamics of agriculture; ethnic territoriality and mapping; modernization contextualized in historical cultural ecology; and the history of geographic ideas and researchers. These themes have been explored in Latin America, with special attention to Andean South America and Ecuador. In addition to publishing on reconstructing prehistoric landscapes and demography in the Andes, Knapp was involved in the first major international study of the impacts of climate change on Andean agriculture, where he argued for policies prioritizing empowerment of local actors, maximizing local adaptive flexibility. His current research focuses on contexts of agricultural modernization in mountains, particularly greenhouse floriculture.

Ryan Alan Sporer received his PhD in 2018 from the University of Illinois at Chicago. He is assistant professor in sociology at Salisbury University in Maryland and is working on a manuscript on the off-grid housing movement.

Kevin Suemnicht is a PhD candidate in anthropology at the University of Illinois at Chicago.

Dan Fischer is a middle school social studies teacher and a volunteer for Food Not Bombs – South Bend. He can be reached at dfischer@riseup.net.

Francisco J. Toro is professor in the Department of Human Geography at the University of Granada, Spain. His 2011 doctoral thesis was entitled "Crisis ecológica y Geografía: Planteamientos y propuestas en torno al paradigma ecológico-ambiental". His main research topics are theoretical and critical approaches to sustainability, the relationship between environmental identity and urban space and radical environmentalism within geographic thought. Along with Federico Ferretti, Gerónimo Barrera de la Torre and Anthony Ince, he coedited *Historical Geographies of Anarchism: Early Critical Geographers and Present-Day Scientific Challenges* (2018). He has been involved in cross-disciplinary research projects such as landscape and infrastructures in Andalusia, Spain; habitability and vulnerability in Andalusian cities; public participation in landscape management in Andalusia and Man and the Biosphere (MAB) UNESCO reports of Spanish-protected areas.